EXPECTATIONS

EXPECTATIONS

A Reader for Developing Writers

SECOND EDITION

ANNA INGALLS
Southwestern College

DAN MOODY
Southwestern College

PEARSON
Longman

New York   San Francisco   Boston
London   Toronto   Sydney   Tokyo   Singapore   Madrid
Mexico City   Munich   Paris   Cape Town   Hong Kong   Montreal

Senior Acquisitions Editor: Susan Kunchandy
Senior Marketing Manager: Melanie Craig
Senior Supplements Editor: Donna Campion
Production Manager: Joseph Vella
Project Coordination, Text Design, and Electronic Page Makeup:
  Shepherd, Inc.
Photo Research: Photosearch, Inc.
Cover Design Manager: John Callahan
Cover Designer: Maria Ilardi
Cover Images: Courtesy of Getty Images, Inc.
Manufacturing Manager: Mary Fischer
Printer and Binder: Courier Corp.—Westford
Cover Printer: The Lehigh Press

For permission to use copyrighted material, grateful acknowledgment is
made to the copyright holders on pp. 289, which are hereby made part of
this copyright page.

Library of Congress Cataloging-in-Publication Data
Expectations: a reader for developing writers/ [compiled by] Anna Ingalls [and]
Dan Moody—2nd ed.
        p. cm.
Includes bibliographical references and index.
ISBN 0-321-14290-X
    1. College readers. 2. English language—Rhetoric—Problems, exercises, etc.
3. Report writing—Problems, exercises, etc. I. Ingalls, Anna. II. Moody, Dan.

PE1417 .E95 2005
808'.0427—dc22

                                        2005042997

Please visit our website at http://www.ablongman.com

ISBN: 0-321-14290-X

2 3 4 5 6 7 8 9 10—CRW—08 07 06

DEDICATION

It is with great respect and affection that we dedicate this book to the phenomenal staff, the talented faculty, and above all, the wonderful students of Southwestern College.

C O N T E N T S

RHETORICAL CONTENTS

Readings are categorized here according to their predominant rhetorical modes. In cases where readings clearly exemplify two or more different modes of thinking and writing, they are listed in more than one category. However, because of the very nature of professional writing, readers will find that many authors have employed a variety of other modes in addition to those listed here.

NARRATION

DESCRIPTION

PERSUASION

EXPOSITION (INFORMATIVE)

PREFACE

Like the first edition of *Expectations: A Reader for Developing Writers*, the second edition features a carefully chosen collection of popular readings for developmental writing students, with questions, discussion topics, and assignments to develop active reading techniques, critical thinking skills, and effective writing strategies. *Expectations* is specifically designed to meet the needs of pre-freshman composition students who can benefit from instruction in reading, critical thinking, and writing skills.

For the second edition, we have retained those readings from the first edition that classroom instructors found most useful and appealing for the target audience of developmental reading and writing students. In addition, the second edition features eleven new readings chosen for their focus on contemporary issues, their literary quality, and their ability to engage students. Well-known authors who are new to the second edition include Paul Rezéndes, David LaGesse, Maya Angelou, and N. Scott Momaday.

READING SELECTIONS

Expectations features a wide variety of readings on topics of interest and value to today's students. Many of the forty readings reflect the multicultural and pluralistic nature of our society, including articles that feature the Japanese American experience, gender issues in the workplace, disabled athletes, and the experience of an African American midwife in the deep South.

In addition to cultural issues, topics range from useful readings on managing time and keeping fit, to nature topics such as observing river dolphins, tracking a bobcat, and climbing Mt. Everest, to timely subjects like cloning, computer addiction, and cellphone tracking. The topics, the lengths, and the difficulty levels of the readings are appropriate for developing writers.

Most of the readings originally appeared in nationally known magazines or contemporary nonfiction books. A few excerpts from textbooks are also included to help students build the kinds of reading skills they will need in order to be successful in college courses across the curriculum. A number of other readings originated as newspaper articles. To enhance students' reading experience and perhaps spark an interest in literature, three examples of fiction and one poem are also included.

The readings exemplify a broad range of rhetorical modes, organizational styles, and effective stylistic techniques that students are encouraged to apply to their own writing. An underlying emphasis on the reading-writing connection is apparent throughout the text.

ORGANIZATION

Expectations is organized by themes that relate to students' lives and personal interests as well as to our society and directions for the future: Social and Cultural Issues, Education and Career, Media and Popular Culture, Fitness and Health, Nature and the Outdoors, and a new, thought-provoking section featured in the second edition, Values and Choices. Within each theme, easier readings are placed first, while readings with a higher vocabulary level, more complicated sentence structure, or a denser text style appear later in the section. To give instructors the flexibility of following either a thematically based instructional outline or a rhetorically based outline, readings are also cross-referenced by their predominant rhetorical modes: narration, description, cause and effect, instructions, comparison/contrast, persuasion, classification, and exposition (informative writing).

STRATEGIES FOR ACTIVE READING

An initial lesson called Strategies for Active Reading introduces such skills as previewing, recognizing audience and purpose, identifying the main idea, discovering meaning through context clues, making inferences, evaluating for logic and bias, reviewing, and reflecting on the reading. These skills are reinforced throughout the book in comprehension questions, critical thinking questions, and language and vocabulary questions.

FEATURES

Within each lesson, pre- and post-reading features make the content and the vocabulary accessible, as well as promoting analysis, discussion, and written expression.

- A short **Introduction** sets the stage for each reading by presenting information about the topic or the source. The second edition features many expanded introductions that provide more information about authors or more background for the reading.

- **Prereading questions** provide a conceptual framework by asking students to start thinking about the topics and issues reflected in the reading.

- A **Vocabulary** list for preview or quick reference provides simple and concise definitions of difficult or unusual vocabulary.

- **Comprehension** questions allow students to check their understanding of the reading.

- **Critical Thinking** questions focus on the author's purpose and audience, the main point of the reading, awareness of bias, and application to society. Skills such as inference, extrapolation, and deductive reasoning are emphasized.

- **Language and Vocabulary** questions range from general, technical, and specific vocabulary of particular fields to broader topics such as synonyms, discovering meaning from context, and figurative language.

- **Style, Structure, and Organization** questions lead students to examine the writers' techniques and to build an awareness of rhetorical methods.

- **Topics for Discussion or Journal Writing** include a selection of creative, imaginative, and personal response topics to stimulate class discussion and informal writing.

- **Writing Topics for Paragraphs or Essays** are based on the topics and the rhetorical modes of the readings, as well as incorporating a variety of other modes. Each lesson includes one or more writing projects that encourage students to use outside sources, such as library materials, oral interviews, and information obtained via the Internet.

TO THE TEACHER

Expectations: A Reader for Developing Writers is designed to be both teacher- and student-friendly. It is our hope that students will find the topics to be interesting and relevant to contemporary society as well as to the improvement of their writing techniques and styles.

Teachers may choose to rely heavily on this reader for classroom use, or use it as an adjunct to a comprehensive writing text—and possibly a basic handbook such as *Check It Out: A Quick and Easy Guide for Writers,* by the same authors.

With forty readings, teachers are able to choose readings to best fit their courses, students, and teaching methods. Some may choose to work extensively with one or more of the themes, or to select readings across several themes, based on the difficulty level. Other teachers will prefer to choose those readings that illustrate a lecture point (or several points) or that match the type of writing that students are engaged in learning. Finally, there will be teachers who allow students to choose their own readings as homework assignments to enrich the core curriculum of the classroom.

This book is intended to be an effective tool in the hands of many capable and creative teachers.

THE TEACHING AND LEARNING PACKAGE

Longman is pleased to offer a variety of support materials to help make teaching developmental English easier on teachers and to help students excel in their coursework. Many of our student supplements are available free or at a greatly reduced price when packaged with a Longman writing textbook. Contact your local Longman sales representative for more information on pricing and how to create a package.

Support Materials for Writing Instructors

Instructor's Manual.   A complete instructor's manual to accompany *Expectations* is available (Instructor / ISBN 0-321-14292-6).

Printed Test Bank for Developmental Writing.   Features more than 5,000 questions in all areas of writing, from grammar to paragraphing through essay writing, research, and documentation (Instructor / ISBN 0-321-08486-1).

Electronic Test Bank for Developmental Writing. Features more than 5,000 questions in all areas of writing, from grammar to paragraphing through essay writing, research, and documentation. Instructors simply choose questions from the electronic test bank, then print out the completed test for distribution OR offer the test online (Instructor / CD ISBN 0-321-08117-X).

Diagnostic and Editing Tests, **Sixth Edition.** This collection of diagnostic tests helps instructors assess students' competence in standard written English to determine placement or to gauge progress (Instructor / Print ISBN 0-321-19647-3; CD ISBN 0-321-19645-7).

The Longman Instructor's Planner. This planner includes weekly and monthly calendars, student attendance and grading rosters, space for contact information, Web references, an almanac, and blank pages for notes (Instructor / ISBN 0-321-09247-3).

For Writing Students

The Longman Writer's Portfolio and Student Planner. This unique supplement provides students with a space to plan, think about, and present their work. In addition to the yearly planner, this portfolio includes an assessing/organizing area (including a grammar diagnostic test, a spelling quiz, and project planning worksheets), a before and during writing area (including peer review sheets, editing checklists, writing self-evaluations, and a personal editing profile), and an after-writing area (including a progress chart, a final table of contents, and a final assessment), as well as a daily planner for students including daily, weekly, and monthly calendars (ISBN 0-321-29609-5).

Longman English Tutor Center Access Card. Unique service offering students access to an in-house writing tutor via phone and/or email. Tutor available from 5 P.M.–12 A.M. Sunday through Thursday (VP: ISBN 0-201-71049-8 or Stand Alone: ISBN 0-201-72170-8).

The Longman Writer's Journal **by Mimi Markus.** Provides students with their own personal space for writing and contains helpful journal writing strategies, sample journal entries by other students, and many writing prompts and topics to get students writing (Student / 0-321-08639-2).

Longman Editing Exercises. Fifty-four pages of paragraph editing exercises give students extra practice using grammar skills in the context of longer passages (Student / ISBN 0-205-31792-8; With Answer Key: ISBN 0-205-31797-9).

100 Things to Write About. This brief book contains more than 100 individual writing assignments, on a variety of topics and in a wide range of formats, from expressive to analytical writing (Student / ISBN 0-673-98239-4).

Research Navigator Guide for English **by H. Eric Branscomb and Doug Gotthoffer.** Designed to teach students how to conduct high-quality online research and to document it properly, Research Navigator guides provide discipline-specific academic resources; in addition to helpful tips on the writing process, online research, and finding and citing valid sources. Research Navigator guides include an access code to Research Navigator™, providing access to thousands of academic journals and periodicals, the *New York Times* Search by Subject Archive, Link Library, Library Guides, and more (Student / 0-321-20277-5).

Penguin Discount Novel Program. In cooperation with Penguin Putnam, Inc., Longman is proud to offer a variety of Penguin paperbacks at a significant discount when packaged with any Longman title. Excellent additions to any English course, Penguin titles give students the opportunity to explore contemporary and classical fiction and drama. The available titles include works by authors as diverse as Toni Morrison, Julia Alvarez, Mary Shelley, and Shakespeare. To review the complete list of titles available, visit the Longman-Penguin-Putnam website: http://www.ablongman.com/penguin.

The New American Webster Handy College Dictionary. A paperback reference text with more than 100,000 entries (Student / ISBN 0-451-18166-2).

Merriam-Webster Collegiate Dictionary. This hardcover comprehensive dictionary is available at a significant discount when packaged with any Longman text (Student / ISBN 0-321-10494-3).

Multimedia Offerings

Interested in incorporating online materials into your course? Longman is happy to help. Our regional technology specialists provide training on all of our multimedia offerings.

MySkillsLab 2.0 (http://www.myskillslab.com). This exciting new website houses all the media tools any developmental English student will need to improve their reading, writing, and study skills, and all in one easy to use place. Resources for Writing include:

- **Writing Voyage Website.** Writing Voyage covers all the stages of the writing process, from brainstorming to final copy preparation. Students begin by taking a diagnostic test to help them assess their skills and place them in the appropriate level of the program. At each level, students visit 12 of the world's most intriguing destinations in the context of a world cruise. As they learn local history and culture at each port, students master a different writing skill with multimedia instruction, tutorials, thousands of exercises with interactive feedback, and mastery tests

- **Grammar Diagnostics and ExerciseZone.** Two diagnostic tests that assess student skills in grammar, mechanics, punctuation, and style. Results pages provide proficiency scores, question-by-question feedback, and direction to appropriate exercises in ExerciseZone. ExerciseZone offers 3,000 self-scoring grammar exercises with new sentence and paragraph editing exercises.

- **ESL ExerciseZone.** ESL ExerciseZone offers over 1,000 self-grading practice exercises for students whose first language is not English.

- **Research Navigator™.** Research Navigator is the easiest way to start a research assignment or research paper. This comprehensive research tool gives users access to four exclusive databases or authoritative and reliable source material.

- **Avoiding Plagiarism Tutorials.** Helping students understand what plagiarism is, these tutorials offer strategies and practices to help students recognize plagiarism and avoid it. The self-guided tutorials combine valuable resources with interactive exercises to help students understand and master skills such as attribution, using quotation marks, citing sources, paraphrasing, and citing images and works.

- **Exchange.** Longman's online peer and instructor writing review program, Exchange allows instructors to comment on student papers at the word, sentence, or paper level or have students review each other's work in peer review groups.

- **Tutor Center.** With MySkillsLab, students also receive complimentary access to Longman's Tutor Center. Students can contact our tutors, who are qualified college instructors, for LIVE help via toll-free phone, e-mail, web, or fax.

- **MyDropBox.** MyDropBox enables instructors to run their students' papers through state-of-the-art plagiarism detection software. The MyDropBox system searches over 4.3 billion web pages, thousands of electronic databases, newspapers, magazines, e-books, online reference sites, and even an archive of student papers from your institution. Originality reports, easy to read and accurate, are turned around within 24 hours. For more information about MyDropBox, please go to their Web site at http://www.mydropbox.com.

Available versions of MySkillsLab 2.0: Website, CourseCompass, WebCT, and Blackboard.

The Writer's ToolKit Plus **CD-ROM.** Offers a wealth of tutorials, exercises, and reference material for writers, including more than 3,000 grammar exercises. It is compatible with either a PC or Macintosh platform, and is flexible enough to be used either occasionally for practice or regularly in class lab sessions (Student / ISBN 0-321-07894-2).

STATE SPECIFIC SUPPLEMENTS

For Florida Adopters

Thinking Through the Test: A Study Guide for the Florida College Basic Skills Exit Test by **D.J. Henry.** FOR FLORIDA ADOPTIONS

ONLY: This workbook helps students strengthen their reading skills in preparation for the Florida College Basic Skills Exit Test. It features both diagnostic tests to help assess areas that may need improvement and exit tests to help test skill mastery. Detailed explanatory answers have been provided for almost all of the questions. *Package item only— not available for sale.* Available Versions:

- *Thinking Through the Test: A Study Guide for the Florida College Basic Skills Exit Tests, Reading and Writing*, Second Edition (ISBN 0-321-27660-4).

- *Thinking Through the Test: A Study Guide for the Florida College Basic Skills Exit Tests, Reading and Writing, with Answers*, Second Edition (ISBN 0-321-27756-2).

- *Thinking Through the Test: A Study Guide for the Florida College Basic Skills Exit Tests, Writing, with Answers* (ISBN 0-321-27755-4).

- *Thinking Through the Test: A Study Guide for the Florida College Basic Skills Exit Tests, Writing* (ISBN 0-321-27745-7).

Writing Skills Summary for the Florida State Exit Exam by D. J. Henry.   FOR FLORIDA ADOPTIONS ONLY: An excellent study tool for students preparing to take Florida College Basic Skills Exit Test for Writing, this laminated writing grid summarizes all the skills tested on the Exit Exam. *Package item only—not available for sale* (Student / ISBN 0-321-08477-2).

CLAST Test Package, Fourth Edition.   These two, 40-item objective tests evaluate students' readiness for the Florida CLAST exams. Strategies for teaching CLAST preparedness are included (Instructor / Print ISBN 0-321-01950-4).

For Texas Adopters

The Longman THEA Study Guide **by Jeannette Harris.**   Created specifically for students in Texas, this study guide includes straightforward explanations and numerous practice exercises to help students prepare for the reading and writing sections of THEA Test. *Package item only—not available for sale* (Student / ISBN 0-321-27240-0).

TASP Test Package, Third Edition.   These 12 practice pre-tests and post-tests assess the same reading and writing skills covered in the Texas TASP examination (Instructor / Print ISBN 0-321-01959-8).

For New York/CUNY Adopters

Preparing for the CUNY-ACT Reading and Writing Test edited by Patricia Licklider.   This booklet, prepared by reading and writing faculty from across the CUNY system, is designed to help students prepare for the CUNY-ACT exit test. It includes test-taking tips, reading passages, typical exam questions, and sample writing prompts to help students become familiar with each portion of the test (Student / ISBN 0-321-19608-2).

ACKNOWLEDGMENTS

First of all, we would like to express our appreciation to Susan Kunchandy, acquisitions editor, and Steve Rigolosi, formerly the senior acquisitions editor at Longman, who have assisted us with the second edition of *Expectations.* They have our sincere thanks, as does Longman's extremely capable and efficient assistant editor, Meegan Thompson, and editorial assistant Erika Lo. They have contributed a great deal to the successful completion of our second edition. Thanks are also due to Joe Opiela, our former editor, whose ideas and pointers aided us greatly in the original design of this reader.

Dan would like to thank his wife Kathleen and his four daughters, Rachel, Sarah, Hannah, and Elizabeth, for the love and support they give him, and his parents for always believing in him. He also owes a debt of gratitude to the many friends and colleagues who have supported him by encouraging him and keeping him in their prayers.

Anna would like to express her appreciation to friends, family, and colleagues who have helped her survive the pressures of writing and editing, especially her traveling companions—Bobbe Tatreau, Meredith Morton, Toni Rowden, Nancy Evans, Donald Pratt, and Frank Giardina—whose wit and generosity of spirit are unsurpassed.

Professor Eliana Santana has our thanks for explaining a Brazilian legend and helping us with Portuguese words in one of the readings.

We also wish to thank the many capable Southwestern College librarians who assisted us in our search for readings and information about authors. Additionally, we wish to acknowledge Dr. Renée Kilmer, dean of the School of Languages and Humanities at Southwestern College, for her enthusiastic and consistent support of our writing projects.

Finally, we would like to thank the astute reviewers who generously took the time to offer their thoughtful, professional suggestions and to rate the interest level and usefulness of the readings in our first edition: Rosie Soy, Hudson Community College; Chris Borglum, Valencia Community College; Jo Ann Buck, Guilford Technical Community College; Kelley Paystrup, Snow College; Alfred Guy Litton, Texas Woman's University; Christine Horan, Oklahoma State University; and Holly Nicholes, Snow College. Their input has been invaluable in shaping and developing the second edition of this text.

ANNA INGALLS
DAN MOODY

STRATEGIES FOR ACTIVE READING

ACTIVE READING

There is a strong connection between reading and writing; in fact, reading is one of the best ways to become an effective writer. Through reading, we can learn, both consciously and subconsciously, how to use language more effectively.

When we read an effective article or story, for example, we often soak up some of the writer's techniques *intuitively*, at a subconscious level, without even being aware of it, and occasionally one of these techniques will surprise us by showing up in our own writing. This can happen even (or especially!) when we are reading for pleasure. We might get caught up in the story and not pay any attention to the writer's techniques or style, but still, at some level, we learn. This is one of the great benefits of reading for pleasure.

In addition to reading for pleasure, those who want to become better writers should learn to read *actively*. Active reading means consciously analyzing the author's techniques to see what works well. By focusing on and evaluating such things as the author's *purpose, point of view, organization, style, vocabulary*, and *grammatical structures*, we can add to our own collection of writing tools and be ready to try them out ourselves in the next papers we write.

Writing is like any other craft: writers have their own specialized tools of the trade. By increasing the number of tools we have to choose from, we can learn to be more effective writers. This book of readings provides a close look at a number of writing tools as they are used by some very effective authors.

The following pages present an illustrated example of active reading. On the left side of each page, you will find a specific strategy for active reading, as well as notes that show how a reader could apply these strategies to the reading on the right, "Tourist Trap."

Active Reading Strategies

By reading actively, you will get the most out of each selection that you read. An active reader interacts with the words on the page (or on the screen), analyzes the reading, and takes note of effective techniques for use in his or her own writing.

There are several methods of active reading. Nearly all of them include the following steps in one form or another:

I. Preview the reading.
Before you read the selection word for word, look ahead to get a general idea of the topic and other important information.

A. Read the title, any introductory writing, and any other information at the top.

TOURIST TRAP
JAMES HEBERT

The idea of time travel is amazingly attractive, partly because it offers the possibility of living another life, in another time. While "real" time travel remains a physical impossibility today, the mind accepts no such barriers. As you read this newspaper article from a special section on *time*, look for the connection between time travel, history, and great literature.

TOURIST TRAP

1 It's difficult to contemplate the concept of time travel without getting into some very serious weirdness.

2 An example: If you hitch a ride into the past on a time machine and prevent your parents from meeting, does that mean you won't be born? And if you weren't born, how could you have gone back in time in the first place?

3 Those who study the idea of time travel have a word for these little hang-ups: paradoxes.

4 There are many of them—not the least of which is that if time travel will ever exist, then it must, in a sense, exist right now. (In fact, there could be time travelers from the future among us at this moment.)

B. Read any notes in the margins, any words that are bolded or in italics, any words inside of quotation marks, and any numbers. ·········

C. Read the first paragraph, the first sentence of each paragraph, and the last paragraph. (If an article has many small paragraphs, like this example, just skim each paragraph by taking a quick glance at it.) ·

5   But no mere paradox has ever kept people from dreaming about traversing time, about going back 400 years to chill with Bill Shakespeare or journeying forward a century or so to play catch with one's own great-grandkids.

6   Ideas about the mechanics of time travel may have changed greatly between, say 1895, when H.G. Wells wrote "The Time Machine," and 1985, when Hollywood made "Back to the Future."

7   But the motivations are no different: To break free from the tyranny of time, to race ahead and see splendors to come, or go back and relive historic events. And maybe, just maybe, even fiddle with a few things.

8   So: Is it possible? Is there a chance that humans will ever travel through time?

9   Well, don't book your vacation for Renaissance Italy just yet. For one thing, you'll need a lot of vaccinations, lest you come back and infect the 20th Century with long-vanquished diseases.

10   For another, no one on Earth is anywhere near ready to build a working time machine right now (a few highly suspect claims on the Internet notwithstanding).

11   But—and this is a very qualified "but"—some physicists believe there is a

II. Understand the reading.

As you read, use several strategies to get more out of your reading.

A. Analyze the selection to understand who the author is writing for—the general public, or a specific target audience. *—general public, college students?*

B. Figure out the author's purpose—to inform, entertain, persuade, a combination of these, or a different purpose. *—to inspire, to persuade?*

C. Look for the main idea of the reading, the key points, and important details and examples.*—Time travel may be possible, science fiction deals with it, great literature offers a kind of time travel.*

D. Try to guess the meaning of new words and unfamiliar expressions from the words around them (the context). Use a dictionary only when it's absolutely necessary in order to understand the key points of the reading.*—paradoxes = "hang-ups," glitches, problems?*

E. Read "between the lines" (make inferences). Look to see if the author makes any points indirectly, even if they are not stated directly.*—We should be reading great literature to expand our minds into the past and future.*

theoretical basis for the possibility of time travel through wormholes—tunnels that, according to quantum physics, could act as "shortcuts" between points in space and time.

12   One problem: No one has ever actually seen a wormhole, although tiny ones are believed to lurk in something called "quantum foam," strange stuff that is believed to exist at the subatomic level—in other words, it's very, very tiny.

13   Another problem: Even if wormholes are real, no one has any idea how one would go about enlarging them or harnessing them for use in time travel.

14   A more straightforward, if as yet unattainable, method of traveling into the future would be simply to hop on a spaceship and accelerate to near the speed of light. Moving at this speed actually slows down time, at least relative to a stationary observer.

15   Thus, when you returned home after a couple of years, time (at least for earthlings) could have advanced by centuries. And everyone here would have forgotten you. Except, of course, for the Internal Revenue Service.

* * *

F. Use your judgment to decide whether the author is presenting unbiased information and using clear logic.—*The author devotes more of the article to great literature than he does to the possibility of scientific time travel. Could he be biased more toward literature than toward science? Or is he just being realistic?*

16   With the time-travel theories of scientists either too hard to grasp or just too darned dry, science fiction has leapt into the void, offering its own notions of how to fool Father Time.

17   Many of the stories and movies on the subject fall into the Barcalounger School of Time Travel: Basically, you plop into a chair attached to a time machine (or car, or spacecraft) of mysterious construction, and—boom! —24th Century, here we come. Think of Wells' "The Time Machine," or the movies "Back to the Future" and "Twelve Monkeys."

18   Other stories have offered more romantic notions of time travel. In both the novel "Time and Again" and the movie "Somewhere in Time" (adapted from a novel), the main characters journey back in time through little but sheer willpower.

19   Both happen to be love stories. "Time and Again" was produced as a musical at San Diego's Old Globe Theatre three years ago. "Somewhere in Time," released in 1981, has amassed such a cult following that its fans hold regular conventions and its Web site offers a range of movie-themed collectibles.

20   Some writers, turning away from the idea of physically traveling through time, have jumped straight ahead to deal with the possible consequences of changing the past. They've spawned a highly popular genre, the alternative history.

21   What if John F. Kennedy had survived his wounds? What if Hitler

III. **Interact with the reading.**

As you read, mark important information with a highlighter, marker, or pen. Then look back over the reading again and mark anything you missed the first time.

A. Make a note in the margin next to the main idea of the reading, or write the main idea in your own words.— *"Real" time travel may be theoretically possible some day, but at the present time we can enjoy another kind of time travel based on the human imagination by reading science fiction stories about the future and great literature from the past.*

B. Highlight the key points that the author makes.

C. Circle or underline important details and examples.

D. Make margin notes of anything you think is important.

could have been stopped before Germany invaded Poland?

22 Alternative historians start with such ideas, and then construct whole new worlds around them—traveling through time into universes that might have been.

interesting to think about

* * *

23 And in a sense, great literature offers a kind of time travel, too. Not only can it transport a reader back to a vividly realized past, but it also can carry the writer forward into our own time, so that he or she speaks to us as if sitting in the same room.

24 No one knew this better than the American poet Walt Whitman. In "Crossing Brooklyn Ferry," one of his most affecting works, Whitman addresses the reader directly, as if to dismiss the very notion of a barrier between his time and ours.

25 He elucidates the bonds between our worldly experiences and his—*Just as you feel when you look on the river and sky, so I felt* — and then says:

What is it then between us?
What is the count of the scores of hundreds of years between us?
Whatever it is, it avails not—
distance avails not, and place avails not.

26 Without wormholes or gizmos or strange devices of any kind—with nothing but words on a page—the poet has broken the shackles of the finite and leaped straight into the present.

27 Human imagination. Now *there's* a time machine.

inspirational!

IV. Review the reading.

After you read, fix the important information from the selection firmly in your mind.

A. Ask yourself or your classmates about the reading, including *who, what, when, where, how,* and *why* questions, and jot down short answers in your notebook.

Who—scientists, science fiction authors, writers of great literature, readers

What—real time travel, science fiction speculations about the future and alternative histories, great literature

When—past, present, future

Where—here, outer space, anywhere

How—scientifically, by reading, or by using the human imagination

Why—to expand our minds; "has broken the shackles of the finite" = has escaped the limits of being stuck in the present time

B. Write a short summary of the selection or make a list of important points. One way to do this is to start with the main idea of the reading, then the main point or topic of each paragraph.

If an article includes many short paragraphs, include the main point of each section instead of each paragraph.

Summary:

"Real" time travel presents some scientific challenges and paradoxes but may be theoretically possible someday. In the meantime, we can enjoy another kind of time travel based on the human imagination.

Many books and movies have been produced from science fiction stories about the future and alternative histories that show the effects of changing the past.

Great literature is another form of time travel—a way of transporting the words and ideas of the past into the present time (and even the future!).

V. Reflect on the reading.
Evaluate if and how the reading can be useful to you for your own writing.

A. Respond to the reading by writing down new ideas that interested you, related thoughts you have on the topic, your opinion of the value of this reading, things to reflect on, or even how you felt when you read it.[1]

B. Observe what types of writing are used and how the selection is organized.

C. Take note of any special techniques or styles that the author uses effectively.

D. Memorize key vocabulary or keep a personal vocabulary list in your notebook.

E. Note any effective grammar structures that might work well in your own writing.

A. *Time travel looks easy in the movies, but I can see it's not going to be that simple. I wonder if people will ever travel in time for real. I want to see some of the movies on time travel that were listed in this article.*

B. *The writing seems to be an honest look at time travel from three points of view. I guess this reading is a combination of explanatory, inspirational, and persuasive writing.*
The three sections are scientific, science fiction, and great literature.

C. *The author gives the meanings of many words from context: paradoxes, traversing, alternative history, wormholes, quantum foam, gizmos. He also includes a number of references to books and movies to illustrate his points.*

D. • *alternative history   a what-would-have-happened-if story.*
• *paradox   a situation that can't exist but it does*
• *quantum physics _____ (I need to look this one up in the dictionary)*

E. *(Past unreal conditional)*
• *What if John F. Kennedy had survived his wounds?*
• *What if Hitler could have been stopped before Germany invaded Poland?*

---

[1]Adapted from *Check It Out: A Quick and Easy Guide for Writers*. Anna Ingalls and Dan Moody, Longman, New York, 2001. Pages 15–16.

CULTURAL AND SOCIAL ISSUES

American Fish

R. A. SASAKI

Each group of immigrants to the United States has made unique contributions to our multiethnic, multicultural society. The following short story is from a collection titled *The Loom and Other Short Stories* by third-generation Japanese-American author R. A. Sasaki.

This story consists almost entirely of a conversation between two Japanese-American women. The story is interesting because of what lies beneath the surface—their attitudes toward each other and how they have both been affected by their experiences in America.

P R E R E A D I N G   Q U E S T I O N S

1. What kinds of things do people talk about when they haven't seen each other for a long time?

2. Do you think that different cultures have different unwritten rules about how one is expected to be polite and courteous to others?

V O C A B U L A R Y

daikon radish a long white radish from Japan

burdock a weedy plant

boasting bragging, glorifying oneself

consoling reassuring, offering comfort

refrained held back, used self-control to resist doing something

aggravating annoying

peeved irritated

shriveled dried out and shrunken

groped tried uncertainly to find

redeem to compensate or make up for something, such as a previous mistake

bumped into met accidentally

AMERICAN FISH

Mrs. Hayashi was inspecting a daikon radish in the American Fish Market in Japantown when she recognized a woman who was heading toward the burdock roots.

2   I know her, she thought. What was her name? Suzuki? Kato? She decided to pretend not to see the woman, and see if the woman recognized her. She put down the radish and picked up another.

3   "Oh . . . hello," said the woman, who was now standing next to her.

4   Mrs. Hayashi looked up and smiled enthusiastically. "Oh, hi!" she said. "Long time no see." Immediately she regretted the remark. What if it was someone she had just seen yesterday?

5   "How've you been?" the woman asked.

6   "Fine, just fine," Mrs. Hayashi said. I should ask her about her husband, she thought. Did she have a husband?

7   "How's your husband?" the woman asked.

8   Mrs. Hayashi's husband had died ten years before. Obviously, the woman was someone she had not seen in quite some time. Thank goodness, she thought. Then it had been appropriate to say "long time no see."

9   "He passed away several years ago," Mrs. Hayashi said.

10   "Oh, so sorry to hear that," the woman said.

11   I should ask her about her children, Mrs. Hayashi thought. But since she still did not know if the woman had a husband or not, she couldn't very well assume that she had children. Wouldn't it be awful if I asked her about her children and it turned out she wasn't even married! And even if she was married, and did have children, what if they had died, or committed crimes? After all, everyone couldn't have a son in law school, and Mrs. Hayashi did not like to appear to be boasting. No, she'd better avoid the subject of children.

12   "How are your kids?" the woman asked.

13   "Oh, Bill is just fine," Mrs. Hayashi replied. She couldn't stand it. "He'll be graduating from law school next spring," she added, consoling herself with the thought that at least she had refrained from mentioning that her son was at the top of his class.

14   "That's nice," said the woman. "And what about your daughter?"

15   "I don't have a daughter," Mrs. Hayashi said stiffly. "Just a son." She was beginning to think that the woman wasn't anyone she knew very well.

16   "Stupid me," said the woman. "I was thinking of someone else."

17   "How are *your* children?" Mrs. Hayashi asked, throwing caution to the wind.

18   "Fine," the woman said. "Emily and her husband live in San Jose and have two little girls."

19   "How nice," Mrs. Hayashi said.

20   There was a pause. Mrs. Hayashi did not know anyone named Emily. Who was this woman?

21   It occurred to her that the woman might be someone she didn't like. How aggravating, she thought, not to be able to remember whether to be pleasant to someone or not.

22   "I'm so sorry," the woman said, "But I have a real bad memory for names. It was Suzuki-san, wasn't it?"

23   "Hayashi," Mrs. Hayashi said, peeved. "Grace Hayashi."

24   "Of course," said the woman, somewhat vaguely. "Hayashi . . ."

25   "And . . . forgive me," said Mrs. Hayashi, seizing the opportunity, "but you're . . .?"
26   "Nakamura," the woman said. "Toshi Nakamura."
27   The name did not even ring a bell.
28   "Is that the family that runs the bakery on Fillmore?" Mrs. Hayashi asked.
29   "No," the woman said, "not that Nakamura."
30   "Then you must be related to Frank Nakamura."
31   "No."
32   "How odd," Mrs. Hayashi said without thinking, and was embarrassed when she realized she had spoken aloud.
33   "My maiden name was Fujii," Mrs. Nakamura said.
34   "Fujii . . ." Mrs. Hayashi said, thinking hard.
35   "Maybe you know my sister Eiko."
36   "Eiko Fujii . . ." Mrs. Hayashi said, frowning.
37   Then a horrible thought occurred to Mrs. Hayashi. Perhaps she did not know this woman at all; perhaps Mrs. Nakamura just looked like someone she knew, or someone she should know— a Japanese-American lady in her late fifties, the same age as Mrs. Hayashi, wearing a somewhat faded but sensible raincoat even though it was not raining outside. But then, Mrs. Nakamura had recognized her, too.
38   "Did I know you in Topaz?" Mrs. Hayashi asked.
39   "Oh, no," Mrs. Nakamura said. Mrs. Hayashi waited, but the other woman said nothing further.
40   "You weren't in Topaz?" Mrs. Hayashi continued.
41   "No."
42   "Where were you—Manzanar?" Mrs. Hayashi asked pleasantly.
43   "No."
44   "Oh, well," Mrs. Hayashi said, becoming flustered. "Perhaps you weren't in camp during the war. I don't mean to pry."
45   "I was in Tule Lake," Mrs. Nakamura said, turning to pick through the burdock roots. She rejected a shriveled bunch of roots and put a fresh bunch in her cart.
46   "Oh," Mrs. Hayashi said. She felt her face go hot. Tule Lake was where all those branded "disloyal" had been imprisoned during the war. "I see," Mrs. Hayashi said, searching for a way to change the topic.

47   "Do you?"

48   Mrs. Hayashi was startled. "I'm sorry," she said. "I don't know what you mean."

49   "And I don't know what you see," Mrs. Nakamura said.

50   "Nothing," Mrs. Hayashi said. "I just meant—oh."

51   "Oh," Mrs. Nakamura said.

52   Mrs. Hayashi by this time was extremely uncomfortable and groped for a way to redeem the situation.

53   "I knew some people who were in Tule Lake," she said. "The Satos. From Watsonville. Did you know them?"

54   "No," Mrs. Nakamura said.

55   "It was the silliest thing, really," Mrs. Hayashi went on. "Mr. Sato was a Buddhist priest, and after Pearl Harbor, his name got on some list, and the FBI picked him up. Imagine that."

56   Mrs. Nakamura was silent.

57   "As if being Buddhist was a crime," Mrs. Hayashi added, trying to make clear where her sympathies lay. She was not a Buddhist herself, but she thought Mrs. Nakamura might be one.

58   "My father said he wanted to go back to Japan," Mrs. Nakamura said suddenly. "That's why we were in Tule Lake."

59   "Oh," Mrs. Hayashi said.

60   "They took his boat away after Pearl Harbor," Mrs. Nakamura continued. "He was a fisherman down in Terminal Island. Without a boat, he couldn't make a living. He thought the only thing to do was to go back to Japan."

61   "I know," Mrs. Hayashi said. "My father was forced to sell his store to the first person who offered to buy. A lifetime of hard work, just thrown away!"

62   "It made my father mad," Mrs. Nakamura went on. "He said why stay in a country that doesn't want us?"

63   "That's perfectly logical," Mrs. Hayashi reassured. "Why indeed?"

64   "Why did *your* parents want to stay?" Mrs. Nakamura asked.

65   "Well," Mrs. Hayashi said, startled. "I don't know." She thought for a moment, then said, "I guess they knew that we, I mean my brothers and sisters and I, would never want to go to Japan. I mean, we were born here. We belonged here. And they wanted the family to stay together."

66   "That's how my mother and I felt," Mrs. Nakamura said. "That's why we said we wanted to go back to Japan, too—so we'd be all together. Except in those days, that made you disloyal."

67   "Well, it was ridiculous," Mrs. Hayashi said firmly. "And it caused so much grief."

68   There was a silence.

69   "Where did you go back to, in Japan?" Mrs. Hayashi asked gently.

70   "Oh, we didn't go back," Mrs. Nakamura replied cheerfully. "My father changed his mind when he remembered that they didn't have central heating in Japan."

71   Both women burst out laughing.

72   Mrs. Hayashi, still laughing, threw a bunch of burdock roots into her cart.

73   "Well, I should be getting along," Mrs. Nakamura said. "I'm so glad I bumped into you . . ." She stopped, embarrassed.

74   "Hayashi."

75   ". . . Hayashi-san," she finished. "Now if I could just remember who you are."

76   They laughed again.

77   "I'm sure it'll come back to us," Mrs. Hayashi said. "Everything does."

78   "Do you go to the Buddhist church?" Mrs. Nakamura asked. "Maybe I've seen you there."

79   "I doubt it," Mrs. Hayashi replied. "I'm Methodist. But I've been to funerals at the Buddhist church, so maybe."

80   "That must be it—we must have met at someone's funeral," Mrs. Nakamura agreed. "I'm sure it'll come to me as soon as I walk out of here with my groceries. Isn't it always like that?"

81   "It can't be that mysterious," Mrs. Hayashi said. "I mean, our lives aren't so terribly complicated. If we didn't know each other in camp, then we knew each other before the war, or after the war. I'm sure I won't be able to sleep until I remember which it was," she added cheerfully. "I hate to forget things. That is, unless they're the sort of things you'd rather not remember."

82   Mrs. Nakamura looked at her watch.

83   "My goodness," she said. "I have to run. I have to be at work in an hour."

84   "Work?" Mrs. Hayashi said.

85   "Yes; I work at Macy's," Mrs. Nakamura said. "I'm in . . ."

86   "Gift wrap!" Mrs. Hayashi said, remembering.

87   The two women stared incredulously at each other for an instant, then broke into raucous laughter. Then they bowed slightly, and continued on their separate ways.

A.   COMPREHENSION

1. At the beginning of the story, why does Mrs. Hayashi have trouble deciding whether or not to speak to Mrs. Nakamura and what to say to her?

2. In what ways do the two women seem to be alike?

3. At what point in the story do the two women seem to be a little bit annoyed with each other, possibly even angry? How does the topic of their conversation affect their feelings?

4. Why do the women laugh together three times near the end of the story? What does their laughter tell us about the change in their relationship?

B.   CRITICAL THINKING

1. If the two women had been Mexican American, African American, Anglo American, or another ethnic combination, do you think their conversation would have been different? How so? Give reasons for your answer.

2. Why does Mrs. Hayashi feel that she ought to be careful about the kinds of questions she asks and the things she says? Give at least two examples from the story.

3. Do the two characters in this short story seem believable and realistic (that is, like real people)? Why or why not?

4. Why is it especially difficult for the two women to talk about the time when their families were in camps? How do you think they feel about that period of their lives?

5. Do you think the women will become friends? Why or why not?

C . LANGUAGE AND VOCABULARY

1. Had you ever heard the expression "throwing caution to the wind" before you read it in the story? What does it sound like it means? Take your best guess at the meaning, and look it up if you need to. Then write a sentence about a time when you or someone else threw caution to the wind.

2. At first, much of the conversation consists of ordinary, everyday comments and questions. Find at least three examples of these routine phrases or sentences near the beginning of the story. Are these typical greetings that Americans exchange with acquaintances or with friends they have not seen in a while?

D . STYLE, STRUCTURE, AND ORGANIZATION

1. Whose point of view is "American Fish" told from? To answer this question, look at the story to see which character's thoughts and feelings are frequently included. How do these thoughts and feelings help us understand the story?

2. Does the ending make the story seem complete? Why or why not?

E . TOPICS FOR DISCUSSION OR JOURNAL WRITING

1. Have you ever had a similar experience of seeing someone you weren't sure you knew? How did you feel?

2. If you were in Mrs. Hayashi's or Mrs. Nakamura's place, how would you have handled the situation? Would you have said or done anything differently?

3. Do you come from a mixed cultural background, or do you know someone else who does? Are you aware of any conflicts or differences between the two cultures?

4. Based on what you learned in this story, do you think Japanese Americans were treated unfairly during World War II? Explain your answer.

F. WRITING TOPICS FOR PARAGRAPHS OR ESSAYS

1. Write about some of the problems that you or someone you know has had in adjusting to a move from one culture to another.

2. Write a short story similar to "American Fish," based on a conversation between two people. Choose two characters who are in an uncomfortable situation or who disagree with each other. Make their conversation, or *dialogue*, sound as real as possible. You may also want to include some of the thoughts of one or both characters.

3. Read another short story by R. A. Sasaki or by another Asian-American author, such as Amy Tan. Write a summary of the story, plus your evaluation and personal response. You may also want to comment on any similarities you see between that story and "American Fish."

4. Look up information about the United States' internment of Japanese citizens and Japanese Americans during World War II. Write a paper about what you learn. Include your opinion about the internment camps.

5. Write an imaginary scene with *dialogue* (conversation) between you and Mrs. Hayashi. How would you get acquainted? What would you talk about? If you wish, you may imagine that you know her son or grandson.

Listen to Me Good

MARGARET CHARLES SMITH
AND LINDA JANET HOLMES

Margaret Charles Smith learned to be a midwife at a time when very few doctors were available in rural areas of the United States, and the overwhelming majority of African-American babies were born at home. As you read this collection of short selections from *Listen to Me Good: The Life Story of an Alabama Midwife*, look for evidence of the conflict between traditional African-American midwives and the medical establishment of doctors and nurses.

PREREADING QUESTIONS

1. In this country, where do most women choose to have their babies, at home or in the hospital? Why do you think that is?

2. Is modern medicine always better than traditional methods of healing people?

VOCABULARY

walk a pain off in this case, walk around until the birth contraction stops again

to get a kick out of something to enjoy something very much

lantern light light from a kerosene lantern (because many houses had no electricity)

incubator in this case, a small tent or box that keeps premature, underweight, or sick babies warm

the pen short form of *penitentiary*, a prison where inmates often serve extended sentences

getting out in this case, becoming known (dialect)

tea in this case, a hot drink made from local plants and herbs that is supposed to help ease a mother's labor pains

clinic a local medical center, not as big as a hospital

LISTEN TO ME GOOD

Listen to me good. Back when I started, it was kind of poor. At that time, the people didn't have nothing. You couldn't get nothing. They had to do the very best they could. Some of them didn't have places to sit. They didn't even have a piece of white sheet, clean or nothing. I'd have to get up sometime and go to the next-door house and ask her to give me some clean rags, if she had 'em. Just barely living.

* * *

2   I took training courses, but the midwife had already trained me, Ella Anderson. I learned everything, learned how to ask the mother if she was ready—does she have all her equipment ready? You know— the newspaper, something to boil the water in, something for the baby. But you just didn't need nothing new for the baby. Somebody else may have some things you could borrow or use. See what I mean? But everything, everything I learned, I learned from Miss Anderson. See, Miss Ella Anderson had done learned me, and I didn't forget it.

* * *

3   Then sometimes, I'd tell the mother to go take a hot bath, and that hot water helps a lot. I sit their feet in hot water or let them sit in that tub, if they got it, a number three tub. I was willing to let them have their way until push comes to shove. Some of them would say, "I don't want to take a bath."

4   I'd say, "Just get in the tub, and I'll bathe you." I was right there to get them out, but some of them just wouldn't do it.

* * *

5   Sometime they want to get up, and I'd help them up. Walk around in the room. Walk a pain off then get back in the bed. A lot of people get a kick out of walking. Go into different rooms and sit in different chairs, or get down on their knees—anywhere they

think they can get ease. But there's no ease for birth till it's over with. It's good to walk, but you'll have to stop sometime.

* * *

6   The houses would be so cold, you would almost freeze sitting beside her bed. The fireplace up here in the front of the house, and you back yonder on the bed. You had to peep to see what's happening down there, and you have to do it by lantern light until the people got to the place where they had better lights.

* * *

7   The nurse would come after the baby was born, if I gave her word to come. If you weighed the baby, and the baby is underweight, then you call your nurse to bring out the incubator. They used to have the one that runs with hot water bottles.

* * *

8   Now, the nurses didn't know what was good and what was bad. You can't take too much of anything. You just need enough to warm you up inside and get those pains a-moving, if you done done everything you can do on the outside.

9   I had to stop fooling with those teas and things in labor because my name was getting out.

* * *

10   They said, "They better not catch nobody giving nobody no tea of no kind. If they do, she was going to jail and from there to the pen."

11   So, I didn't figure I wanted to go to the pen, but they had a couple midwives that still gave a woman teas. They had the nurses to come and the doctor that was the head of the clinic, and a couple more white ladies. I don't know who they were or where they were from. But they sure got that midwife ripped about them teas. They told her the best thing you do when you go home, get your bag and come back to town. Bring your bag in because you're going to kill somebody.

12   You know, they're quick to think teas and things are going to kill somebody. One midwife told the nurse when we had the meeting, she just told her, "I think I'll bring my bag in and give it to you all because you all are not there when this labor is going on. You don't know how it goes. Rubbing helps and teas help. If I can't give them some hot teas which I know will help, I just as well ought to give it up."

* * *

13   All they wanted was the midwives off. Training was the last thing they wanted. They wrote me at the health department that I couldn't be no more midwife. I had to bring my bag and my equipment in, not only me, but all of them that was delivering.

* * *

14   Everybody goes to the hospital now. Some of them feel pretty good about it, and some don't. But if you go to the hospital, you're going to pay some money.

15   The doctors have made them so much money. They take two thousand, three thousand for delivering one baby. That's a lot of money, and you're doing all the work.

16   I think it's just better to stay home than to go to the hospital. Go to the hospital, have your baby, get up and go home the next day? I'd have the baby at home and let that do.

17   You can have your way more at home. You can have your own freedom at home. You won't have to lay down until your time come. You can get up and do things. The baby won't have to be drugged before birth from giving you those shots to knock you out.

* * *

18   I'm worth millions of dollars for what I've done done. I thought I was doing a big thing. I was proud of it. The lives that I've saved, going to deliver all these babies, till I got something to be thankful for. The children have grown so. Some of them have to bend their heads down to hardly get in that door. They have grown just that way. I am thankful, yeah.

A .   C O M P R E H E N S I O N

1.   How did Margaret Smith learn to be a midwife?

2.   What things did a midwife need in order to deliver a baby?

3.   Why did a nurse sometimes come to the house after a baby was born?

4.   According to the selection, what are some benefits of having a baby at home?

B . CRITICAL THINKING

1. Based on the reading, what social and economic changes led to fewer midwives delivering babies?

2. How does the author, Margaret Smith, feel about doctors, nurses, and hospitals? Find at least two examples in the reading to support your answer.

3. Do you think the author's viewpoint might be biased against modern medicine?

4. Do you think that the doctors and nurses in this selection were biased against traditional midwives and delivering babies at home?

C . LANGUAGE AND VOCABULARY

1. What does the author mean when she writes, "But they sure got that midwife ripped about them teas"?

2. Using her rural dialect, the author writes, "At that time, the people didn't have nothing. You couldn't get nothing." In the past, even well-known authors such as William Shakespeare used double negatives. Is it acceptable to use double negatives in academic writing today, such as in papers for college classes?

D . STYLE, STRUCTURE, AND ORGANIZATION

1. The author of these selections writes in her own voice, the dialect of one area of the rural South. Does using dialect make the selections feel richer and more authentic?

2. This reading consists of selections taken from various places in the book. Do you think these selections give a good picture of a midwife's job in the mid 1900s in a poor area of the country?

3. How does the conclusion wrap up the topic and make the selection feel finished?

E. TOPICS FOR DISCUSSION OR JOURNAL WRITING

1. Do you believe in natural methods of healing and childbirth, or do you think that births should take place in hospitals?

2. What is alternative medicine? Is it as effective as modern medical practices, such as surgery and drugs?

3. In your opinion, what are some benefits of having a baby in a hospital? What are some benefits of having a baby at home?

4. Why do you think the doctors and nurses in the story didn't want the midwives giving herbal teas (made from local plants) to expectant mothers? Do you agree?

5. Some religions do not approve of certain medical techniques, such as blood transfusions. Should people have the right to refuse medical treatment that they don't want?

F. WRITING TOPICS FOR PARAGRAPHS OR ESSAYS

1. Describe a hospital experience you have had, or interview someone else who has been a patient in a hospital.

2. If you have had a baby, give some advice to an expectant mother or father.

3. Look up information in a library or on the Internet about one or more of the following health professionals: osteopaths, chiropractors, homeopaths, and acupuncturists. Then write a report about what you learn. How well are they accepted by the medical establishment? What is your opinion about them?

4. Interview a midwife, a nurse, an obstetrician, an anesthesiologist, or any other person who helps deliver babies. Prepare a list of questions in advance. After the interview, write about what it's like to help babies come into this world.

5. Choose one of the following health-related topics. Find out more
about the topic by searching online or in a library; then write about it.

    a. What is alternative medicine? Are some types of alternative
medicine as effective as modern medical methods?

    b. Compare two different methods of labor and delivery, such as
Lamaze, Bradley, Leboyer, or Waterbirth (underwater delivery).

Boomer Parents

SANDY BANKS

The baby boomer generation grew up with events such as the Vietnam War protests, the Civil Rights Movement, and the assassination of President John F. Kennedy. A popular saying, "Don't trust anyone over 30," showed that many boomers questioned all forms of authority.

Now that boomers are raising their own teenagers, they must deal with being authority figures themselves. As you read this newspaper article, think about how strict—or how lenient—parents should be with their teenage sons and daughters.

PREREADING QUESTIONS

1. Who are the "baby boomers"?
2. Do most parents share the same standards for raising their children?

VOCABULARY

catered food party food delivered and served by a restaurant or catering service

bellied up came forward and stood close (slang)

swig swallow quickly, gulp

grimaced made a face, frowned

adhered stuck

disabuse (oneself) of stop believing something false

thicket in this case, a large number (of difficult choices), tangle

blissfully very happily

off-guard with one's defenses down

SATs Scholastic Aptitude Tests, a widely used college entrance exam

unwittingly without meaning to, without realizing

albeit although

risqué daring and possibly offensive

spill out my contrition tell them how sorry I am

obscenity-laced full of offensive language

schlep carry, transport

ambivalence lack of enthusiasm

lyrics words

28

BOOMER PARENTS

They were new neighbors, decent enough people with nice cars, a well-maintained home, one handsome, well-behaved young son. Their housewarming party was an all-night affair, with good music, catered food, a poolside bar.

2   It was long past midnight when the kids began crowding the patio bar. A bunch of 12-year-olds, arms outstretched, paper cups in hand. "Can you put a little vodka in this, please," the young son of the hostess politely inquired.

3   The bartender eyed him suspiciously. "For you?" she asked. "You must be kidding."

4   "For me," he said, thrusting his cup toward her. "C'mon . . . my mom said it's OK." The bartender shook her head and put the vodka bottle away. "I don't serve children." Then mom breezed up, uncapped the bottle and poured a short stream of vodka into her son's cup. "Just a capful," she announced resolutely, as if she were handing out candy on Halloween. Her son's buddies bellied up to the bar . . . capfuls of vodka all around.

5   A few party-goers raised voices in protest: Aren't they a little young? Isn't that illegal? But we grew quiet when Mom waved us off, as if she were guilty of nothing more serious than serving cake before dinner. "Oh, it's not going to hurt them. It's just a capful . . . what's the big deal?"

6   I rose to leave, feeling heartsick as I watched these little boys swig vodka. They grimaced as they choked it down, then slapped high-fives to celebrate. And I couldn't help but think about their mothers, blissfully ignorant at home, never dreaming that a sleepover would make social drinkers of their preteen sons.

7   Or maybe not. Maybe they serve their kids liquor too.

* * *

8   It was easy when my three children were small to imagine that every family was just like ours, followed the same conventions, adhered to the same set of parenting rules. But the older they get, the more I realize how little I know about what goes on in homes that once seemed very much like my own.

9   I have had to disabuse myself of the notion that every "good" parent is raising his or her kids just like I am, that there is one

universal set of behavioral standards that guides us all through this thicket of parenting choices.

10   Still, I am caught off-guard by what I see and hear:

11   An 11-year-old lets loose with a string of swear words. Her mother shushes her gently with this admonition: "Now you know you're not to talk that way in public." How can that be? These are good parents, responsible, well-educated. Mom stays at home with her kids, sends them to Catholic school . . . and lets them curse around the dinner table.

12   My baby-sitter opens her mouth to show my daughters her birthday present—a giant gold stud pierced through her tongue. She is 16, still wears braces on her teeth, is deemed by her mom too young to date. Yet piercing her tongue seems somehow not extreme. "My mom got hers pierced too," she tells us. "And if I do well on my SATs, she might let me get a tattoo for Christmas."

13   I question their choices, then suddenly, unwittingly, I land on the outlaw mother side.

14   I've invited my daughters' friends to join us for a movie. They are 9- and 11-years-old—suburban girls like mine, sheltered, but not naive. The movie—"Nutty Professor II"—is PG-13.

15   It is raucously funny, albeit a little risqué. I laugh but cringe at the off-color gags and four-letter words. But the theater is full of children, so how bad can this be? Very bad, I realize later, when I'm confronted by a disapproving 11-year-old. "Did you guys like the movie," I ask, as we gather our things to leave.

16   My daughter glances at her friend, who shakes her head and looks away. "It was inappropriate, Mommy," my daughter says firmly. "I didn't think you'd let us watch something with so many bad words."

17   Our guests are quiet as I drive them home. Could it be this is unlike anything their own mothers would have let them see? I rehearse in my mind the apologies I'll have to deliver. And when I drop them off and spill out my contrition, I see in the eyes of their mothers disappointment, and this unspoken question:

18   "What kind of mother is she?"

·   * * *

19   They are not the "family values" politicians crow about, these micro issues we confront in the day-to-day raising of our kids. But they are the choices that go to the heart of who we are as parents and families today.

20   How much freedom is too much for our children? At what age do you let them go off alone to Magic Mountain? Is a 9-year-old too young for a second hole in her ear? Should I let my 15-year-old see an R-rated movie, my 11-year-old listen to her friend's obscenity-laced rap CD?

21   I imagine I am no different than many parents, caught in a muddle of confusion over shifting standards and sensibilities.

22   "It's not hard to know how we feel about the big issues," says USC sociology professor Constance Ahrons. "What's harder is the small stuff that comes up day to day, the decisions that raising children forces you to make. That's where we're bombarded with pressures, and every parent is not going to respond the same way."

23   Surveys show that more than half of parents today think they are doing a worse job raising kids than their parents did. They admit that they're often confused by the choices they face, and disappointed in the course they take.

24   "The problem is not neglectful parents," says David Blankenhorn, director of the research group the Institute for American Values.

25   "It's us—the baby boomers . . . folks with nice homes, two cars in the garage, who love our kids, schlep them to soccer practice and piano lessons, make enormous sacrifices to give them the best we can," yet shortchange them in a very important way.

26   "Because we were raised to be skeptical of authority, we have this fundamental ambivalence about being authoritative," he says. "Remember, 'Don't trust anybody over 30'? . . . Well, now here we are, middle-aged people with teenage kids and young children, and we don't want to tell them what to do. So we don't."

27   So before we blame the lyrics in the music, the trash on TV, the violence of video games, perhaps we ought to look in the mirror and ask ourselves: Who is really in charge? Are we leading or following, guiding or giving up? Are we making our children choose on their own which road to stumble down?

A. COMPREHENSION

1. What did the bartender tell the children when they wanted some vodka?

2. In some of today's families, certain standards of behavior are different from the standards that most families had in the past. What are two examples from the reading?

3. How did the author's daughter and her friends feel about the PG-13 movie that the author took them to see?

4. Besides parenting styles, what other influences on children are listed in the article?

B. CRITICAL THINKING

1. Who is the author's intended audience—in other words, who is the writer primarily directing this article to?

2. What is the main idea of the reading?

3. According to the article, who is responsible for the way children turn out?

4. How do you think the author feels about her own parenting skills?

5. How do you think the generation called "baby boomers" got that name? How old are the baby boomers now?

C. LANGUAGE AND VOCABULARY

1. What does "mom breezed up" mean (in the fourth paragraph)? Besides the basic meaning, what impressions does the expression "breezed up" give the reader?

2. One of the sentences in this article says that the girls are "sheltered, but not naive." What is the difference between *sheltered* and *naive* in this sentence?

D. STYLE, STRUCTURE, AND ORGANIZATION

1. In this article, the author uses many personal examples to *show* the reader what she means rather than just *tell* her points. Do these personal examples make the article more effective? Why?

2. The author includes a lot of *questions* in this article. Find and underline at least five of the author's questions. How does using so many questions help set the *tone* (or *feel*) of the reading?

3. There are many short paragraphs in this reading, each with a small chunk of meaning. How is this style, which is commonly used in newspaper articles, different from the style used in papers written for college classes?

E. TOPICS FOR DISCUSSION OR JOURNAL WRITING

1. What would you do if you learned that your child had been exposed to something you don't approve of at a friend's house?

2. Is raising children more difficult today than it was in the past? Why?

3. People need a license to drive a car, open a business, or teach school, but anyone can have children. In a perfect world, what qualifications would parents have before they started raising children?

4. Do you think the author of this article is a strict parent? Is that good or bad?

5. In your opinion, will raising children in the future be easier or harder? Why?

F. WRITING TOPICS FOR PARAGRAPHS OR ESSAYS

1. What is the best way to raise children? Provide some advice for new parents.

2. Write about some things your parents did well in raising you or that you have done well in raising your own children.

3. Describe some of the bad or dangerous influences on children in today's society, and recommend a way for parents and young people to deal with these influences.

4. Compare a typical day in the life of two children, one in the 1960s or 1970s and one today.

5. Choose one of the following topics. Find out more about the topic by searching online or in a library; then write a short paper on the effects of that activity.
   a. How can learning to drink alcohol at a young age affect a person later in life?
   b. What effect does watching violence on TV, in movies, and in video games have on children?

Spanglish Spoken Here

JANICE CASTRO

The United States contains an exciting mix of people from all over the world, each group contributing to our unique culture. The fastest-growing immigrant group in recent decades has been the Hispanic population; as a result, many Spanish words have entered mainstream English and added to its richness. Likewise, many English words are used by Spanish speakers on a daily basis. As you read this article that was first published in 1988, think about which facts may have changed since then (such as statistics) and which situations have not changed.

PREREADING QUESTIONS

1. Do most people in the United States know at least a few words of Spanish? What other languages are spoken in your area of the country?

2. Immigrant groups have always faced prejudice from some people. Do you think that Hispanics face more, less, or about the same levels of prejudice as previous waves of immigrants, such as Africans, Italians, Irish, and Germans?

VOCABULARY

bemused puzzled

miss a beat hesitate

personnel officer a person who accepts job applications and sometimes interviews applicants

free-form without specific rules or boundaries

mode in this case, a way of speaking

syntax grammar, especially word order

handier easier to use

melting pot the idea that the United States "melts" all cultures together into one common culture

Anglo English-speaking

Hispanic of Spanish-speaking origin or family background

Latinos in this case, people of Latin-American origin or background; often used to mean Hispanics

gaffes, blunders, goofs mistakes

inadvertently without intending to, accidentally

mangled badly mistreated

SPANGLISH SPOKEN HERE

In Manhattan a first-grader greets her visiting grandparents, happily exclaiming, "Come here, *siéntate!*" Her bemused grandfather, who does not speak Spanish, nevertheless knows she is asking him to sit down. A Miami personnel officer understands what a job applicant means when he says "*Quiero un* part time." Nor do drivers miss a beat reading a billboard alongside a Los Angeles street advertising CERVEZA—SIX-PACK!

2   This free-form blend of Spanish and English, known as Spanglish, is common linguistic currency wherever concentrations of Hispanic Americans are found in the U.S. In Los Angeles, where 55% of the city's 3 million inhabitants speak Spanish, Spanglish is as much a part of daily life as sunglasses. Unlike the broken-English efforts of earlier immigrants from Europe, Asia, and other regions, Spanglish has become a widely accepted conversational mode used casually—even playfully—by Spanish-speaking immigrants and native-born Californians alike.

3   Consisting of one part Hispanicized English, one part Americanized Spanish and more than a little fractured syntax, Spanglish is a bit like a Robin Williams comedy routine: a crackling line of cross-cultural patter straight from the melting pot. Often it enters Anglo homes and families through the children, who pick it up at school or at play with their young Hispanic contemporaries. In other cases, it comes from watching TV; many an Anglo child watching *Sesame Street* has learned *uno dos tres* almost as quickly as one two three.

4   Spanglish takes a variety of forms, from the Southern California Anglos who bid farewell with the utterly silly "*hasta la* bye-bye" to the Cuban-American drivers in Miami who *parquean* their *carros.* Some Spanglish sentences are mostly Spanish, with a quick detour

for an English word or two. A Latino friend may cut short a
conversation by glancing at his watch and excusing himself with
the explanation that he must "*ir al* supermarket."

5   Many of the English words transplanted in this way are
simply handier than their Spanish counterparts. No matter how
distasteful the subject, for example, it is still easier to say "income
tax" than *impuesto sobre la renta.* At the same time, many Spanish-
speaking immigrants have adopted such terms as VCR, microwave
and dishwasher for what they view as largely American
phenomena. Still other English words convey a cultural context
that is not implicit in the Spanish. A friend who invites you to
lonche most likely has in mind the brisk American custom of
"doing lunch" rather than the languorous afternoon break
traditionally implied by *almuerzo.*

6   Mainstream Americans exposed to similar hybrids of German,
Chinese or Hindi might be mystified. But even Anglos who speak
little or no Spanish are somewhat familiar with Spanglish. Living
among them, for one thing, are 19 million Hispanics. In addition,

more American high school and university students sign up for
Spanish than for any other foreign language.

7   Only in the past ten years, though, has Spanglish begun to turn
into a national slang. Its popularity has grown with the explosive
increases in U.S. immigration from Latin American countries.
English has increasingly collided with Spanish in retail stores,
offices and classrooms, in pop music and on street corners. Anglos
whose ancestors picked up such Spanish words as *rancho, bronco,
tornado* and *incommunicado,* for instance, now freely use such
Spanish words as *gracias, bueno, amigo* and *por favor.*

8   Among Latinos, Spanglish conversations often flow easily from
Spanish into several sentences of English and back again. "It is done
unconsciously," explains Carmen Silva-Corvalan, a Chilean-born
associate professor of linguistics at the University of California who
speaks Spanglish with relatives and neighbors. "I couldn't even tell
you minutes later if I said something in Spanish or English."

9   Spanglish is a sort of code for Latinos: the speakers know
Spanish, but their hybrid language reflects the American culture in
which they live. Many lean to shorter, clipped phrases in place
of the longer, more graceful expressions their parents used. Says
Leonel de la Cuesta, an assistant professor of modern languages at
Florida International University in Miami: "In the U.S., time is
money, and that is showing up in Spanglish as an economy of
language." Conversational examples: *taipiar* (type) and *winshi-wiper*
(windshield wiper) replace *escribir a máquina* and *limpiaparabrisas.*

10   Major advertisers, eager to tap the estimated $134 billion in
spending power wielded by Spanish-speaking Americans, have
ventured into Spanglish to promote their products. In some cases,
attempts to sprinkle Spanish through commercials have produced
embarrassing gaffes. A Braniff airlines ad that sought to tell Spanish-
speaking audiences that they could settle back *en* (in) luxuriant
cuero (leather) seats, for example, inadvertently said they could fly
without clothes (*encuero*). A fractured translation of the Miller Lite
slogan told readers the beer was "Filling, and less delicious." Similar
blunders are often made by Anglos trying to impress Spanish-
speaking pals. But if Latinos are amused by mangled Spanglish, they
also recognize these goofs as a sort of friendly acceptance. As they
might put it, *no problema.*

A. COMPREHENSION

1. What is Spanglish? How does it reflect the culture of those who speak it?

2. What Spanish words listed in the article are commonly used among English speakers in the United States? List at least five.

3. How much spending power did Spanish-speaking Americans control in 1988, when this article was written?

4. What is the most popular foreign language among U.S. high school and university students?

B. CRITICAL THINKING

1. How do you think the author feels about Latino immigration and Spanglish? Is her attitude negative or positive?

2. Is the author's purpose only to inform or also to entertain? How informative is the article and how entertaining?

3. The author's name is Janice Castro. What might that tell you about her family background? Do you think having a Hispanic background could give someone a special insight into the topic of this article?

4. Is this article objective (based on facts and numbers), subjective (based on personal experience and opinion), or both?

C. LANGUAGE AND VOCABULARY

1. In this article, the author uses many *adjectives*—words that describe a noun (person, place, thing, animal, or idea). In the final paragraph, the first five adjectives are *major, eager, spending, Spanish-speaking,* and *embarrassing.* Highlight or underline five more adjectives in the final paragraph. Do these adjectives make the reading more interesting?

2. The author uses many Spanish words as examples in this article. If you are unsure of the meaning of any of these Spanish words, look them up in a Spanish-English dictionary.

D. STYLE, STRUCTURE, AND ORGANIZATION

1. Who do you think the author is writing for (who is her intended audience)? Why do you think so?

2. The author uses several quoted phrases and sentences throughout the article, such as "Come here, *siéntate!*" How do these quotations help make the article interesting?

3. The conclusion of this article ends with an example of Spanglish: "*no problema.*" How does this technique support the author's point by *showing* rather than *telling*?

E. TOPICS FOR DISCUSSION OR JOURNAL WRITING

1. What are some benefits of learning and speaking a second language?

2. Do you speak any other languages? Which ones? Do any of your relatives or friends speak another language? What languages did your ancestors speak?

3. Have you ever used any Spanish words while speaking English? What are some examples?

4. Have you ever spent time in a foreign country where a different language is spoken or in an area of the United States where Spanish is commonly spoken, such as California, Texas, Florida, or New York City? Describe your experience.

5. What languages have you heard spoken in the United States? What foods from other countries have you eaten? Describe your experiences.

F. WRITING TOPICS FOR PARAGRAPHS OR ESSAYS

1. Is the United States more like a melting pot of different cultures or more like a salad bowl? Why?

2. Write about a trip you took to another place, or write about a trip you would like to take. Include information about language and customs.

3. Write about your own experience studying and practicing a foreign language. How did you feel when you were learning it? How do you feel about your ability to speak it now?

4. Write an instructions paper that gives useful tips on learning to speak another language. How can a second language learner become really proficient?

5. Choose one of the following topics. Find out more about the topic by searching online or in a library; then write a paragraph or short essay.

    a. Compare how many languages (and which languages) are spoken by schoolchildren in your area with the number of languages that are spoken by schoolchildren in a large city, such as New York or Los Angeles. Give examples and information on where the students in each area have come from.

    b. Find updated information to replace the 1988 statistics in the reading. Compare how the statistics have changed and how these numbers have affected the society in the United States.

Saffron Sky

GELAREH ASAYESH

Gelareh Asayesh is a talented and respected journalist who has written for a number of major newspapers in the United States. She grew up in Iran and immigrated to this country with her parents when she was a young teenager. In her book *Saffron Sky*, which this reading is taken from, she vividly portrays her experiences as an immigrant and her connections with other Iranian Americans.

PREREADING QUESTIONS

1. What problems do you think an Iranian woman might experience living in the United States with her American husband?

2. To what extent do you think people who immigrate to another country should try to maintain the customs and traditions of their home country?

VOCABULARY

emerged came out

feat accomplishment

Norooz the Persian/Iranian new year festival, celebrated at the time of the spring equinox

mike microphone

tar in this case, a stringed musical instrument

launching into beginning

reconcile to accept, to make compatible

infighting disagreement among members of a group

exiles people who for one reason or another cannot move back to their native land

Sizdah-bedar the thirteenth day of the new year

dawned on occurred to

reclusiveness a preference for isolation rather than socializing

schisms divisions

pits puts people or groups in opposition to each other

colloquialisms informal conversational phrases used by native speakers

consign to assign, to place permanently in that situation

spurious false

disenfranchisement loss of privileges or rights

ambivalence uncertainty, mixed feelings

invokes summons, calls for

angst strong anxiety, apprehension

cemented bonded, held together

SAFFRON SKY

April 1, 1998 (Farvardin 12, 1377)

My friend Forough is going to Tehran on Saturday.

2   I rush down to the outlet mall near Sarasota. After an hour in the dressing room of Westport Woman, I emerge with a cobalt blue outfit for my cousin Maryam and a red one for my cousin Soodi. This is no easy feat, finding long-sleeved clothes (short sleeves are not permitted in Iran in public) in Florida in Spring.

3   I call Forough to find out when I can bring by the clothes, which she will take to Iran for me. We make a date, then compare notes on Norooz parties. Forough and her husband, Ali, went to the one at the University of South Florida in Tampa—a less formal affair than the dinner my family and I chose to attend. "How was your party?" Forough wants to know. "I heard it was dreadful."

4   "I thought it was great," I tell her, surprised. "There were some problems with the mike and the dancing started too late for us, but I was impressed. So were my parents. They're used to pretty fancy parties in Toronto."

5   "I heard the *tar* player had a real attitude," Forough says, launching into the list of criticisms she heard from friends who attended our party. We keep talking, trying to reconcile these differing reports of the same event. We conclude that the problem is the tendency toward infighting that so often exists among exiles. I'm not sure what causes it, but suspect it has something to do with feeling threatened. I've noticed that groups under stress tend to pull apart—the losing side in a game of Pictionary, the passengers of the

Titanic, the underclass in any society. Perhaps this is why the two Iranian cultural groups in Tampa Bay have devoted a fair bit of time, and a couple of mailings, to putting each other down.

6   Ali is trying to get the two groups to meet and work together, maybe even merge, Forough tells me. "I can't see it," I say. "Their styles are totally opposite. Besides, there's nothing wrong with having two groups, two events, two choices. If only they could get along."

7   Before we say good-bye, she asks me if I'm going to the Sizdah-bedar picnic. "The Sizdah-bedar picnic!" I say enthusiastically. "I'd like to go but I'm not sure. I'll have to talk to Neil."

8   I hang up the phone, vaguely ashamed. I know in my heart that we will not go to the picnic. Although our reasons vary from event to event, Neil and I rarely attend the picnics, concerts, and poetry nights sponsored by Iranians here.

9   Years ago, it dawned on me that just because someone was Iranian did not mean I had much in common with them. We have little enough leisure time as a family that we guard our weekends closely. But there is more to my reclusiveness.

10   Iranians in America, like many immigrants, are a troubled group. Take away the financial problems, language barriers, and emotional challenges of immigration, take away the political schisms that cause mutual distrust, and you are still left with the central dilemma of assimilation. The need to belong is a powerful thing. It pits those of us who are children of other worlds against ourselves and one another.

11   It made the Iranian clerk I encountered a few years ago at Bloomingdale's, in Rockville, Maryland, stare coldly when I spoke to her in Farsi. She rang up my sale without a word. A few months later, when an Iranian handed me the numbered tag I took into the dressing room of another department store, I was careful to thank her in English. I pretended that I did not recognize the almond skin, arched eyebrows, and glossy hair of a countrywoman.

12   A memory surfaces, one I haven't summoned in years. I am twenty-something, working at the *Miami Herald.* I fly up to Washington, D.C., to get a new passport. I stay at the Kalorama Guesthouse, near the zoo, and wake early in the morning to go to the Iranian Interests Section on Wisconsin Avenue. The Interests Section requires that applicants wear Islamic dress. Waiting on the steps of the guesthouse for a cab, I am painfully conscious of the

scarf on my head. I try to catch the eyes of people passing by, hungry for an opportunity to show them that, despite my appearance, I am not one of *them*. Let me speak a sentence loaded with colloquialisms. See, I am fluent in English! I have no accent! I'm like *you*. Don't consign me to the trash heap, where the unforgivably different belong. Don't look at me as if I were an animal at the zoo, an object of curiosity and spurious compassion.

13   This inner dialogue fills me with shame, yet I am helpless against it. I have become a party to my own disenfranchisement. The worst part of being told in a thousand ways, subtle and not, that one is inferior is the way that message worms itself into the heart. It is not enough to battle the prejudice of others, one must also battle the infection within.

14   I have struggled for years with my own ambivalence. Socializing with other Iranians invokes my angst in painful ways. Yet despite my discomfort, in every city I have lived I have sought out my countrymen and tried to establish meaningful connections with them.

15   Only in St. Petersburg, with our children as a common bond, have I succeeded. Only in Iran—or in Toronto, where relationships are cemented by family ties—is it easy to be with other Iranians. My closest friends, including my husband, are American.

16   Sometimes I get tired of the struggle.

17   So it is that each year I go to great lengths to travel to Iran. Each week I spend hours preparing our Farsi lesson.

18   Yet I won't make the effort to go to a picnic half an hour away in Clearwater.

A .   C O M P R E H E N S I O N

1. Why is it difficult for Gelareh Asayesh to find appropriate gifts of clothing for her cousins in Tehran?

2. How does the author explain the existence of two different Iranian cultural groups in Tampa Bay?

3. What happened when the author spoke Farsi to an Iranian clerk in Bloomingdale's?

4. How did the author feel when she wore Islamic dress on the streets of Washington, D.C., on her way to get a new passport?

B . C R I T I C A L T H I N K I N G

1. Why isn't the author planning to attend the Sizdah-bedar picnic?

2. Why does the author say that "Iranians in America, like many immigrants, are a troubled group"?

3. Does the author still feel strong ties to Iran, or does she feel stronger ties to the United States? Give reasons for your answer.

4. Do you think that Gelareh Asayesh and Forough are close friends? Why or why not?

5. Do you think the author has experienced prejudice and discrimination in the United States? In what kinds of situations?

C . L A N G U A G E A N D V O C A B U L A R Y

1. What do you think *dilemma* and *assimilation* mean? (Consult a dictionary if necessary.) After you know the meaning of these two key words, consider the meaning of the author's phrase "the dilemma of assimilation." Express in your own words the dilemma she is referring to.

2. What are *colloquialisms?* Why did the author say, "Let me speak a sentence loaded with colloquialisms"? Do you think it's important for immigrants from other cultures to learn American colloquialisms? Why or why not?

D . STYLE, STRUCTURE, AND ORGANIZATION

1. Find the one paragraph that is written completely in the *past tense.* Why do you think the author chose to put this particular paragraph in the past tense?

2. A good conclusion often leaves readers with something to think about. Is that true of the conclusion for this reading? What issue does it leave readers thinking about?

E . T O P I C S F O R D I S C U S S I O N O R J O U R N A L W R I T I N G

1. Which ethnic minority groups live in your area? What kinds of problems or conflicts do you think they experience because of cultural differences?

2. What can we do to reduce prejudice and discrimination against different ethnic groups?

3. Based on what you read in this selection from *Saffron Sky,* how do you think the position of women in Iran differs from the position of women in the United States?

4. Have you ever been in a situation where you had ambivalent feelings about something or felt pulled in two directions at the same time? How did you feel? How did you resolve the conflict?

5. Do you agree with the author that groups of people who are experiencing stress have a tendency to pull apart (in paragraph 5)? Why or why not? What examples can you think of?

F. WRITING TOPICS FOR PARAGRAPHS OR ESSAYS

1. Write a personal narrative about a time when you experienced discrimination or felt that you didn't fit in with a group.

2. Interview someone from another country. Ask about cultural differences between that person's native country and the United States, as well as about any difficulties he or she has had in adjusting to life in this country. Write a paper about the experiences of the person you interviewed.

3. Write about your own national origins. What country (or countries) did your parents or your ancestors come from? In what ways do you still feel a connection with that culture (or those cultures)?

4. Access a Web site that features information about Iranian culture, such as the Iranian Cultural Information Center at **http://tehran. stanford.edu/** or **http://netiran.com** or **www.persia.org/**. You may also want to follow links to other related sites. Then write a paper about something you have learned through your research.

5. Using library resources or the Internet, find out more about the Iranian celebrations of Norooz and Sizdah-bedar. Write a paper about what you learned, or compare and contrast Norooz with Western celebrations of the new year.

A Song Flung
Up to Heaven

MAYA ANGELOU

Maya Angelou, one of today's foremost American writers, has published five volumes of poetry, six autobiographical books, including *I Know Why the Caged Bird Sings* and *A Song Flung Up to Heaven*, magazine articles, screenplays, and documentaries. In addition to being a civil rights activist, a historian, and an educator, Angelou is also a producer and director for stage and screen. In fact, she was the first black woman director in Hollywood. In 1993, Maya Angelou's reading of her poem "The Pulse of the Morning" at the inauguration of President William Clinton brought her worldwide recognition. One of her volumes of poetry, *Just Give Me a Cool Drink of Water 'Fore I Diiie*, was nominated for a Pulitzer Prize.

A Song Flung Up to Heaven, which was published in 2002, begins with Maya Angelou's return from Africa in 1965, shortly before the assassination of Malcolm X, with whom she had intended to work. In 1968, while she was involved in civil rights work as the northern coordinator for Martin Luther King, Jr., he too was assassinated. The book covers these devastating periods of her life, as well as other events of the 1960s. In the following excerpt from *A Song Flung Up to Heaven*, Angelou vividly recalls scenes of rioting in the Watts area of Los Angeles in August 1965. During the six days of riots, thirty-four people died, more than 1,000 were injured, and almost 4,000 people were arrested.

PREREADING QUESTIONS

1. Do you know of any times in recent history when race riots occurred somewhere in the United States or elsewhere?

2. Which form of writing do you think conveys thoughts and feelings more effectively, *poetry* or *prose* (regular sentences and paragraphs)?

V O C A B U L A R Y

conflagration a huge fire

stench a bad smell

tumult commotion or disturbance

interspersed distributed at intervals

unscathed unaffected, not damaged

talking out of their hats not telling the truth, not giving an accurate picture (idiomatic expression)

blared in this case, broadcast loudly

colonialists people who establish a colony to take control of a new area

exploit take advantage of

putrid rotten

conspiratorial as if participating in a conspiracy

keen sharp-sounding, intense

mesmerizing fascinating, spellbinding

in tandem together

foray an advance or venture

din loud noise

heckled taunted, harassed

zircons blue-white gems resembling diamonds but less valuable

cornpone cornmeal bread (Southern U.S.); may also mean a folksy, down-home manner

novae the plural of nova, a star that suddenly increases in brightness

A SONG FLUNG UP TO HEAVEN

The uproar in Watts taught me something I had not known. Odor travels faster and farther than sound. We smelled the conflagration before we heard it, or even heard about it. The odor that drifted like a shadow over my neighborhood was complex because it was layered. Burning wood was the first odor that reached my nose, but it was soon followed by the smell of scorched food, then the stench of smoldering rubber. We had one hour of wondering what was burning before the television news reporters arrived breathlessly.

2   There had been no cameras to catch the ignition of the fire. A number of buildings were burning wildly before anyone could film

them. Newscasters began to relay the pictures and sounds of the tumult.

3   "There is full-blown riot in Watts. Watts is an area in southeast Los Angeles. Its residents are predominately Negroes." Pictures were interspersed with the gasps of the newscasters.

4   That description was for the millions of whites who lived in Los Angeles but who had no idea that Watts existed and certainly no awareness that it was a parcel of the city and only a short ride from their own communities.

5   Policemen and politicians, all white, came on the television screens to calm down the citizenry in the unscathed regions.

6   "You have nothing to fear. The police have been deployed to Watts, and in a few hours we will have everything under control."

7   Those of us who watched the action live on television over the next few days knew that the officials were talking out of their hats.

8   The rioters had abandoned all concern for themselves, for their safety and freedom. Some threw rocks, stones, cans of beer and soda at police in cars and police on foot. Heavily burdened people staggered out the doors of supermarkets, followed by billows of smoke. Men and women carried electrical appliances in their arms, and some pushed washers and dryers down the middle of the street.

9   However, nothing—not the voices trained to relay excitement nor the images of unidentifiable looters entering and leaving unlighted shops—could capture the terrifying threat of a riot like the stench of scorched wood and burning rubber.

10   Radios blared, "Watts is on fire." Television cameras filmed a group of men turning over a car and a young woman throwing a bottle at a superstore window. The glass seemed to break in slow motion. In fact, throughout the duration of the explosion, every incident shown on television seemed acted out at a pace slower than real time.

11   Sirens screamed through the night, and television screens showed gangs of young men refusing to allow fire trucks a chance to put out fires.

12   "Burn, baby, burn." The instruction came clear over the radios: "Burn, baby, burn." Certain political analysts observed that the people were burning their own neighborhood. Though few houses

were set afire, the rioters considered the stores, including supermarkets, property of the colonialists who had come into the neighborhood to exploit them and take their hard-earned money.

13   Two days passed and I could wait no longer. I drove to Watts and parked as near the center of the uprising as possible, then I walked. The smell had turned putrid as plastic furniture and supermarket meat departments smoldered. When I reached a main street, I stopped and watched as people pushed piled-high store carts out of burning buildings. Police seemed to be everywhere and nowhere, watching from inside their cars.

14   A young boy, his arms laden, his face knotted in concentration, suddenly saw me.

15   "You want a radio?"

16   I was amazed that there was no guilt in his voice. I said, "No, not yet. Thanks anyway."

17   Ordinarily I would have read in the boy's face, or felt, an "Uh-huh, this woman knows I've been stealing." There would have been at least an ounce of shame. But his approach had been conspiratorial,

as if to say, "We're in this together. I know you not only know what I am doing, you approve of it and would do it yourself if you could."

18   Smoke and screams carried in the air. Someone behind me was cursing long, keen streaks of profanity. It became hard to discern if the figures brushing past me were male or female, young or old.

19   The farther I walked, the more difficult it was to breathe. I had turned and started back to my car when a sound cut the air. The loud whine of police sirens was so close it stabbed into my ears. Policemen in gas masks emerged out of the smoke, figures from a nightmare. Alarm flooded me, and in a second I was dislocated. It seemed that the sirens were in my nose, and smoke packed my ears like cotton. Two policemen grabbed a person in front of me. They dragged the man away as he screamed, "Take your hands of me, you bastards! Let me go!"

20   I ran, but I couldn't see the pavement, so it was nearly impossible to keep my footing. I ran anyway. Someone grabbed for me, but I shrugged off the hand and continued running. My lungs were going to burst, and my calves were cramping. I pushed myself along. I was still running when I realized I was breathing clean air. I read the street signs and saw that I was almost a mile away from my car, but at least I wasn't in jail. Because I had run in the opposite direction from where I had parked, I would have to circle Watts to find my car, but at least I wasn't in Watts.

21   When I returned home, the television coverage was mesmerizing. The National Guard was shown arriving in Watts. They were young men who showed daring on their faces but fear in their hearts. They were uncomfortable with new, heavy responsibilities and new, heavy guns.

22   After three days the jails began to fill. The media covered hundreds of looters being arrested. Frances Williams said that the rumor in the neighborhood beauty salons and barbershops was that the police were arresting anyone black and those suspected of being black.

23   Watts was all anyone could think of. The fact of it, the explosion of anger, surprised and befuddled some: "I've driven through Watts many times. It's very nice." Some people were furious: "The police should have the right to shoot at will. If a few of

these looters were shot, the rest would get the message soon enough." Watts went on burning. It had not had enough, and I hadn't had enough.

24   Curiosity had often lured me to the edge of ruin. For years, I had known that there is nothing idle about curiosity, despite the fact that the two words are often used in tandem. Curiosity fidgets, is hard to satisfy, looks for answers even before forming questions. Curiosity wants to behold, to comprehend, maybe even to become.

25   Two days after my tentative foray into the war zone. I had to go again, but this time I wouldn't allow fear any control over me. This time I would not run.

26   The combustion had spread, so my previous parking space was now only a block from the riot. I parked there anyway and walked directly into the din.

27   Burglar alarms continued to ring in the stores that had no front doors or windows. Armed civilians stood in front of ravaged businesses, guarding against further looting. They were heckled.

28   "Hey brother, you guarding Charlie's thing. You must be a fool."

29   "I sure wouldn't risk my life for somebody else's stuff. If they care that much for it, they ought to come down here and look after it themselves."

30   "Ain't that much money in the world make me lose my life . . ."

31   The National Guard was heckled, too, but not as pointedly.

32   "Hey, man, you drew some lame duty."

33   "Don't you feel like a fool standing in front of a supermarket?"

34   I heard this in front of a pawnshop: "Hey, man, don't you feel stupid keeping people from stealing something that was already stole in the first place?"

35   The soldiers worked at keeping straight faces.

36   The devastation was so much broader. On the second day of the riot, and my first day visiting Watts, there was a corridor of burned-out buildings and cars, but on the fourth day, the corridor had widened substantially.

37   That night I sat down at my kitchen table and wrote on a yellow pad my description of the events I had seen in Watts and the uprising as it was reported on television.

Our
YOUR FRIEND CHARLIE pawnshop
was a glorious blaze
I heard the flames lick
then eat the trays
of zircons
mounted in red-gold alloys
Easter clothes and stolen furs
burned in the attic
radios and TVs
crackled with static
plugged in
only to a racial outlet

Hospitality, southern-style
cornpone grits and you-all smile
whole blocks novae
brand-new stars
policemen caught in their
brand-new cars
Chugga chugga chigga
git me one nigga
lootin' n burnin'
he won't git far

Lighting: a hundred Watts
Detroit, Newark and New York
Screeching nerves, exploding minds
lives tied to
a policeman's whistle
a welfare worker's doorbell
finger

A .   C O M P R E H E N S I O N

1. During the riots, what did the author learn about smells? Which smells bothered her the most?

2. What news of the riots did the author and millions of other people across the country hear on radio and television? Did Angelou think that all of the news was accurate?

3. According to the author, which people were heckled by some of the rioters? What kinds of things did the hecklers say?

4. What changes or differences did Angelou observe the second time she visited the area of the riots?

B .   C R I T I C A L   T H I N K I N G

1. Why do you think the author drove into the Watts area herself in spite of the danger?

2. Which images and scenes of the riots seemed to be the most shocking to Angelou?

3. Why did people burn and loot stores in their own neighborhood?

4. Why do you think Maya Angelou included a poem in this passage from *A Song Flung Up to Heaven*? How does it add to your understanding of the situation in Watts?

5. Does the poem portray the same events and situations that the rest of the reading does? Are any new ideas or images introduced? If so, what are they and how did you react to them?

C .   L A N G U A G E   A N D   V O C A B U L A R Y

1. Angelou's poem uses the word "nigga." Earlier in the reading, the word "Negroes" is used. Why do you think she used these two different word choices in two different situations? How do you feel about the appropriateness of these words as they are used in the reading? Would either term be considered socially acceptable today? Explain your answer.

2. The last stanza of Angelou's poem begins with the words "Lighting: a hundred Watts." What are the two possible meanings of these words? Does the double meaning of this line add to the effectiveness of the poem?

D. STYLE, STRUCTURE, AND ORGANIZATION

1. Paragraphs 3 and 6 contain words in quotation marks, such as "You have nothing to fear," but the speaker of the words is not identified. Who do you think is speaking? Why didn't the author identify the speaker?

2. In the poem at the end of the reading, find five pairs of lines that rhyme, or end with the same sound (not necessarily the same spelling). In some cases, the rhyming lines are consecutive; in other cases, they are separated by another line that does not rhyme.

E. TOPICS FOR DISCUSSION OR JOURNAL WRITING

1. In the area where you live, do conflicts between people of different ethnic backgrounds occur frequently, sometimes, or almost never? Why?

2. Have you ever witnessed an event that was violent, shocking, or disturbing in some other way? Tell the story of the event, being sure to include descriptive details.

3. How do you think you would have felt if you had been in Watts in August, 1965? What do you think you would have done?

4. What do you think can and should be done to prevent race riots like the ones that occurred in Watts?

5. Do you think that calling up the National Guard during the riots was a good idea or not? What other kinds of situations can you think of when the National Guard has been used to stand guard or to provide protection in civilian areas?

F. WRITING TOPICS FOR PARAGRAPHS OR ESSAYS

1. Write a short paper about a frightening or shocking event that you saw or heard about. Then, as Maya Angelou did, write a poem (at least ten lines long) that includes striking images of the event. You may want to rhyme a few lines, or you may decide to write the poem in free verse (that is, with no particular pattern of rhythm or rhyme).

2. Because of improvements in television technology, people all over the world can often witness events as they happen. Write about a serious, intense, real-life event that you saw happen on television. Include details of the event itself, as well as your feelings while watching.

3. Beginning with paragraph 14, the author tells us about a young boy who was carrying items he had stolen and who offered her a radio. Using your imagination, write the story of where the boy goes and what he does after that. Include some dialogue: the exact words that he and others say.

4. Read a book by Maya Angelou and write a review of it. Include a summary of the book, why you liked it or didn't like it, and a description of the part that you enjoyed the most. Also include at least one significant quotation from the book and explain why it is important to the author's message.

5. Using the Internet or library resources, look up more information about the Watts riots in Los Angeles in 1965 and write an informative paper about the causes of the riots, events during the riots, effects after the riots, the Watts district today, or more than one of these topics combined.

Suspect Policy

RANDALL KENNEDY

Racial profiling is the practice by law enforcement officers of stopping and questioning people because of their race or ethnicity. It is a controversial issue, and many people have very strong feelings about it. In this excerpt from an article that originally appeared in *The New Republic* magazine, Randall Kennedy, a professor at Harvard Law School, examines various perspectives on the issue.

PREREADING QUESTIONS

1. What are some of the challenges faced by law enforcement officers in ethnically diverse neighborhoods?

2. How do law enforcement officers decide which people to stop and question?

VOCABULARY

flooding in this context, providing very large quantities

made a beeline went quickly and directly (an idiomatic expression)

deplaning getting off a plane

trafficking sales, dealing (of drugs, in this case)

v. abbreviation for *versus*, used in naming the two sides of a court case

constitutionality legality according to the Constitution of the United States

presumptively based on a presumption, not on actual evidence

detain in this context, hold for questioning

bona fide genuine, real

harassment systematic persecution, repeated threats or demands

hooligans troublemakers or
lawbreakers

profile in this context, a general
description of a likely suspect
for certain crimes

rackets illegal businesses

empirically based based on
statistics

denunciations strong
criticisms, condemnations

corrosive destructive

undercuts undermines or takes
away support for an idea

SUSPECT POLICY

An officer from the Drug Enforcement Administration stops and
questions a young man who has just stepped off a flight to Kansas
City from Los Angeles. The officer has focused on this man for
several reasons. Intelligence reports indicate that black gangs in Los
Angeles are flooding the Kansas City area with illegal drugs, and the
man in question was on a flight originating in Los Angeles. Young,
toughly dressed, and appearing very nervous, he paid for his ticket
in cash, checked no luggage, brought two carry-on bags, and made
a beeline for a taxi upon deplaning. Oh, and one other thing:
the officer also took into account the fact that the young man
was black.

* * *

2   How should we evaluate the officer's conduct? Should we
applaud it? Permit it? Prohibit it? Encounters like this take place
every day, all over the country, as police attempt to battle street
crime, drug trafficking, and illegal immigration. And this particular
case study happens to be the fact pattern presented in a federal
lawsuit of the early '90s, *United States v. Weaver*, in which the U.S.
Court of Appeals for the Eighth Circuit upheld the constitutionality
of the officer's action.

3   "Large groups of our citizens," the court declared, "should not
be regarded by law enforcement officers as presumptively criminal
based upon their race." The court went on to say, however, that
"facts are not to be ignored simply because they may be
unpleasant." According to the court, it made sense for the officer to
regard blackness, when considered in conjunction with the other

factors, as a signal that could be legitimately relied upon in the decision to approach and detain the suspect.

4   Other courts have agreed with the Eighth Circuit that the Constitution does not prohibit police from routinely taking race into account when they decide whom to stop and question, as long as they do so for purposes of bona fide law enforcement (not racial harassment) and as long as race is one of several factors that they consider.

* * *

5   Some police officers note that racial profiling is race-neutral in that various forms of it can be applied to persons of all races, depending on the circumstances. In predominantly black neighborhoods and other places in which white people stick out in a suspicious fashion (as potential drug customers or racist hooligans, for example), whiteness can become part of a profile. In the southwestern United States, where Latinos often traffic in illegal immigrants, apparent Latin American ancestry can become part of a profile. In a Chinatown where Chinese gangs appear to dominate certain criminal rackets, apparent Chinese ancestry can become part of a profile. Racial profiling, then, according to many cops, is good police work: a race-neutral, empirically based, and, above all, effective tool in fighting crime.

6   But the defenders of racial profiling are wrong.

7   Indeed, ever since the Black and Latino Caucus of the New Jersey State Legislature held sensational hearings a few months ago, complete with testimony from victims of the New Jersey State Police force's racial profiling, the air has been thick with public denunciations of the practice. In June, at a forum organized by the Justice Department on racial problems in law enforcement, President Clinton condemned racial profiling as a "morally indefensible, deeply corrosive practice." Vice President Al Gore has promised that, if elected president, he would see to it that the first civil rights act of the new century would end racial profiling.

* * *

8   Racial profiling undercuts a good idea that needs more support from both society and the law: that individuals should be judged by public authority on the basis of their own conduct and not on the basis—not even *partly* on the basis—of racial generalization.

A . C O M P R E H E N S I O N

1. Why do many law enforcement officers consider racial profiling an effective crime-fighting tool?

2. In the court case *United States v. Weaver*, which the author refers to, what decision did the judge make about racial profiling? What reasons did the judge give for his decision?

3. In what kinds of neighborhoods is whiteness likely to be part of a racial profile for criminal suspects?

4. According to Randall Kennedy, why should racial profiling be abolished?

B . C R I T I C A L T H I N K I N G

1. Reread the first paragraph, which tells the story of a Drug Enforcement Administration officer stopping and questioning a young African-American man in Kansas City. Why did the officer decide to stop him? Do you think the officer's decision was reasonable? Give reasons for your answer.

2. Why do many police officers consider racial profiling "good police work"?

3. Do you think Randall Kennedy is well qualified to write on the topic of racial profiling? Why or why not?

4. If witnesses report seeing a white woman in her early thirties, about 5′6″ tall, with blonde hair, running from the scene of a murder, should the police question every woman in the area who fits that description? Why or why not?

C . L A N G U A G E A N D V O C A B U L A R Y

1. What do you think the author means by the term *racial harassment* in paragraph 4?

2. Because of the nature of the topic, the author uses a number of fairly technical words that relate to the legal system or law enforcement, such as *constitutionality* and *intelligence reports*. Find at least two other technical words or phrases related to law

enforcement or the legal field. What do you think they mean? If you are not sure of the meaning, consult a dictionary.

D. STYLE, STRUCTURE, AND ORGANIZATION

1. At what point in the reading does Kennedy reveal that he is against racial profiling? Did you suspect his real stand on the issue earlier in the reading?

2. In which paragraphs does the author present evidence in favor of racial profiling? Label these paragraphs *Pro.* In which paragraphs does he argue against it? Label these paragraphs *Con.* Do you think this pattern of organization is effective?

E. TOPICS FOR DISCUSSION OR JOURNAL WRITING

1. Have you ever experienced discrimination because of your race or ethnicity? If so, how did you react?

2. Do you think that the law enforcement officers in your community usually treat people of different races and ethnicities fairly or unfairly?

3. What do you think would be the hardest part of being a police officer? Why?

4. How do you think someone who was falsely accused of a crime would feel?

5. What advice do you think Neighborhood Watch groups should give residents about keeping an eye out for strangers in their neighborhood? Should race or ethnicity be considered as a factor?

F. WRITING TOPICS FOR PARAGRAPHS OR ESSAYS

1. Look up information about the job of being a police officer in the *Occupational Outlook Handbook* online or in a library, or interview a police officer. Then write a paper about a police officer's duties and responsibilities. Also include several advantages and disadvantages of the job.

2. Write a short dramatic scene between a police officer making an arrest and an innocent suspect who is African American, Hispanic, Native American, or Asian. Try to create a believable story about what happens. Be sure to include realistic *dialogue*—that is, words that the two people might actually say to each other.

3. Watch a police drama on television. Notice how the police officers identify and question suspects and whether they use racial profiling. Then write a paper about the program, including your observations and your opinion of the program.

4. Have you ever been falsely accused of something by your parents, a teacher, a friend, or someone else? Write the story of what happened. Be sure to include your feelings and descriptive details, so that readers can picture what happened.

PART

3

EDUCATION
AND CAREER

Stop!

SAM QUINONES

Sam Quinones is a freelance writer who has been based in Mexico City since 1994. His work includes numerous articles for magazines and newspapers, including the *Los Angeles Times*, the *San Francisco Chronicle*, the *Houston Chronicle*, and the *Baltimore Sun*, and a *FRONTLINE/ World* report on the problems of Central American coffee farmers. He has also written a book titled *True Tales from Another Mexico: The Lynch Mob, the Popsicle Kings, Chalino, and the Bronx*, a special collection of true stories about little-known aspects of Mexican life and culture.

This article about women in the Mexico City police force originally appeared in *Ms.*, a magazine published in New York and intended primarily for women. However, the article deals with an issue that involves both men and women—gender roles in law enforcement.

PREREADING QUESTIONS

1. What special qualities do you think a good police officer should have?

2. Are male and female police officers capable of doing the same kinds of jobs equally well?

VOCABULARY

screws up makes a mess of something, makes a mistake (slang)

image in this case, the public perception

task an assigned duty or job

corruption immoral or dishonest activity

pyramid a structure with a broad base that narrows at the top

SOURCE: "*Stop!*" by Sam Quinones, from *Ms. Magazine*, Vol. X, Num. 1. Reprinted by permission of *Ms. Magazine*, copyright © 1999–2000.

purportedly supposedly

commute traffic going to or from work

chaos confusion

apathy lack of interest, indifference

peso the monetary unit of Mexico

infraction minor violation of the law

root in this case, primary; the basic core of something

notoriously well-known in a negative way

empowered given power

extortion illegal use of one's official position to obtain money by means of intimidation

tailgating following too closely behind (usually referring to one vehicle closely following another)

STOP!

What a man screws up, a woman will do right. This appeared to be the philosophy at work when Mexico City Police Chief and Secretary of Public Safety Alejandro Gertz Manero announced last August that only female officers would have the authority to write traffic tickets—in the belief, and hope, that women are more honest than men.

2   There are 950 women officers in the so-called Grupo Cisne, or Swan Group. (Each unit in the Mexico City Police Department is named after a bird. The swan was chosen for the women's traffic unit because it's "feminine.")

3   These birds are charged not only with issuing tickets, but with changing the image of traffic cops, which is no easy task. The Mexico City traffic cop is a worldwide symbol of police corruption, routinely stopping drivers to take a bribe, known as a *mordida*, or bite.

4   Traffic cops have always been at the lowest level in Mexico City's pyramid of police corruption. Each cop is rumored to have a daily quota of bribe money to meet. He purportedly keeps part for himself, then pays off his sergeant, who pays off the lieutenant, and so on.

5   And while cops are taking bribes, drivers are taking risks—running red lights, changing lanes without signaling, making illegal U-turns, making right turns from the left lane—all in a single commute.

6   Into this chaos step the women of Grupo Cisne. The officers are part of teams—including both men and women—that direct traffic, tow cars, and remove license plates from offending vehicles. Only the women, however, are allowed to write tickets.

7   "Why only women?" asks Raul Tovar, Mexico City police spokesman. "Because women are more dedicated and less able to be corrupted."

8   Officer María del Carmen García agrees. "I think it's because at some point women are more energetic," she told *Ms.* "We do work the way it should be done. There's a little more apathy in men."

9   Whatever the reason may be, Grupo Cisne is doing too well for the taste of many drivers who now find that, faced with the possibility of a 300-peso fine, a quick 50-peso bribe looks pretty good.

10   "When they commit some infraction, they'll immediately argue," says García. "They get out and say, 'Here, take this [money],' when we've never asked for anything.

11   "You'll pull someone over for an illegal U-turn, and he'll stand there watching to see who else does it. He'll say, 'Why are you stopping me? Look at him. Stop him.' I just say, 'Sir, we're all adults. We each have to correct our own behavior.' They never want to accept their error."

12   The women won't be able to do much about the root cause of corruption: officers' notoriously poor pay. García is typical of male and female officers. After eight years on the force, she takes home only about $53 a week. If the city officials can't improve that, then these newly empowered women might surrender to temptation just as easily as the men have.

13   "First, the people asked for this because there was extortion," says Officer Erika Alcaraz. "Now, they've seen they can't get away with anything with us, so they complain to our superiors!"

14   No female officer has yet been accused of demanding bribes. But then again, maybe it's just another case of women having to catch up with the men. So far, they're not even tailgating.

A. COMPREHENSION

1. According to the Mexico City police chief and Officer Maria del Carmen García, why has the job of writing traffic tickets been assigned only to women?

2. Why is the women's traffic unit called the Grupo Cisne?

3. What problems have Officers Maria del Carmen García and Erika Alcaraz encountered while issuing traffic tickets?

4. According to the author, what reputation do the Mexico City police have? Why have they acquired this reputation?

B. CRITICAL THINKING

1. Do you think that the female police officers will be more honest and less likely to accept bribes than the male police officers in Mexico City? Why or why not?

2. Does author Sam Quinones present a fair and accurate picture of the differences between male and female police officers in Mexico City? Give reasons for your answer.

3. Why is it important to ensure that police officers are paid a good salary?

4. Do you agree or disagree with the differences between men and women that are mentioned in the article? Give reasons for your answer.

C .   L A N G U A G E   A N D   V O C A B U L A R Y

1. Who is the writer referring to in paragraph 3 when he says "these birds"? Why does he call them birds?

2. Explain the term *daily quota* in paragraph 4. If necessary, use a dictionary to find the meaning of *quota*. Can you think of any kinds of jobs that have legitimate daily quotas?

D .   S T Y L E ,   S T R U C T U R E ,   A N D   O R G A N I Z A T I O N

1. How does the author capture readers' attention with his first sentence? Do you think he believes that this statement is completely true? If not, why did he use it?

2. Newspaper articles and many magazine articles tend to use shorter paragraphs than academic writing requires. Why do you think this is so? Count the number of sentences in each of the first eight paragraphs. Which one has the most sentences?

3. In what ways do you think that the author's intended audience affected his style and his choices of what information to include? (Remember that he originally wrote the article for a women's magazine.)

E .   T O P I C S   F O R   D I S C U S S I O N   O R   J O U R N A L   W R I T I N G

1. Do you think that male and female police officers should be given different types of job assignments or exactly the same assignments? Why?

2. What are some of the major types of problems that law enforcement officers in any large city might experience?

3. What do you think are the hardest or most challenging parts of being a police officer? What are the most rewarding parts?

4. Do you think that people react differently to being issued a traffic ticket by a female officer than by a male officer? Why or why not? Would it make any difference to you personally?

F. WRITING TOPICS FOR PARAGRAPHS OR ESSAYS

1. Do you think there are any basic differences between men and women in the areas of personality, values, communication, and/or ability to deal with people? Think through the topic before you begin writing so that you can compose a clear main idea statement, and then illustrate your main idea with examples from your own experience.

2. What are the requirements to become a police officer, a border patrol agent, a marshal, an FBI agent, or some other type of law enforcement officer? If your college has a career center, you can find information there about one of these careers. You can also inquire at a local law enforcement agency or use library resources.

3. Have you ever gotten a traffic ticket or been in the car with someone who did? How did the police officer treat you? How did you feel? Write a personal narrative about your experience.

4. Are there periods of heavy rush-hour traffic in your area when people are commuting to and from work? Are drivers generally polite, or do you see instances of road rage? Do most drivers obey speed limits and other laws? Choose one of the following writing topics about traffic in your area:
    a. Describe a typical drive in one of the worst traffic areas.
    b. Suggest ways to improve the traffic situation.
    c. Classify the kinds of drivers on the road into at least three categories and describe each category, giving specific examples of how drivers in each group act.

One Man's Kids

DANIEL MEIER

Daniel Meier is a first grade elementary school teacher. In this article, he shares his love of teaching and discusses the reactions he has encountered as a male teacher of young children. He has written several other articles and books on teaching and learning, including *Learning in Small Moments: Life in an Urban Classroom.*

As you read this article, notice the enthusiasm that he shows for his job.

PREREADING QUESTIONS

1. What are some personal qualities that are important for a good elementary school teacher to have?

2. Why do you think there aren't more men teaching kindergarten, first, and second grade elementary school?

VOCABULARY

stale no longer fresh

transact to conduct or carry out a business deal

singular exceptional

pursuit occupation or job

wheeling and dealing transactions important and complicated negotiations and agreements

consoling comforting

shudder to shiver, often with fear or disgust

hilarity good spirits, cheerfulness, laughter

intellectual matters topics involving the brain rather than the emotions

altered changed or adapted

the career stepladder a series of promotions in a particular field of work

merit pay a system of paying some teachers more than others based on their performance evaluations

trappings in this case, symbols

lull pause

riddle brainteaser

ONE MAN'S KIDS

I teach first graders. I live in a world of skinned knees, double-knotted shoelaces, riddles that I've heard a dozen times, stale birthday cakes, hurt feelings, wandering stories and one lost shoe ("and if you don't find it my mother'll kill me"). My work is dominated by 6-year-olds. It's 10:45, the middle of snack, and I'm helping Emily open her milk carton. She has already tried the other end without success, and now there's so much paint and ink on the carton from her fingers that I'm not sure she should drink it at all. But I open it. Then I turn to help Scott clean up some milk he has just spilled onto Rebecca's whale crossword puzzle.

2   While I wipe my milk- and paint-covered hands, Jenny wants to know if I've seen that funny book about penguins that I read in class. As I hunt for it in a messy pile of books, Jason wants to know if there is a new seating arrangement for lunch tables. I find the book, turn to answer Jason, then face Maya, who is fast approaching with a new knock-knock joke. After what seems like the 10th "Who's there?" I laugh and Maya is pleased.

3   Then Andrew wants to know how to spell "flukes" for his crossword. As I get to "u," I give a hand signal for Sarah to take away the snack. But just as Sarah is almost out the door, two children complain that "we haven't even had ours yet." I stop the snack mid-flight, complying with their request for graham crackers. I then return to Andrew, noticing that he has put "flu" for 9 Down, rather than 9 Across. It's now 10:50.

4   My work is not traditional male work. It's not a singular pursuit. There is not a large pile of paper to get through or one deal to transact. I don't have one area of expertise or knowledge. I don't have the singular power over language of a lawyer, the physical force of a construction worker, the command over fellow workers of a surgeon, the wheeling and dealing transactions of a businessman. My energy is not spent in pursuing, climbing, achieving, conquering or cornering some goal or object.

5   My energy is spent in encouraging, supporting, consoling and praising my children. In teaching, the inner rewards come from without. On any given day, quite apart from teaching reading and spelling, I bandage a cut, dry a tear, erase a frown, tape a torn doll

and locate a long-lost boot. The day is really won through matters of the heart. As my students groan, laugh, shudder, cry, exult and wonder, I do too. I have to be soft around the edges.

6   A few years ago, when I was interviewing for an elementary-school teaching position, every principal told me with confidence that, as a male, I had an advantage over female applicants because of the lack of male teachers. But in the next breath, they asked with a hint of suspicion why I chose to work with young children. I told them that I wanted to observe and contribute to the intellectual growth of a maturing mind. What I really felt like saying, but didn't, was that I loved helping a child learn to write his name for the first time, finding someone a new friend, or sharing in the hilarity of reading about Winnie the Pooh getting so stuck in a hole that only his head and rear show.

7   I gave that answer to those principals, who were mostly male, because I thought they wanted a "male" response. This meant talking about intellectual matters. If I had taken a different course and talked about my interest in helping children in their emotional development, it would have been seen as closer to a "female" answer. I even altered my language, not once mentioning the word "love" to describe what I do indeed love about teaching. My answer worked; every principal nodded approvingly.

8   Some of the principals also asked what I saw myself doing later in my career. They wanted to know if I eventually wanted to go into educational administration. Becoming a dean of students or a principal has never been one of my goals, but they seemed to expect me, as a male, to want to climb higher on the career stepladder. So I mentioned that, at some point, I would be interested in working with teachers as a curriculum coordinator. Again, they nodded approvingly.

9   If those principals had been female instead of male, I wonder whether their questions, and my answers, would have been different. My guess is that they would have been. At other times, when I'm at a party or a dinner and tell someone that I teach young children, I've found that men and women respond differently. Most men ask about the subjects I teach and the courses I took in my training. Then, unless they bring up an issue such as merit pay, the conversation stops. Most women, on the other hand, begin the

conversation on a more immediate and personal level. They say things like "those kids must love having a male teacher" or "that age is just wonderful, you must love it." Then, more often than not, they'll talk about their own kids or ask me specific questions about what I do. We're then off and talking shop.

10   Possibly, men would have more to say to me, and I to them, if my job had more of the trappings and benefits of more traditional male jobs. But my job has no bonuses or promotions. No complimentary box seats at the ball park. No cab fare home. No drinking buddies after work. No briefcase. No suit. (Ties get stuck in paint jars.) No power lunches. (I eat peanut butter and jelly, chips, milk and cookies with the kids.) No taking clients out for cocktails. The only place I take my kids is to the playground.

11   Although I could have pursued a career in law or business, as several of my friends did, I chose teaching instead. My job has benefits all its own. I'm able to bake cookies without getting them stuck together as they cool, buy cheap sewing materials, take out splinters, and search just the right trash cans for useful odds and ends. I'm sometimes called "Daddy" and even "Mommy" by my students, and if there's ever a lull in the conversation at a dinner party, I can always ask those assembled if they've heard the latest riddle about why the turkey crossed the road. (He thought he was a chicken.)

A . C O M P R E H E N S I O N

1. Immediately after the introduction (the first three sentences), the author describes a number of activities that he does with children. How much time goes by while he is doing all of these things?

2. What four "typical male jobs" does the author mention in the article? Why did he choose teaching rather than one of these jobs?

3. How do men and women that the author meets in social situations react when they find out that he is a teacher?

4. How did the principals react to a man wanting to teach young children?

B . C R I T I C A L T H I N K I N G

1. What qualities does a good teacher for young children need? Are other qualities more important for teaching older children?

2. Why do you think people react the way they do to a male first-grade teacher? Why do men and women react differently?

3. Why do you think more men do not choose careers as elementary school teachers? Try to come up with more than one reason.

4. What are some differences between "typical men's jobs" and "typical women's jobs"? Do you think it is OK for there to be more men in some professions and more women in others? Why or why not?

C . L A N G U A G E A N D V O C A B U L A R Y

1. How do you think Daniel Meier feels about his job? What are some specific words or expressions he uses to show his feelings to readers?

2. This article contains several noun phrases that contain hyphenated adjectives (adjectives that consist of more than one word connected by a hyphen). These include "milk- and paint-covered hands," "long-lost boot," and "elementary-school teaching position." Why do you think the writer uses these hyphenated adjectives?

D . S T Y L E , S T R U C T U R E , A N D O R G A N I Z A T I O N

1. Read the introduction, which consists of the first three sentences. Do you think it is an effective introduction? Does this introduction give the reader an accurate idea of what the article is about?

2. In paragraph four, the author uses a series of negative sentences that tell what his job *isn't* like and what he *doesn't* do. Go back and read them again. Do these negative sentences give the reader some idea of what his job is like?

E . TOPICS FOR DISCUSSION OR JOURNAL WRITING

1. Would you be interested in teaching young children? Why or why not?

2. List several jobs that more men work in and make another list of jobs that more women work in. Do the "typical men's jobs" have some things in common? What about the "typical women's jobs"?

3. What is the most difficult part of being a good elementary school teacher? Can you think of some strategies to make the job easier?

4. Are you satisfied with your present job, or are you interested in finding a better job? Why? What do you like most about your present job?

5. If you could choose any type of career or profession, what sort of job would you choose? Why does this career or profession appeal to you? Are there more men or women in this kind of job?

F . WRITING TOPICS FOR PARAGRAPHS OR ESSAYS

1. Access the Web site of a college or university near where you live that offers education courses, or find a copy of its catalog. Find out the requirements to get a teaching credential and write an informative paper that describes the requirements to become a teacher.

2. Write a résumé for yourself, either to meet your current job needs or to meet your future needs after you have finished college. Include your career goal, education and training, work experience, and anything else that may relate to your job qualifications.

3. Write at least ten questions that you would ask if you were hiring an elementary school teacher, and explain the reason that you would ask each of these questions.

4. Use the library or do an online search on the percentage of men and women in different types of careers. Write a cause-and-effect paper analyzing why more men or more women work at one or more of these jobs.

5. Write a comparison/contrast paper about two different teachers you have had. Include information about their personalities as well as their teaching styles.

How to Write with Style

KURT VONNEGUT, JR.

Kurt Vonnegut, Jr., is well known for his satirical novels, which incorporate fantasy and science fiction, as well as for his collections of short stories and a variety of articles and essays. Vonnegut's first novel, *Player Piano*, published in 1952, portrays a futuristic society where automation is gradually taking over everything. His most famous novel is *Slaughterhouse Five* (1969), which is based on his experiences as a prisoner of war in Dresden, Germany, during World War II. Other novels by Vonnegut include *Cat's Cradle* (1963), *Slapstick* (1976), *Hocus Pocus* (1990), and *Timequake* (1997).

Now in his eighties, Kurt Vonnegut, Jr., still makes speeches and public appearances. In "How to Write with Style," he offers practical advice about how to write effectively. As you read this article, think about which of his suggestions you can apply to your own writing.

PREREADING QUESTIONS

1. Who are some popular modern authors? Why do people like to read their writing?

2. Do most people know how to write effectively? Where can they learn how to write better?

VOCABULARY

wretches miserable beings

chowderhead blockhead, dummy

compelling engaging, extremely interesting

SOURCE: "How to Write with Style" by Kurt Vonnegut, Jr., from the *Power of the Printed Word* series, copyright © 1982 by International Paper Company. Reprinted by permission of International Paper.

ramble to go on and on without a clear purpose

profound deep

frisky light-hearted and energetic

reputable well thought of

illuminate to shed light on

piquant colorful or spicy

locutions language expressions, especially those from a particular time period

vehemently angrily and forcefully

dialect a particular variety of a language

unambiguously very clearly

HOW TO WRITE WITH STYLE

Newspaper reporters and technical writers are trained to reveal almost nothing about themselves in their writings. This makes them freaks in the world of writers, since almost all of the other ink-stained wretches in that world reveal a lot about themselves to readers. We call these revelations, accidental and unintentional, elements of style.

2 These revelations tell us as readers what sort of person it is with whom we are spending time. Does the writer sound ignorant or informed, stupid or bright, crooked or honest, humorless or playful—? And on and on.

3 Why should you examine your writing style with the idea of improving it? Do so as a mark of your respect for your readers, whatever you're writing. If you scribble your thoughts any which way, your readers will surely feel that you care nothing about them. They will mark you down as an egomaniac or a chowderhead—or worse, they will stop reading you.

4 The most damning revelation you can make about yourself is that you do not know what is interesting and what is not. Don't you yourself like or dislike writers mainly for what they choose to show you or make you think about? Did you ever admire an empty-headed writer for his or her mastery of the language? No.

5 So your own winning style must begin with ideas in your head.

1. Find a Subject You Care About

6   Find a subject you care about and which you in your heart feel others should care about. It is this genuine caring, and not your games with language, which will be the most compelling and seductive element in your style.

7   I am not urging you to write a novel, by the way—although I would not be sorry if you wrote one, provided you genuinely cared about something. A petition to the mayor about a pothole in front of your house or a love letter to the girl next door will do.

2. Do Not Ramble, Though

8   I won't ramble on about that.

3. Keep It Simple

9   As for the use of language: Remember that two great masters of language, William Shakespeare and James Joyce, wrote sentences which were almost childlike when their subjects were most profound. "To be or not to be?" asks Shakespeare's Hamlet. The longest word is three letters long. Joyce, when he was frisky, could put together a sentence as intricate and glittering as a necklace for Cleopatra, but my favorite sentence in his short story "Eveline" is this one: "She was tired." At that point in the story, no other words could break the heart of a reader as those three words do.

10   Simplicity of language is not only reputable, but perhaps even sacred. The *Bible* opens with a sentence well within the writing skills of a lively fourteen-year-old: "In the beginning God created the heaven and the earth."

4. Have the Guts to Cut

11   It may be that you, too, are capable of making necklaces for Cleopatra, so to speak. But your eloquence should be the servant of the ideas in your head. Your rule might be this: If a sentence, no matter how excellent, does not illuminate your subject in some new and useful way, scratch it out.

5. *Sound Like Yourself*

12   The writing style which is most natural for you is bound to echo the speech you heard when you were a child. English was the novelist Joseph Conrad's third language, and much that seems piquant in his use of English was no doubt colored by his first language, which was Polish. And lucky indeed is the writer who has grown up in Ireland, for the English spoken there is so amusing and musical. I myself grew up in Indianapolis, where common speech sounds like a band saw cutting galvanized tin, and employs a vocabulary as unornamental as a monkey wrench.

13   In some of the more remote hollows of Appalachia, children still grow up hearing songs and locutions of Elizabethan times. Yes, and many Americans grow up hearing a language other than English, or an English dialect a majority of Americans cannot understand.

14   All these varieties of speech are beautiful, just as the varieties of butterflies are beautiful. No matter what your first language, you should treasure it all your life. If it happens not to be standard English, and it shows itself when you write standard English, the result is usually delightful, like a very pretty girl with one eye that is green and one that is blue.

15   I myself find that I trust my own writing most, and others seem to trust it most, too, when I sound most like a person from Indianapolis, which is what I am. What alternatives do I have? The one most vehemently recommended by teachers has no doubt been pressed on you, as well: to write like cultivated Englishmen of a century or more ago.

6. *Say What You Mean to Say*

16   I used to be exasperated by such teachers, but am no more. I understand now that all those antique essays and stories with which I was to compare my own work were not magnificent for their datedness or foreignness, but for saying precisely what their authors meant them to say. My teachers wished me to write accurately, always selecting the most effective words, and relating the words to one another unambiguously, rigidly, like parts of a machine. The

teachers did not want to turn me into an Englishman after all. They hoped that I would become understandable—and therefore understood. And there went my dream of doing with words what Pablo Picasso did with paint or what any number of jazz idols did with music. If I broke all the rules of punctuation, had words mean whatever I wanted them to mean, and strung them together higgledy-piggledy, I would simply not be understood. So you, too, had better avoid Picasso-style or jazz-style writing, if you have something worth saying and wish to be understood.

17   Readers want our pages to look very much like pages they have seen before. Why? This is because they themselves have a tough job to do, and they need all the help they can get from us.

7. Pity the Readers

18   They have to identify thousands of little marks on paper, and make sense of them immediately. They have to *read*, an art so difficult that most people don't really master it even after having studied it all through grade school and high school—twelve long years.

19   So this discussion must finally acknowledge that our stylistic options as writers are neither numerous nor glamorous, since our readers are bound to be such imperfect artists. Our audience requires us to be sympathetic and patient teachers, ever willing to simplify and clarify—whereas we would rather soar high above the crowd, singing like nightingales.

20   That is the bad news. The good news is that we Americans are governed under a unique Constitution, which allows us to write whatever we please without fear of punishment. So the most meaningful aspect of our styles, which is what we choose to write about, is utterly unlimited.

8. For Really Detailed Advice

21   For a discussion of literary style in a narrower sense, in a more technical sense, I commend to your attention *The Elements of Style,* by William Strunk, Jr., and E. B. White [the most recent edition is published by Longman, 2000]. E. B. White is, of course, one of the most admirable literary stylists this country has so far produced.

22   You should realize, too, that no one would care how well or badly Mr. White expressed himself, if he did not have perfectly enchanting things to say.

A .   C O M P R E H E N S I O N

1. How many tips for writing effectively does the author provide? What are they?

2. What did Vonnegut's English teachers want him to be able to do?

3. What reason does the author give for saying that we need to "simplify and clarify" our writing? Why can't we just express ourselves any way we want in everything we write?

4. According to the author, what is the single most important requirement for writing well?

B .   C R I T I C A L   T H I N K I N G

1. Is Vonnegut's advice useful for everyone, or will some readers find it more helpful than others? Why?

2. Do you think Vonnegut is really interested in helping other writers? What is there in this article that makes you think so?

3. How do you think Kurt Vonnegut became such an expert on writing?

4. How much information about himself did Vonnegut reveal in this article? Do you think it was intentional or accidental?

C .   L A N G U A G E   A N D   V O C A B U L A R Y

1. Under point 7, "Pity the Readers," the author uses the expression "singing like nightingales." What does he mean when he says this?

2. The author uses a number of specialized words, such as *piquant* and *locutions*. Would Vonnegut's writing still be helpful if he used only everyday words, such as *colorful* for *piquant* and *expressions* instead of *locutions*? Would it be as interesting as it is now?

D. STYLE, STRUCTURE, AND ORGANIZATION

1. What does the author say about the necessity for writing standard English? Does his own writing style follow this advice?

2. This article contains several *similes*—expressions that compare one thing to something that is similar in a very specific way. One of these is "singing like nightingales." Choose two or three more similes that use *like* or *as*. What idea does each simile communicate?

3. Reread the concluding sentence of the article. Does it emphasize the author's main point effectively?

E. TOPICS FOR DISCUSSION OR JOURNAL WRITING

1. Is it more important to write with your own voice or to write so that the reader will easily understand your message? Is it possible to do both?

2. How do you feel about your own writing ability? What writing skills would you like to improve?

3. Would you enjoy being a professional writer—making a living by selling your writing to publishers?

4. Which of Vonnegut's tips do you like the best? Why?

F. WRITING TOPICS FOR PARAGRAPHS OR ESSAYS

1. What steps do you follow when you write a paper? List each step and briefly describe it.

2. Rewrite a paper you wrote earlier, using some of Vonnegut's tips this time. Then write a paragraph telling which tips you used and how they seemed to work for you.

3. Write about how you felt when you had to write a paper for one of your college classes. If your feelings about writing have changed, compare your feelings now and in the past.

4. Give some practical advice about college to a new student. Include a short introduction, several points in the body, and a conclusion. Try to follow some of Vonnegut's tips for writing with style.

5. Check out a book by Kurt Vonnegut, Jr., from your local library, and choose one of the following topics to write about:

   a. In your opinion, does Vonnegut follow his own rules for writing? Include several examples from one chapter of his book.

   b. Write a critique of at least one chapter of the book. Include the author, title, page numbers, publisher, and year and date of publication; a short summary of the story; a few comments on the author's style; and your own reaction to the story.

Possible Lives

MIKE ROSE

As a professor of social research methodology at the University of California in Los Angeles, Mike Rose writes about the realities of American education today—the failures as well as the successes. His best-known book is probably *Lives on the Boundary: A Moving Account of the Struggles and Achievements of America's Educationally Underprepared.*

In these selections from his book *Possible Lives: The Promise of Public Education in America,* he credits the successful elementary and high school programs in the low-income desert community of Calexico, California, to three factors. As you read, try to identify these factors.

PREREADING QUESTIONS

1. Do you think that most people learned a lot in their K–12 schooling? How well does K–12 education prepare most students for college?

2. Do you know of some things that the school system in your local area does well? Can you think of some things that could be improved?

VOCABULARY PREVIEW

kiosk booth

bicultural sharing elements of two cultures

surveying mapping of landscape features and property boundaries

dropout rate the percentage of students who do not finish high school

Latino Latin-American, Hispanic; often used to mean Spanish-speaking people

unanimity complete agreement

district administration the management, those whose job it is to manage a school district on a daily basis

school board the elected officials who oversee the management of a school district and establish policies and guidelines for the administration to follow

bilingual education education in two languages (in this case, English and Spanish)

satellite campus a small campus that is not independent from a main campus

four-year degree the standard bachelor's degree, which usually takes at least four years to earn

rocanrol rock and roll (an attempt to represent the Mexican pronunciation)

precariously dangerously (in this case, in danger of falling)

listlessly without any excitement, interest, or energy

fecund fertile

empathetic understanding

La Maestra the teacher (Spanish)

poverty line the income level that the U.S. government sets to officially decide who is "poor"

parcel out divide up

gender male or female

factored into played a part in

unilateral one-sided

cohesiveness sticking together

role part to play

POSSIBLE LIVES

I drove out of Los Angeles on the 405, two hours or so, curving through San Diego, close to the Mexican border, heading east onto Highway 8, where the road narrowed from four lanes to two. I passed an abandoned government kiosk, various twists of scrap metal, and a thousand configurations of rock and brush, and began the slow descent onto the desert floor of the Imperial Valley. There were signs for—but no sight of—Lake Moreno, Kitchen Creek Road, the Tecate Divide, Manzanita, Jacumba, and Ocotillo. The sky was clear, deep blue, and the sun played off the rockface in the distance. I was the only car on the road. The air was warm and dry. In the distance: ROAD 98. The road that takes you along the border to Calexico.

2   Calexico is an American city that speaks two languages, a truly bicultural city. Border culture. Of the 21,000 residents, most are of Mexican ancestry, and the majority of Anglos speak so-so-to-fluent Spanish. This whole area of the Imperial Valley was converted from desert to arable land through water diverted from the Colorado River. The project began just after the turn of the century. Calexico was the surveying camp on the Mexican border—the name blends *Cali*fornia and *Mexico*—and in 1908 was incorporated as a city. A few of the early buildings still stand on First Street, just this side of Mexicali.

3   Though many families in Calexico are poor—income is low and seasonal—and the school district is always scrambling for funds, the elementary schools exceeded the Imperial County average on recent statewide tests of language arts, mathematics, and science, and the high schools have the lowest dropout rate of any predominantly Latino school district in California. In fact, they are 9 percentage points below the statewide average for *all* schools. A significant number of graduates go on to two- and four-year colleges. One explanation has to do with the unanimity of goals between district administration and school board. Another with an effective bilingual education program. And a third has to do with the way teacher education develops out of respect for local history.

                                      * * *

4   The Imperial Valley Campus of San Diego State University took up one square block of land six short blocks from the Mexican border. It was located on the site of the old Calexico High School, which had been boarded up and broken into for a long time. The campus retained three original, though refurbished, buildings— archways, white stucco, tile roofs—and had built a few classrooms and brought in some portable structures for administration, student services, and faculty offices. There were plans in the works for a complete reconstruction, but for over twenty-five years this small satellite campus, with its patchwork of buildings and bungalows, has served as the only means for Valley residents to get a four-year degree. Walking down Seventh Street, you came upon it like a park or a historical preserve, nestled between houses and parked cars and an occasional delivery van. Maybe you'd hear the buzz of a lawn mower. Little more.

5   Students at the campus would usually begin their work at IVC, Imperial Valley College, a two-year school about twelve miles north of Calexico, right up Highway 111, and transfer over to complete degrees in humanities or social science. They majored in liberal studies or Latin-American studies, English or Spanish or criminal justice administration, psychology or history, to prepare themselves for careers in business or law enforcement or education. Many hoped to teach. They were a serious student body—numbering four or five hundred in any given year—and they came to school in order to lead a better life here in the Valley. Most worked, and night courses were popular. Hardly anyone hung out. So unless you walked across campus right at those times when classes were starting up or winding down—noon, say, or four or seven or ten— you might, in fact, think the place *was* a historical monument. There would be the shade and rustle of Mexican fan palms and date palms and eucalyptus, and you might stop to hear the birds chirping in the trees and cooing in the red tile. As you made your way toward the north side of campus—it's a short walk—you'd begin to hear faint music from behind the closed doors of the service bungalows: the hectic advertisements of the Mexican *rocanrol* stations or trumpets and guitars or the lyrics of North American oldies—"Angel Baby" or "Blue Velvet." A little farther, over toward the plywood and corrugated metal, and you'd come upon the faculty offices, faded and baking in the sun.

* * *

6   Evangelina Bustamante Jones sat in front of gray metal bookcases wedged tight against her brief office wall. The shelves were crammed with books on the teaching of writing, bilingual education, reading, and teacher education—her responsibilities here. Student papers and projects from semesters past were boxed or bundled or rolled up and stacked precariously on shelves or placed safely in a corner on the floor. Newspaper clippings about former students—weddings and awards—were taped to the wall. "It's such a small community," she said, leaning forward and loosely folding her hands on the desk, "that you kinda keep track of everyone."

7   We had just come from visiting a student teacher she was supervising—teaching over in Heber, a little agricultural town about three miles northwest of Calexico. Anthony Heber was one of the

early developers of the Imperial Valley—many of the cities in the Valley and the streets within them were named after developers and civil engineers—and the town that bore his name had twenty-five hundred people, two schools, and a lot of cattle that listlessly regarded you as you drove in. The air was heavy and fecund. "You don't notice it," a local told me, "until you leave. Then when you return, it's well, it's the smell of home." Lori, the young teacher, was born in Heber and wrote in the journal Evangelina asked her to keep, "I am so happy and so lucky to be working in this school where I grew up."

8   "She's really good," Evangelina continued. "She's very creative, very responsible, and she's empathetic. She may not stay in Heber, but it's important for her to be there now." Evangelina absentmindedly touched a streak of silver in her hair. "You know, some of the teachers Lori had as a little girl are still there—and her principal, too. They gave her a lot of support." A pause here. "And in the eyes of her old neighbors. Imagine! 'Look at Lori. She's come back.' *La Maestra.*"

9   Education was highly valued in places like Heber and Calexico, as it was generally in Mexican culture. Teachers were respected, and school was seen as a place where children could learn the skills that would enable them to do better than their parents had done. This support of education played out, however, amid a complex of forces. Many of the families in the Valley were poor—35 percent of the residents lived below the poverty line— and sometimes had to make decisions between work and school. As Evangelina put it, "Poverty forces you to parcel out your human resources." So some children would be selected to pursue their education, and others sent out to make money. "I was the oldest and had to work," one man explained, "but my brother was able to go to college." Traditional beliefs about gender factored into these decisions, but not in the unilateral way commonly portrayed. Some families still believed that girls don't need schooling as much as boys do, but I also heard from a number of professional women that it was their working-class fathers who urged them toward achievement. Such achievement could, though, conflict with other beliefs about family cohesiveness and a woman's role in maintaining it—and this could become a source of awful tension if a college-bound woman decided to leave the area

to pursue her education. The local San Diego State campus made higher education possible for women who could not easily leave the Valley.

A . C O M P R E H E N S I O N

1. According to the author, what three factors explain the success of the high school program in Calexico?
2. Why did some residents of the Imperial Valley have to choose between school and work?
3. Who is Evangelina Bustamante Jones? What is her job?
4. How do the people in this region feel about education and teachers?

B . C R I T I C A L T H I N K I N G

1. The author gives several details about the performance of students in Calexico schools. Do these facts support his point that the schools are successful?
2. Do you think there are still some parents in Calexico who don't want their daughters to go to college as much as they want their sons to go to college? What statement in the reading gives you that idea?
3. In another book, *Lives on the Boundary*, author Mike Rose talks about struggling college students whose K–12 educations left them underprepared for college. In *Possible Lives*, he focuses on successful educational programs. Do these book titles match the author's message?
4. What do you think is the author's purpose in writing about educational programs?

C . L A N G U A G E A N D V O C A B U L A R Y

1. Had you ever read or heard the expression "arable land" before you read it in the second paragraph of this selection? Can you figure out the meaning by reading the other words around it?
2. In this reading, the author uses many adverbs that end in -ly. An *adverb* is a word that describes or changes the meaning of verbs,

adjectives, and other adverbs, such as "Education was *highly valued* . . ." Find and underline at least 8 -*ly* adverbs in the reading. (Do not underline four other words that end in -*ly* but are not used as adverbs—*early, only, hardly,* and *family*.)

D. STYLE, STRUCTURE, AND ORGANIZATION

1. Mike Rose includes a lot of background information about Calexico and the Imperial Valley in this selection. Find and list six or seven details about the community. Does this background information make the reading seem more interesting and realistic?

2. Of the three reasons for the successes of Calexico's schools, the author focuses on two of them. Why do you think he wrote more about those two reasons than about the other reason?

3. There are eight paragraphs in this selection. For each paragraph, write down one or two words (or at most a few words) that tell what its main topic is. Does each paragraph concentrate on one main point?

E. TOPICS FOR DISCUSSION OR JOURNAL WRITING

1. What is it like to grow up very poor? In what ways can poverty prevent students from learning, getting a high school education, and going on to college?

2. What are the advantages and disadvantages of growing up in a small town compared with living in or near a city?

3. Would you like to be a teacher? Why or why not?

4. Reread the last section, about Evangelina Bustamante Jones and Lori, the student teacher. Do you think you would enjoy being in a class taught by either of these women? Do they remind you of any teachers you have known?

F.   WRITING   TOPICS   FOR   PARAGRAPHS   OR   ESSAYS

1. Write about a particular class that you learned a lot from or about another learning situation that was important in your life.

2. What are your educational goals or dreams?

3. Investigate what kind of tutorial and small-group help is available to students at your college. Write a short report telling when, where, and how students can access these services.

4. Make a list of several classes in which you learned a lot and another list of classes in which you didn't learn as much. What did the more effective classes have in common that the other classes didn't?

5. Read all or part of a book by Mike Rose, such as *Lives on the Boundary* or *Possible Lives*. Then choose one of the following writing assignments:

    a. Imagine that you are one of the characters in the book. Then write about your educational experiences. What worked and what didn't?

    b. Write a short summary of the author's main points.

Breaking Through
the Barriers

JAMES M. HENSLIN

Jaime Escalante, a high school calculus teacher in East Los Angeles, is well known for his ability to motivate and inspire students. A popular 1987 movie, *Stand and Deliver*, brought Escalante's success story to the attention of the public. As you read the following selection from a college sociology textbook, consider why Jaime Escalante has been so effective in motivating students.

PREREADING QUESTIONS

1. What qualities should a teacher have in order to motivate and inspire students?

2. What kinds of problems would you expect to find in an inner-city school?

VOCABULARY

plagued with severely affected by

recruitment persuading people to join

motto a brief statement of someone's ideals or principles

tracked in this context, placed in certain kinds of classes, usually based on grades or standardized tests

barrio a Spanish-speaking area of a city, where most families have limited incomes

SOURCE: "Breaking Through the Barriers" by James M. Henslin. From James M. Henslin, *Sociology, a Down-to-Earth Approach*, Fourth Edition, copyright © 1999 by Allyn & Bacon. Reprinted by permission.

rigorous strict

binds obligates or requires

foundation an organization that provides money for special purposes

sociological about or related to society

BREAKING THROUGH THE BARRIERS

Called "the best teacher in America," Jaime Escalante taught in an East Los Angeles inner-city school plagued with poverty, crime, drugs, gangs, and the usual miserably low student scores. In this self-defeating environment, he taught calculus. His students scored so highly on national tests that test officials, suspecting cheating, asked his students to retake the test. They did. Again they passed—this time with even higher scores.

2   Escalante's school ranks fourth in the nation in the number of students who have taken and passed the Advanced Placement SAT Calculus examination. For students to even take the test, they must complete Algebra I, Geometry, Algebra II, Trigonometry or Math Analysis, and Calculus for first-year college and/or Calculus for second-year college.

3   How did Escalante overcome such odds? His success is *not* due to a recruitment of the brightest students. Students' poor academic performance does not stand in the way of being admitted to the math program. The *only* requirement is an interest in math. What did Escalante do right, and what can we learn from his approach?

4   "Success starts with attitude" could be Escalante's motto. Few Latino students were taking math. Most were tracked into craft classes and made jewelry and birdhouses. "Our kids are just as talented as anyone else. They just need the opportunity to show it. And for that, they must be motivated," he said. "They just don't think about becoming scientists or engineers."

5   Here are the keys to what Escalante accomplished. First, teaching and learning can't take place unless there is discipline. For that the

teachers, not gangs, must control the classroom. Second, the students must believe in themselves. The teacher must inspire students with the idea that they *can* learn (remember teacher expectations). Third, the students must be motivated to perform, in this case to see learning as a way out of the barrio, the path to good jobs.

6   Escalante uses a team approach. He has his students think of themselves as a team, of him as the coach, and the national exams as a sort of Olympics for which they are preparing. To stimulate team identity, the students wear team jackets, caps, and T-shirts with logos that identify them as part of the team. Before class, his students do "warmups" (hand clapping and foot stomping to a rock song).

7   His team has practice schedules as rigorous as a championship football team. Students must sign a contract that binds them to participate in the summer program he has developed, to complete the daily homework, and to attend Saturday morning and after-school study sessions. To get in his class, even the student's parents have to sign the contract. To keep before his students the principle that self-discipline pays off, Escalante covers his room

with posters of sports figures in action—Michael Jordan, Jerry West, Babe Ruth, and Tiger Woods.

8   "How have I been successful with students from such backgrounds?" he asks. "Very simple. I use a time-honored tradition—hard work, lots of it, for teacher and student alike."

9   The following statement helps us understand how Escalante challenges his students to think of what is possible in life, instead of problems that destroy the possible:

> The first day when these kids walk into my room, I have a bunch of names of schools and colleges on the chalkboard. I ask each student to memorize one. The next day I pick one kid and ask, "What school did you pick?" He says USC or UCLA or Stanford, MIT, Colgate, and so on. So I say, "Okay, keep that in mind. I'm going to bring in somebody who'll be talking about the schools."

10   Escalante then has a college adviser talk to the class. But more than this, he also has arranged foundation money to help the students get to the colleges of their choice.

11   The sociological point is that the problem was *not* the ability of the students. Their failure to do well in school was not due to something *within* them. The problem was the *system*, the way classroom instruction is arranged. When Escalante changed the system of instruction, both attitudes and performance changed. Escalante makes this very point—that student performance does not depend on the charismatic personality of a single person, but on how we structure the learning setting.

A . C O M P R E H E N S I O N

1. What kinds of problems did Escalante encounter as a teacher in East Los Angeles?

2. What was Escalante's greatest achievement as a teacher?

3. According to the author, there are three key factors that account for the success of Escalante's program. What are they, and why is each one important?

4. What did Escalante do to get students interested in going to college?

B . CRITICAL THINKING

1. Why do you think Jaime Escalante's approach has been so successful? Would this approach work well in other high schools? Why or why not?

2. What is the main point that the reading makes about our educational system?

3. What are some of the biggest challenges that teachers like Jaime Escalante face?

4. Why were only a few Latino students enrolled in math classes before Escalante's program began?

C . LANGUAGE AND VOCABULARY

1. Were you familiar with the word *charismatic* before you read it in the last sentence of the reading? What do you think it means? Why does the author say, "Student performance does not depend on the *charismatic* personality of a single person"?

2. In paragraph 6, Escalante's "team approach" is compared to training for the Olympics. Does this comparison make sense? Why or why not?

D . STYLE, STRUCTURE, AND ORGANIZATION

1. How does the introductory paragraph (the first paragraph of the reading) capture readers' attention?

2. Look for three places in the reading where the author includes statements made by Jaime Escalante himself. How do these statements make the reading more interesting and effective?

3. Which paragraph expresses the author's main point about our educational system?

E . T O P I C S   F O R   D I S C U S S I O N   O R   J O U R N A L   W R I T I N G

1. What do you think students liked best about Escalante's program?

2. Do you think that schools today are still experiencing the same kinds of problems that Escalante encountered in East Los Angeles?

3. Would you like to be a teacher? Why or why not? What grades or subjects would you like to teach?

4. Do you think that students should be *tracked*, or placed in certain kinds of classes, on the basis of their grades and test scores? Why or why not?

5. Have you ever encountered ethnic stereotyping in school or elsewhere?

F . W R I T I N G   T O P I C S   F O R   P A R A G R A P H S   O R   E S S A Y S

1. Write about a special teacher or someone else who inspired you to achieve something.

2. Compare and contrast Jaime Escalante's math program with the math classes at the high school you attended. In your paper, explain the most important similarities and differences.

3. Imagine that a friend of yours is thinking about dropping out of school. Using some ideas from the reading and some ideas of your own, persuade your friend to stay in school. Write either a personal letter to your friend or a persuasive paragraph.

4. Interview a favorite teacher or a person you admire. Use a tape recorder or take good notes, so that you can accurately quote some of the person's most interesting statements. Then write a paper about the person you interviewed, including at least two quotations.

5. Watch the movie *Stand and Deliver* to learn more about Jaime Escalante and some of his students. Then choose one of the following writing assignments:
   a. Write about Jaime Escalante. Explain why he is a good teacher.
   b. Write about one of the students featured in the movie. How did the experience of being in Escalante's class change this person's life?

Online Schools Provide New Education Options

THE ASSOCIATED PRESS

According to professional educators, an estimated two million students were being homeschooled in the United States in 2001–2002, with large increases every year since then. This Associated Press article discusses online schooling, one of the newest methods of learning at home. Online students learn from the Internet, e-mail, and computer software, either from an online school or independently.

P R E R E A D I N G   Q U E S T I O N S

1. Do you think that most students receive a good education in their kindergarten through twelfth grade classes in public schools?

2. Do you think that students could learn as well from computers as from attending class? Is your answer the same for all ages?

V O C A B U L A R Y

formal education schooling

backers supporters

software computer programs

uncharted unknown and not mapped out

cyberspace the world of interconnected computer networks

skeptical doubting

spiraling in this case, rapidly increasing

the dot-com world the world of Internet-based computer companies

secondary schools high schools

charter schools experimental schools granted more flexibility than traditional schools

Web the part of the Internet where pages are displayed (World Wide Web)

fax to transmit pages over telephone lines (as graphics)

void empty place

attention deficit/hyperactivity disorder a disorder that can make people impulsive, inattentive, and excessively active

interactive lessons lessons that include student participation

hacked into the system broke into a computer or computer network electronically

racked up caused (or scored)

knocking the school offline causing the school to disconnect from the Internet

congressional panel a group of congressional representatives that examines a particular topic

hands-on learning learning by doing

model in this case, a way of doing something

ONLINE SCHOOLS PROVIDE NEW EDUCATION OPTIONS

A generation growing up on the Internet may now get its formal education there—from new schools offering kindergarten through 12th grade online.

2   Backers of education technology say the Internet can help children isolated from traditional schoolhouses by distance or disabilities or benefit children already schooled at home by their parents.

3   "Education is what America cares about the most, and technology is what we do best," said former Education Secretary William Bennett, introducing a new online school Thursday. The for-profit school, K12, begins enrollment next fall in kindergarten through second grade and promises eventually to offer lessons in all grades from math and science to arts and sex education. Costs would range from $25 for skill tests to about $2,000 for full lesson plans and software for a year.

4   As a past critic of education technology, Bennett once gave schools' efforts to increase use of computers in teaching an "F−." Yet he is joining companies and school districts willing, even eager, to sail into uncharted cyberspace despite skeptical child development experts and the spiraling business failure rate in the dot-com world.

5   There's no exact count of public and private elementary and secondary schools that have followed the lead of Web-based colleges; the nonprofit, Orlando-based Florida Online High School has offered online courses since 1997 for grades 9 to 12 nationwide. Public charter schools from California to Pennsylvania teach children online. At the state-funded Valley Pathways online school based in Palmer, Alaska, roughly 300 students take one to six courses a semester on the Web.

6   "We wouldn't do it if we didn't think it could produce an equal education—or better," said Pathways teacher Kathi Baldwin. "I know my students online and in detail. They tell you things in writing they would never tell you face-to-face."

7   Classes are held by computer, teachers and staff work from a central office, and students sign in from their home desktop or laptop computers. Standards for teachers ideally are the same as those of traditional schools.

8   It's not all reading, writing and arithmetic. In gym class over the Web, pupils keep daily logs of their exercises. They learn music theory online, then go to a designated campus for piano or guitar

lessons. They can fax, email or bring in art projects completed at home. Parents even dial in for an online PTA meeting.

9   Linda Deafenbaugh said online schooling has filled a void for her son, a third-grader with attention deficit/hyperactivity disorder. Each morning, despite his behavioral disorder, Douglas Meikle, 8, signs on to the Western Pennsylvania Cyber Charter School and downloads his reading, science and math assignments himself. He completes the lessons, working with online teachers, including a special-education expert, to keep him focused.

10   "He definitely had a bad school experience, to the point teachers were not letting him in the door of the classrooms," said Deafenbaugh, a cultural anthropologist who works for the federal government. "Not only was his social life falling apart, but his academics were, too."

11   Douglas, who stays home with his father in Pittsburgh, socializes with other children at after-school sessions, sporting events and church groups, she said.

12   The going has been bumpy for some online schools. Teachers have to keep up student interest with interactive lessons, guard against student cheating and do without body language or verbal cues to tell them whether students understand lectures.

13   And in October, a 15-year-old in an online charter school in California hacked into the system and racked up $18,000 in damage, knocking the school offline for two days and destroying homework assignments, lesson plans and attendance records.

14   "There simply is not enough research," said William Rukeyser, coordinator of the nonprofit Woodland, California-based Learning in the Real World. "Too often, people say 'Let's spend the money and maybe the wisdom will miraculously transfer from the computer to the child.'"

15   Schools spent more than $5 billion on education technology last year, and a congressional panel concluded last week that 70 percent of America's classrooms are connected to the Web.

16   But the marriage of education and technology is needed, say educators who believe teaching is becoming more difficult in today's environment. Growing enrollments and shrinking budgets are leaving less room for one-on-one, hands-on learning at the side of an attentive teacher.

17   "We shouldn't be stuck with one model," Bennett said.

A . C O M P R E H E N S I O N

1. According to the article, what types of children can online learning help?

2. According to former Education Secretary William Bennett, what does America care about the most?

3. What types of online classes are mentioned in the article?

4. How much did schools spend on educational technology the year before this article was written?

B . C R I T I C A L   T H I N K I N G

1. Do you think online classes would be easier or more difficult than classroom learning? In what ways?

2. One of the biggest questions about homeschooling or online classes is how those students can socialize with other young people. Do you think this is a valid question? What does the article say on this topic?

3. Should online teachers be required to have the same qualifications as teachers in traditional classrooms? Do you think they need to have any additional qualifications to teach online? Why?

4. Can the Internet be dangerous? How?

C . L A N G U A G E   A N D   V O C A B U L A R Y

1. This article includes several examples of figurative language— expressions that mean something different from the literal meaning of the words. These include "the going has been bumpy," "the marriage of education and technology," "hacked into the system," and "racked up." Do you think these expressions add something to the article? If so, in what way?

2. This article contains many adjectives—words that describe nouns. The first three examples are *formal* education, *new* schools, and *educational* technology. List at least ten other adjectives from the article. How does the use of adjectives contribute to an effective article or essay?

D. STYLE, STRUCTURE, AND ORGANIZATION

1. Find at least eight *numbers* in the article. Does the use of numbers and statistics make the article seem more professional? Why or why not?

2. Find at least three statements by education professionals that are quoted in the reading. Does the use of quotations make the reading more effective? In what way?

E. TOPICS FOR DISCUSSION OR JOURNAL WRITING

1. What kinds of schools did you go to (public, private, charter, homeschool, or other)? Are you satisfied with the quality of education that you received?

2. Would you enjoy taking college classes online? What would be some advantages and disadvantages?

3. How comfortable are you with computers and the Internet? Would you be comfortable enrolling your own children in an online school?

4. Near the end of this article the writer states, "Growing enrollments and shrinking budgets are leaving less room for one-on-one, hands-on learning at the side of an attentive teacher." Did you have this kind of one-on-one attention in your kindergarten through twelfth grade classes? Why or why not?

5. In what ways have you used computers (playing games, finding information, writing papers, communicating with other people, learning, etc.)? What different software programs have you used? Would any of these be useful in online education?

F. WRITING TOPICS FOR PARAGRAPHS OR ESSAYS

1. What experience have you had with computer-assisted instruction (CAI)? Write a narration paper describing your experience in using computers for educational purposes.

2. Find a newspaper article or magazine article about homeschooling or online schooling in *Time* magazine or another source. Write a summary of the article and include your own evaluation of the article.

3. Write ten questions that you would ask if you were considering online classes for yourself or your children, and explain why you would ask each question.

4. Use the library or do an online search on the different types of homeschooling, such as through the public schools, private schools, charter schools, online schools, or independent homeschooling. Write a classification paper on the different types of homeschooling available.

5. Use library resources or the Internet to find out more about attention deficit disorder and hyperactivity. Write an informative paper about the information you find.

How to Win the College Game

BARBARA KANTROWITZ

Barbara Kantrowitz, a senior editor for *Newsweek* magazine, has written many articles about education and the family for *Newsweek*, as well as articles for the *New York Times*, the *Philadelphia Inquirer*, and numerous popular magazines. Her many awards include the National Education Reporting Award from the Education Writers Association, the Benjamin Fine Journalism Award from the National Association of Secondary School Principals, and the Distinguished Achievement Award from the Educational Press Association.

Kantrowitz holds a bachelor's degree from Cornell University and a master's degree in journalism from Columbia. She is well qualified to write about current issues and trends in education. The issue that she explores in "How to Win the College Game" is the intense competition for admission to top colleges and universities, and what some high school students are doing to make their resumés more appealing to prestigious schools.

PREREADING QUESTIONS

1. Which colleges and universities in your area are the most popular and the most prestigious? Is there a lot of competition for admission to these schools?

2. Do you think high school grades are a good predictor of how well someone will do in college?

VOCABULARY

brisk invigorating (in this case, cool and windy)

elite having a superior intellectual or social status

top of the food chain the highest point in a progression (slang)

SATs Scholastic Aptitude Tests

daunting intimidating, discouraging

alleviate to relieve, to make something less severe

decal in this case, a college sticker or label

burgeoning growing

shell out pay money (slang)

holy grail in this case, the objective of a "quest" or extensive search

spiel a lengthy talk or speech

royal flush an excellent poker hand; in this case, a winning combination

Third World relatively undeveloped countries in Africa, Asia, and Latin America

holistic overall, based on the whole picture rather than specific details

savviest the most perceptive or shrewdest

lukewarm in this case, lacking enthusiasm

alumni people who graduated from a particular college or university

HOW TO WIN THE COLLEGE GAME

On a brisk afternoon in late March, I follow several dozen nervous parents and teenagers into a lecture room in the basement of Byerly Hall at Harvard University. We are engaged in a uniquely American ritual: the college tour. I am just an observer, the only adult without a prospective student in tow. But as the mother of a high-school junior, I understand the anxiety as we await the start of an "information session." On the floor above us, in a room with photographs of Nelson Mandela and Winston Churchill receiving honorary Harvard degrees, admissions officers are deciding who will be offered a place in the class of 2006. Around 19,500 seniors have applied; only about 2,110 will make the cut.

2   Who will get in? With a record number of well-qualified seniors, the outcome at Harvard and other selective schools has become increasingly unpredictable. Even the strongest student is advised not to buy the sweat shirt until the envelope is actually in hand. I've been covering higher education for more than a decade,

but as a parent, I am just as bewildered as anyone else. The whole process has begun to seem like some kind of mysterious game. And, "as a game," says former Duke admissions officer Rachel Toor, "college admissions is kind of like Americans watching a cricket match. You think you can sort of follow it, but basically you have no idea, really, what is going on."

3   A generation ago, fewer than a third of high-school seniors were college-bound; now more than twice as many say they're shooting for a bachelor's degree. Although most will attend public universities, students from a much wider range of social and economic backgrounds now aim for elite schools. The problem is that they are competing for basically the same number of places as students did 30 years ago when Harvard, for example, had just 7,885 applicants, all male, and accepted 19 percent.

4   Even universities at the top of the food chain, alarmed about the spectacle of seventh graders cramming for their SATs, are looking for ways to make the admissions process seem less daunting—although without actually letting more people in. University of California president Richard Atkinson made headlines

when he called for abandoning the SAT I, which is supposed to test reasoning skills, because he thinks students spend too much time studying for it instead of actually learning math or history.

5   But these efforts haven't done much to alleviate parents' and students' concerns—especially in upper-middle-class communities in the Northeast and California, where decal envy is the most intense. "There are an increasing number of people who think that if their child does not go to a certain level of school, they won't make it in life," says Bruce Poch, dean of admissions at Pomona College, which had a 14 percent increase in applications this year. "We even have parents of sixth graders calling us and asking what courses their children should take." The result is a burgeoning industry of private college counselors, test-prep courses and books (including Toor's recent account of her three years at Duke, called "Admissions Confidential"). Private counselors can cost as much as $25,000 for four years of advice, but there are plenty of parents willing to shell out. Of the 90 seniors currently in the top 10 percent of the class at New Trier High School in Winnetka, Illinois, which regularly sends many students to elite schools, more than a quarter sought advice from an outside consultant, says Jim Conroy, who runs the school's college counseling department.

6   Even if you get into one of these schools, there's no evidence that a name-brand degree guarantees anything except a steady stream of requests for alumni donations. "In today's world, there's no one college that's the only place to go," says independent counselor Howard Greene, author of a popular series of college guides including "The Public Ivies" and "The Hidden Ivies." What really matters, Greene says, is finding a college that's a good fit for a particular student—either because of the courses it offers, the location, or the size.

7   That's a hard message to sell to a generation of parents who have put so much energy into providing the "best" of everything for their kids. Although the most obsessive start worrying in preschool, the game really begins in earnest during spring vacation of junior year. That's when parents start to drag their offspring from campus to campus. At Harvard, the holy grail for many top students, admissions officer Jenny Rifkin tries to put a

friendly spin on her spiel. "Good afternoon," she says. Silence. She smiles encouragingly. "You can respond. I won't bite." Tentative laughter. Then she asks for names, schools, and hometowns. Most of the students are juniors, although there are a couple of seniors. They're from all over the country: Massachusetts, Indiana, California, New York, Texas, Maryland.

8   About the only thing these students have in common is that they probably won't get into Harvard. Many of today's applicants boast accomplishments that were rare a generation ago. And that makes it even harder for the colleges to distinguish between them. At high schools all over the country, students take Advanced Placement courses and compete for awards in a wide range of national contests to encourage future engineers, artists, scientists, and writers. The prosperous '90s meant many parents had money to nurture their youngsters' talents in everything soccer or Shakespeare.

9   Students believe they need something that really sets them apart, a "hook," like being an Intel finalist or winning a national honor in the Scholastic Art and Writing Awards. Summers have become particularly critical. The most affluent students look for community service, preferably in the Third World, like digging ditches in a remote village in South America.

10   While genuine accomplishments and a passion for something definitely boost an applicant's chances, "packaging" just to look good doesn't really work on the savviest admissions officers. Karl Furstenburg, Dartmouth's dean of admissions, says his staff of 14 can easily pick out a packaged kid. What Dartmouth is looking for, he says, is a consistent image of a student from the transcript, test scores, essays, recommendations (two from teachers, one from a counselor and one from a peer) and interviews. "When you read all this material, you see patterns," Furstenburg says. "You get a holistic view of the student. It's not a system that lends itself to being gamed." A great essay from a student with C's in English would be a red flag, for example, as would lukewarm teacher recommendations.

11   Of course, there are students who do generally have an edge: underrepresented minorities, children of alumni (called legacies), recruited athletes and applicants whose families have given substantial sums to a school. The boost these students get—

especially the legacies—depends on the school. But the special categories make it even harder for what Toor calls BWRKs (bright, well-rounded kids) to stand out. Some schools want BWRKs. Others look for "angular" kids who've made a mark in a particular area, like art or science. Unfortunately, colleges don't usually post this information on their Web sites, so unless you have a well-connected guidance counselor, you may not know which is which.

A. COMPREHENSION

1. In the year this article was written (2002), how many high school seniors had applied for admission to Harvard University? How many would actually be admitted? Thirty years ago, how many applied to Harvard and how many were accepted?

2. Why do some parents pay a lot of money to hire private college counselors or consultants?

3. According to the article, how early do some obsessive parents start worrying about their children's success in college?

4. What are some of the unusual activities or special projects that applicants at Harvard (and other universities) often do in hopes of making a good impression on the admissions officers?

B. CRITICAL THINKING

1. Why does the author describe the college admissions process as "some kind of mysterious game"?

2. What is the author's opinion of parents who push their sixth or seventh graders to start preparing and competing for college admissions? Do you agree or disagree?

3. Do you think the requirements for transferring from a community college to a four-year college or university are similar to the admission requirements for freshmen that are examined in this article? What do you think are the most important qualities that colleges and universities look for in transfer students?

4. Why do many students apply to prestigious universities like Harvard when they know that most applicants will not be admitted?

5. What do you think is the author's main point or overall view of the admissions process? Do you agree or disagree with her way of thinking?

C . L A N G U A G E A N D V O C A B U L A R Y

1. What does the abbreviation BWRKs stand for? Why do you suppose admissions officers sometimes use this abbreviation?

2. The author discusses "packaging" of students to increase their chances for college admission. What does she mean by this term used in this way? Do you think the term is effective and appropriate?

D . S T Y L E , S T R U C T U R E , A N D O R G A N I Z A T I O N

1. Is the opening paragraph effective? How does it capture your attention? Why is this paragraph written in the first person (using "I")?

2. Does the second paragraph do a good job of expressing the author's main idea about the college admissions process? Which other paragraph also emphasizes the author's main point? (Hint: Look near the end of the article.)

E . T O P I C S F O R D I S C U S S I O N O R J O U R N A L W R I T I N G

1. Why are you attending college? Do you think that your college degree will be an important asset in finding a job that you enjoy?

2. How do community colleges differ from four-year colleges and universities? What kinds of admission requirements do community colleges in your area generally have?

3. What are the advantages of attending a community college first and then transferring to a four-year college or university? What are the advantages of starting out as a freshman at a four-year college or university instead of attending a community college?

4. Do you think that students who did not have high grades in high school can sometimes be very successful in college? Why? What kinds of opportunities are available for these students to prove their ability?

5. How do you feel about your progress and success in college so far? How can you continue to be successful? Are there things you can do to improve your success and increase your satisfaction with your educational progress?

F. WRITING TOPICS FOR PARAGRAPHS OR ESSAYS

1. Find out what the admissions requirements (or transfer requirements) are for a college or university that you would like to attend, and report on your findings. You can look up the college or university online, call or write to the admissions office, visit the college or university in person, or ask for assistance at your school's transfer center or counseling office (if one is available).

2. Choose two colleges or universities, or a community college and a university, and write a comparison/contrast paper about their similarities and differences.

3. Write a paper about how college has changed or affected your life.

4. Write about your goals for the future, including how graduating from college is important to achieving your goals.

5. Write a persuasive or instructional paper aimed at high school students who are preparing to attend college. Based on what you read in this article as well as on your own experience, give your audience helpful tips and suggestions about what they should do and what they should not do in their last years of high school. If you wish, you may also include advice about which colleges or universities they should consider.

MEDIA AND POPULAR CULTURE

Taking Potluck

TOM BODETT

Tom Bodett is well known as an American humorist. Although he grew up in Michigan, he now divides his time between the Seattle area and Homer, Alaska. Much of his humor is about life in Alaska.

At one time, Tom Bodett hosted a radio variety show from Homer, Alaska, and he has been a radio commentator and the host of a television travel show. He is also the author of six books, including collections of his radio shows and a novel for children called *Williwaw!* Listeners and readers alike have enjoyed his casual humor based on ordinary people and everyday situations.

P R E R E A D I N G   Q U E S T I O N S

1. Why do people enjoy potluck dinners and picnics?
2. Can you think of some foods that are popular in certain parts of the country but not in other areas?

V O C A B U L A R Y

potluck a meal or party where each guest brings a food dish

staple a basic food

foodfest a feast; an event with lots of food

entrée the main course

splayed spread out

constitution in this context, the way something is made; structure or composition

cod a type of fish

hover remain nearby

slinks moves quietly, trying not to be noticed

trough in this case, a V-shaped feeding dish like those used for farm animals

lingering remaining

ravaged destroyed; in this context, meaning that most of the food has been partially eaten

dispirited without much spirit, lacking enthusiasm

TAKING POTLUCK

Of all the wonderful distractions that summer has to offer, none is quite as wonderful as the potluck. I know it isn't strictly a summer event, but a potluck takes on much broader dimensions in the warmer months. It's held outdoors, usually accompanied by horseshoes or volleyball. The children run circles around each other, and the fish is fresh.

2   Fish is a staple of the Alaskan potluck, and I've never been to one that didn't have at least three species of it on hand in one form or another. Back in the Midwest where I first sat down to one, you could ruin a good potluck by bringing fish to it. People are suspicious of fish back there, and I'm sure the expression "smells fishy to me" originated at a community feed somewhere in northern Indiana. Fried chicken is the heart of the Great Plains foodfest, but outside the entrée, the ingredients of a good potluck are pretty universal.

3   Start with a large folding table on an uneven lawn and invite a bunch of people over. No matter what happens someone always brings too much fish, so there's no need to worry about the main course. Then wanders in a pot of beans and weenies and a relish tray with rolled-up cold cuts splayed around a radish-and-celery arrangement. Someone always brings marshmallows so the kids have something to get stuck in their hair, and a bachelor or two will show up with a six-pack and a bag of Doritos.

4   No fewer than five potato salads will appear in rapid succession. You have to like potato salad if you're going to like potlucks. In fact, I think the "pot" in "potluck" is an abbreviation for "potato salad," and the luck refers to those few fortunate individuals who can get through the meal and not wear some of it home.

5   Everything is served up on paper plates with the constitution of flour tortillas and eaten with little plastic forks that couldn't pry a bone from a cooked cod let alone penetrate your neighbor's lasagna.

6   Potlucks are hardest on those who do the cooking. They hover around the food table to see what's going over the best. "Now, no one has touched the three-bean salad. What's the matter with you people?" The builder of the salad turns the color of the red-cabbage clam dip and slinks toward the beer cooler. The hero of any

potluck is the one who brings the deviled eggs. They are usually devoured before the other folks can even get the tin foil off their casseroles.

7   After one or two courses your plate has become something of a trough folded in the palm of one hand. An amazing blend of flavors is then inevitable. The juice from the fruit-and-nut salad seeps in under your uncle's world-famous beef-and-bean burritos, and the hot sauce from that makes an interesting topping for the fresh apple crumb cake you discovered while going back for one more bratwurst.

8   In a while most folks will have had their fill and will wander off sleepily in small groups to toss horseshoes or slap mosquitoes. There's always one or two guys who linger to graze at the table, but their picking has no real spirit behind it. A survey of the ravaged spread will reveal a half-dozen potato salads with one scoop out of each and a large basket of wholly untouched fruit.

9   I got an idea from this. You see, in this season of multiple potlucks it's not unusual to be invited to more than one on a single day. You can't make a different dish for each of them, so I recommend you make a potato salad and take the paprika shaker

along with you. When you leave the first party, just smooth over your salad with a spoon and put some fresh paprika on top. No one will know the difference, and you'll be able to gracefully enter potluck after potluck.

10   To be prepared for the improbable—like if someone actually eats all your salad—keep a basket of plastic fruit in the car at all times. This will get you into the next party and it's perfectly safe, as no one ever eats the fruit. I glue them all together in case those lingering grazers get nosy and try to get them out of the basket. They usually give up after a few dispirited tugs and wander off to test the potato salads.

11   Of course, I don't recommend everyone follow my advice on this. *Somebody's* gotta bring the fish.

A. COMPREHENSION

1. How is an Alaskan potluck different from a Midwest or Great Plains potluck?

2. Which potluck menu items named by the author are universal (common at potlucks in all parts of the country)?

3. According to the author, which potluck food item is the most popular, judging by the fact that it is eaten first?

4. If a person is invited to more than one potluck on the same day, how does Tom Bodett suggest handling the situation?

B. CRITICAL THINKING

1. Do you think the author really believes that "the 'pot' in 'potluck' is an abbreviation for 'potato salad'"? How can you tell whether he is serious?

2. Find at least four negative things that the author says about potlucks. Why does he mention these things? Do you think he is really being critical of potlucks, or is he trying to be humorous? How can you tell?

3. Do you think the author enjoys living in Alaska? Why or why not?

4. What do you think was the author's main purpose in writing this essay—to inform or to entertain?

C . L A N G U A G E   A N D   V O C A B U L A R Y

1. Had you ever heard an expression like "graze at the table" to describe a style of eating at a potluck or buffet dinner? What do you think it means? Describe what a person does when he or she is *grazing.*

2. Find at least two statements that made you smile or laugh while you were reading this selection. What is there about the author's word choices that makes these statements humorous?

D . S T Y L E ,   S T R U C T U R E , A N D   O R G A N I Z A T I O N

1. In some parts of the essay, the author seems to be giving instructions. For example, in paragraph 3, he says, "Start with a large folding table on an uneven lawn . . . ," as if he is telling readers how to organize a potluck. Find another place where the author tells readers what to do in a certain potluck situation. Does this part of the essay use a somewhat different style than other parts in order to give instructions to readers?

2. The author's style includes a lot of visual details, as well as some details that involve the senses of touch, smell, and taste. Highlight or underline at least five visual details that you think are especially effective and at least two details that use one of the other senses.

E . T O P I C S   F O R   D I S C U S S I O N O R   J O U R N A L   W R I T I N G

1. What are the advantages and disadvantages of a potluck, compared with other types of parties?

2. Would you feel comfortable at a potluck in Alaska like the one the author describes? Why or why not?

3. What kinds of difficulties might a person experience while adjusting to the customs and way of life in a different part of the country?

4. Plan a potluck that includes your favorite foods and activities. How is it different from the one described in the reading?

5. Would you enjoy listening to a radio show hosted by Tom Bodett? Why or why not?

F. WRITING TOPICS FOR PARAGRAPHS OR ESSAYS

1. Have you ever attended a potluck? Describe your experience. Include some humorous details if you would like to.

2. Write a humorous paper about an ordinary event, such as a birthday party, a date, a workout at the gym, or a visit to the dentist. Try to use some of the same kinds of techniques that Tom Bodett did in order to create humor.

3. Using library resources or the Internet, look up information about Homer, Alaska, or another town in Alaska. What are the most interesting things about that town? How is it different from the area where you live? Write a paper about that town aimed at persuading readers to visit the area or to move there.

4. Interview someone who has lived in another country or another state. Ask questions about the way of life there, including how people usually socialize and what types of food people prefer. Then write a paper comparing the way of life in that country or state with the lifestyle in your own area.

5. Find a magazine article, a newspaper column, a comic strip, or a web page that you think is humorous. (Be sure to select something in good taste that would be appropriate for everyone in your class to read.) Share the item with a workshop group or with the class to find out if others also appreciate the humor. Then write a paper explaining the author's purpose, how the author used humor, why it appeals to people, and anything else you would like to comment on.

Breaking the Habit

MIKE DUFFY

The TV-Turnoff Network is an organization with the goal of getting people to *reduce* the number of hours they watch television and to *increase* the time they spend reading, relating to family and friends, and exercising. Just before the sixth annual National TV-Turnoff Week began in April 2000, the following newspaper article appeared in the *Detroit Free Press*. To publicize TV-Turnoff Week, television critic and journalist Mike Duffy encouraged readers to think about their own television viewing habits.

PREREADING QUESTIONS

1. Do you think that most people spend too much time watching television?

2. How would people spend their free time if they weren't watching television?

VOCABULARY

carved out in this case, set aside time for

heresy a view that goes against accepted beliefs

media-saturated overly full of the media (television, movies, videos, etc.)

endorsed approved

Gutenberg Johann Gutenberg, fifteenth-century inventor of movable type for printing

affords provides

Red Wings Detroit hockey team

snooty stuck up, snobbish

elitism an attitude of superiority

underpinning support or rationale

sedentary sitting too much, not getting exercise

sensationalistic containing shocking or lurid details

degrading lowering

common denominator in this context, something that people have in common

effigy a lifelike model

misbegotten having an improper origin

samba a dance

oodles a lot

glutted flooded with an excess of something

BREAKING THE HABIT

Once upon a time, Anne Trudeau had a TV life.

2   She watched "L.A. Law" and lots of PBS shows. She tuned in "ER" when it came on. And she carved out daily guilty pleasures with a favorite soap opera.

3   "I was hooked on 'General Hospital,' I'm embarrassed to say," recalls Trudeau, 42, a Ferndale resident.

4   But three years ago, Trudeau and her husband, Reilly Shea, kicked the TV habit; they dropped their cable subscription. Two years ago, they stored their one TV set on a cart in a closet.

5   Now they and their 3½-year-old daughter, Natalie, have virtually no TV life. And they love it.

6   "We're outdoors more. We go on walks. We go to the library three times a week," says Trudeau. "I don't even know what 'Ally McBeal' is about."

7   Heavens to Homer Simpson, that's heresy in a media-saturated American culture where a TV set is on 7 hours, 12 minutes a day in the average household.

8   But the next few days belong to the Trudeau family and others looking for alternatives to living in Couch Potato Nation.

9   The sixth annual National TV-Turnoff Week begins Monday.

10   Its observance has had little or no impact on the Nielsen TV ratings, but it has been growing ever so slowly, attracting an estimated six million participants last year. It's sponsored by

TV-Turnoff Network, formerly TV-Free America, a Washington-based organization that "encourages children and adults to watch less television in order to promote healthier lives and communities," according to a recent press release.

11   "We've done an exceptional job of getting into schools," says Frank Vespe, executive director of TV-Turnoff Network. "If you go to school, you've probably heard of TV-Turnoff Week."

12   The unplugged TV week has the support of the U.S. Surgeon General and 61 national organizations, including the American Medical Association, the National Education Association, the American Pediatric Association, the Girl Scouts and the YMCA. The governors of 31 states, including Michigan, have endorsed the week.

13   Numerous schools in the Detroit area are participating.

14   "Our community is very TV-oriented," says Ernestina Iglesias, a teacher at Maybury Elementary School in southwest Detroit. "There are a lot of families from lower socioeconomic backgrounds. And TV is the baby-sitter in many homes. So it's going to be tough."

15   Maybury students are being asked to sign pledges not to watch television this week. And a letter being sent to parents asks for their participation.

16   Each day this week, Iglesias says, Maybury students will take home suggested family activities as possible replacements for TV watching: Read a book, take a walk with your parents, play a board game, bake cookies. And at the end of the week, students are to do a homework report on how they spent TV-Turnoff Week.

Results?

17   Does it work? Do kids change their relationship with the tube after turning it off for a week?

18   "I've had various levels of success," says Micki Sanders, a teacher for 20 years who has participated in TV-Turnoff Week at several independent and charter schools, including Waldorf Schools in Detroit and Southfield.

19   "Most kids can't have a real conversation anymore. They're so limited because their life experience is the television and movies

they're watching," says Sanders, who teaches at Detroit Community High School and Kindergarten, a 3-year-old charter school on Detroit's west side.

20 Because her school is on spring break, Sanders isn't doing TV-Turnoff Week 2000. But she doesn't limit her philosophy about television to one week a year.

21 "I'm always telling them, 'Turn it off and wake up your brain. Mrs. Sanders doesn't like TV because it makes your brain go to sleep,'" she says. "The problem is that most of my parents are in their 20s and 30s and they're very addicted to TV themselves. It's a very addictive drug."

The Other Side

22 Of course, not everyone's wild about TV-Turnoff Week.

23 "Oh, what a stupid idea. That's like putting out your eyes if you had Gutenberg waiting in the lobby," says Jerry Herron, a pop culture scholar and head of the American studies program at Wayne State University.

24 "Turning off your TV set is like living in a house with a picture window and always having the shade drawn," adds Herron, a big fan of such smart, conversation-provoking television as "The West Wing" and "The Simpsons." He praises television as "a system of global literacy that Americans invented." Not watching it, Herron says, is like "refusing knowledge."

25 But the idea of National TV-Turnoff Week isn't to abolish television, says TV-Turnoff Network's Vespe.

26 "In general, most people are going to go back to watching TV. But this week affords them an opportunity to re-engage in activities that make life richer and fuller, whether it's reading a book, talking to your children or going to a city council meeting," says Vespe.

27 "And when people go back to TV, hopefully they'll watch smarter. Maybe they'll only turn on the TV for the specific shows they want to watch."

28 That's exactly what happened to Matt Likins, 31, a physical therapist who lives in St. Clair Shores. He learned about TV-Turnoff Week last year when the American Physical Therapy

Association sent literature about the event to his Grosse Pointe Woods office.

29   "I was not completely successful. I ran afoul of the Red Wings playoff games last year," jokes Likins. "So I didn't go totally without TV. But the biggest difference for me is that after the week was over, I had a better awareness of how much I was actually watching each week.

30   "I was probably watching 20 or 25 hours of sports and movies every week. It's a habit I wasn't aware of because I'd just come home every night and pop on the TV."

31   Likins also found some positive marital vibrations to watching less television.

32   "My wife (Sharisse) was pretty pleased. She gets a lot more attention from me. And I'm doing more things around the house," says Likins, who still plans to watch Red Wings games during his modified TV-Turnoff Week.

Is It Television's Fault?

33   There is a faint tone of snooty elitism to some of TV-Turnoff Week's philosophical underpinning.

34   "The fundamental message of all TV is, 'You should consume,'" says Vespe. "That's not a message that encourages civic participation. It's a message that encourages going to the mall."

35   Television, of course, is always taking the blame for cultural ills.

36   Too fat and sedentary? It's TV's fault. Too much violence and too many gun killings? It's TV's fault. Too many sexually active teens? It's TV's fault.

37   "In the 19th Century, you could have found Victorians who felt Charles Dickens' writing was sensationalistic, degrading the popular taste and appealing to the lowest common denominator," says Wayne State's Herron.

38   Television, where Dickens' classic works now wind up on "Masterpiece Theatre," has become modern society's chosen pop culture effigy.

39   Liberals and conservatives alike love to take whacks at it. In the 1950s, it was comic books and rock 'n' roll that were ruining the nation's youth. Now it's television and its sitcoms, cartoons and misbegotten reality carnivals like "Who Wants to Marry a Multi-Millionaire?"

40   Except that even an intelligent television enthusiast like Herron knows too much of anything is not a good thing. "If you make your life a one-note samba, whether it's with TV or movies or drugs," he says, "you'll degrade your life."

41   And any temporary break from television that might get children and families walking, talking, baking cookies, interacting, playing games—how bad can that be?

42   "I don't think people who watch TV are bad," says former "General Hospital" fan Trudeau. "I just think the nature of media is addictive. I just think TV pulls you in and makes you slack-jawed."

43   Not that everyone who watches oodles of television and enjoys it is automatically transformed into a remote control zombie. But in a satellite-delivered, cable channel-glutted world of wall-to-wall channel-surfing, maybe less really is more. And smarter. Click.

A. COMPREHENSION

1. How many hours per day is a television set turned on in the average American household?

2. Who sponsors TV-Turnoff Week, and what is its purpose?

3. What does the other side say in defense of television?

4. What problems in society is TV often blamed for?

B. CRITICAL THINKING

1. Do you agree with Anne Trudeau and teacher Micki Sanders, who are quoted in the article, that TV is addictive?

2. Do you think that participating in National TV-Turnoff Week is a good idea?

3. Why do Americans spend so much time watching television?

4. In what ways could family life be improved if people spent less time watching TV?

5. To what extent do you think that sex and violence shown on television have an effect on young viewers?

C. LANGUAGE AND VOCABULARY

1. Jerry Herron, a pop culture scholar at Wayne State University, is quoted as saying, "Turning off your TV set is like living in a house with a picture window and always having the shade drawn." What does he mean by this comparison?

2. Had you heard the term *couch potato* before reading it in this article? What do you think it means? Would it be possible to be a couch potato without television?

D. STYLE, STRUCTURE, AND ORGANIZATION

1. Mike Duffy quotes several people in this article, including ordinary TV viewers. Choose one of the people whom he quotes and scan (look through) the reading to locate everything that person said. Which of this person's statements do you think is most effective?

2. Why does the author begin with "Once upon a time . . ."?

3. Why are most of the paragraphs in this article shorter than the paragraphs in an academic essay? (Hint: Consider the format in which the article originally appeared.)

E. TOPICS FOR DISCUSSION OR JOURNAL WRITING

1. If you didn't watch television for a week, how would you spend the time you saved?

2. Are there any television programs that you disapprove of or that you think are a waste of time? Why?

3. Are there any ways in which television can be a valuable learning resource?

4. Do you think that parents should supervise their children's television viewing? Why or why not?

5. Keep a journal of your television viewing for a week and rate each of the programs you watch by giving them one, two, three, or four

stars. At the end of the week, evaluate your viewing habits. How many four-star programs did you see? Which programs rated only one or two stars? Do you think that you should consider eliminating some of those programs from your viewing schedule?

F. WRITING TOPICS FOR PARAGRAPHS OR ESSAYS

1. Defend one of your favorite TV programs. If possible, show that it offers some cultural or social value in addition to providing entertainment.

2. Write a cause and effect paper about the effects of TV violence on children. Be sure to mention some specific programs as examples. You may also want to look for articles about this topic at the library or on the Internet in order to add some factual information to your paper.

3. What real-life events have you watched on television that had an impact on you? Using some of these events as examples, write a paper about how television enables us to share important happenings.

4. Imagine that you are preparing a time capsule to be opened 50 years in the future, and you decide to include videotapes of two television programs that represent today's society. Write a paper that tells which two programs you would choose and why.

5. Do you think that families need to spend more quality time together? Why? How would you suggest that families improve the way they spend their time? Write a paper that answers these questions.

Shoeless Joe

W. P. KINSELLA

This reading comes from W. P. Kinsella's fictional book about a man who builds a baseball diamond in his cornfield because he sees a vision of a baseball stadium and hears the message, "If you build it, he will come." "*He*" refers to Shoeless Joe Jackson, one of eight Chicago White Sox players who were involved in the biggest scandal in baseball history many years before this story takes place. Shoeless Joe and the others were accused of accepting money to intentionally lose the 1919 World Series to the Cincinnati Reds, but many loyal fans believed that Shoeless Joe was innocent.

PREREADING QUESTIONS

1. Why are baseball fans so dedicated to the game?
2. What special qualities do dreamers and visionaries have?

VOCABULARY

rashly foolishly, without thinking

vow promise

smock a long, loose shirt, generally worn over other clothes

surreptitiously secretly, trying not to be noticed

spinster a woman who has never been married

optimists people who always expect things to turn out well

dissolve in this case, to be overcome by

birthed in this case, created

bleacher a section of raised seats

deaden reduce the power or force of

cud a wad or lump of something held in the mouth and chewed

recalcitrant uncooperative

rutted having deep tracks from frequent use

curry in this case, groom or comb

deflect cause to turn in a different direction

hurled thrown, pitched

shutout a baseball game in which the opposing team scored no runs

beveled shaped to a certain angle

128

bunt a ball hit by tapping it lightly so that it won't roll past the infielders

aerated exposed to air

sheepishly with a feeling of embarrassment

SHOELESS JOE

1 We have been trading promises like baseball cards, Shoeless Joe and I. First I had to keep my rashly given vow to finish the baseball field. As I did, Shoeless Joe, or whoever or whatever breathed this magic down onto my Iowa farm, provided me with another live baseball player each time I finished constructing a section of the field: another of the Unlucky Eight who were banished for life from organized baseball in 1920 for supposedly betraying the game they loved.

2 I completed the home-plate area first. In fact I was out there the very next morning digging and leveling, for besides being the easiest part to do, it was the most important to me. Home plate cost $14.95 at my friendly sporting-goods store in Iowa City. It surprised me that I could buy a mass-produced home plate, although I don't know why it should have, considering that one can custom-order a baby nowadays. But somehow I had pictured myself measuring and cutting a section from a piny-smelling plank, the sawdust clinging like gold to my jeans. I installed it carefully, securely, like a grave marker, then laid out a batter's box and baselines.

3 But nothing happened.

4 I continued to work on the rest of the field, but less enthusiastically. Bases cost $28.95 for a set of three, starched and glazed white as the smock of a fat baker. It was weeks before the stadium appeared again in the cornfield. Each evening I peered surreptitiously through the kitchen curtains, like a spinster keeping tab on her neighbors, waiting and hoping. All the while Annie kept reassuring me, and I would call her a Pollyanna and tell her how I hated optimists. But I find it all but impossible to be cross with Annie, and we would end up embracing at the kitchen window where I could smell the sunshine in her snow-and-lemon-drop curtains. Then

Karin would drag a chair close to us, stand on it, and interrupt our
love with hers, a little jealous of our attention to each other. Annie and
I would stare in awe at the wonder we had created, our daughter.

5   Karin is five going on sixty; the dreamer in me combined with the
practicality and good humor of Annie. We would both kiss her soft
cheeks and she would dissolve in laughter as my mustache tickled her.

6   "Daddy, the baseball man's outside," Karin said to me.

7   It was still daylight, the days longer now, the cornfield and
baseball diamond soaked warm with summer. I stared through the
curtains where Shoeless Joe softly patrolled the left field I had birthed.

8   I swept Karin into my arms and we hurried to the bleacher
behind the left-field fence. I studied the situation carefully but
nothing appeared to have changed from the last time. Shoeless Joe
was the only player with any substance.

9   "What about the catcher?" I call down.

10   Joe smiles. "I said we'd look at him, remember?"

11   "I've finished home plate. What else do you need?"

12   "I said *we*," reminds Joe, "After the others are here, we'll give
him a tryout. He'll have a fair chance to catch on."

13   "All the others?" I say.

14   "All the others," echoes Joe. "Get the bases down and sand and
level that ground around first base. It'll deaden the hot grounders
and make them easy for old Chick to field."

15   But I have more questions than a first grader on a field trip: "Why
have you been away so long?"; "When will you come back again?";
and a dozen more, but Joe only shifts the cud of tobacco in his cheek
and concentrates on the gray-uniformed batter 300 feet away.

16   I did sand the first-base area, sometimes cursing as the
recalcitrant wheelbarrow twisted out of my hands as if it had a life of
its own, spilling its contents on the rutted path leading to the
baseball field. My back ached as if someone were holding a welding
torch against my spine, turning the flame on and off at will. But I
sanded. And raked. I combed the ground as I would curry a horse,
until there wasn't a pebble or lump left to deflect the ball. And as I
finished I ignored my throbbing back, triumphant as if I'd just
hurled a shutout. I'd stand on my diamond, where just beyond the
fence the summer corn listens like a field of swaying disciples, and
I'd talk to the sky.

17 "I'm ready whenever you are," I say. "Chick Gandil, you've never played on so fine a field. I've beveled the ground along the baseline so that any bunt without divine guidance will roll foul. The earth around the base is aerated and soft as piecrust. Ground balls will die on the second bounce, as if they've been hit into an anthill. You'll feel like you're wearing a glove ten feet square." I wave my arms at the perfect blue Iowa sky, and then, as I realize what I'm doing, I turn sheepishly to look at the house. Annie has been watching, and she flutters her fingers at me around the edge of the curtains.

18 The process is all so slow, as dreams are slow, as dreams suspend time like a balloon hung in midair. I want it all to happen now. I want that catcher to appear. I want whatever miracle I am party to, to prosper and grow: I want the dimensions of time that have been loosened from their foundations to entwine like a basketful of bright embroidery threads. But it seems that even for dreams, I have to work and wait. It hardly seems fair.

A. COMPREHENSION

1. Who were the "Unlucky Eight"? What happened to them?
2. What are the first three things that the narrator (the person telling the story) does to begin building the baseball field?
3. Where and when does the stadium appear?
4. When Shoeless Joe shows up, what instructions does he give about finishing the baseball field? What questions does he leave unanswered?

B. CRITICAL THINKING

1. How does the man feel about building the baseball field? Do his feelings change at any points in the story?
2. How do his wife, Annie, and his daughter, Karin, feel about the project?
3. Why does the man talk to Chick Gandil? Who do you think Chick Gandil is?

4. Reread the last paragraph. Is the narrator thinking these words or saying them to someone? What does he mean by his final comment, "It hardly seems fair"?

C. LANGUAGE AND VOCABULARY

1. Had you ever heard anyone called a *Pollyanna* before reading the word in this selection? What do you think it means? Look up *Pollyanna* in a dictionary to see if your guess is accurate. Also look for the origin of the term—who was the original Pollyanna?

2. Are you familiar with all of the baseball terms that the author uses, such as *home plate, batter's box, baselines, grounders,* and *bunt?* Make a list of all the baseball terms in the reading and look up the meanings of any that you don't know.

D. STYLE, STRUCTURE, AND ORGANIZATION

1. Why does the author include an actual conversation between the man building the baseball field and Shoeless Joe? How does this affect readers' view of the reality of the situation?

2. The author uses *personification*—giving human qualities or abilities to something nonhuman—when he writes, ". . . just beyond the fence the summer corn *listens* like a field of swaying disciples . . .." Do you think this wording is effective? Why or why not?

E. TOPICS FOR DISCUSSION OR JOURNAL WRITING

1. Are you a baseball fan? If so, what do you especially like about the game, and who are your favorite players?

2. Which sports do you enjoy watching? Are there any special sports figures from the past that you would like to see in action?

3. Have you heard or read about any recent sports scandals or any accusations against a well-known sports figure? Based on what you know about the situation, do you think the accusations are true? Why or why not?

4. Have you ever had a dream or a vision that seemed real? If so, did it affect any of your actions in real life?

5. Do you believe that Shoeless Joe really appeared? Why or why not?

F.   WRITING   TOPICS   FOR PARAGRAPHS   OR   ESSAYS

1. Why do you think sports heroes are so admired in our society? As you answer this question, mention at least two or three popular sports figures (past or present) as examples.

2. Watch the 1989 movie *Field of Dreams,* which is based on the book *Shoeless Joe* by W. P. Kinsella. Then write a review of the movie. Include a summary of what happens, your evaluation of the movie, and details about which parts you liked best.

3. Using library resources or the Internet, find out more about Shoeless Joe Jackson, his baseball career, and the part he may have played in the 1919 World Series scandal. Then write an informative paper about Shoeless Joe Jackson.

4. Write a paper about one of your favorite sports. In your paper, answer at least two of the following questions: Why do you like to watch or participate in this sport? What is unique and special about this sport? What qualities or skills does it take to be successful in this sport? Who are a few of the most popular professional players? What is one of your most memorable experiences with this sport, either as a player or as a fan?

5. Write an imaginative story about meeting someone from the past— for example, a sports figure, a movie star, a legendary hero, or a political or religious leader. Describe the scene and include a conversation between the two of you.

Wolfman in Farsi?

DAN GILGOFF

The following article appeared in the Culture and Ideas section of *U.S. News & World Report* magazine in late January of 2003, when a new radio station called Radio Farda began broadcasting in Iran. Featuring a mixture of Persian songs and contemporary Western pop, such as music by top performers like Britney Spears and Enrique Iglesias, Farda's programming is aimed primarily at young people under the age of thirty. Dan Gilgoff, author of numerous articles for *U.S. News & World Report* and other major magazines, looks at the issues involved and raises the question of whether American-sponsored programming will actually influence its Iranian audience's way of thinking.

PREREADING QUESTIONS

1. Do you think music can influence people's ideas and ways of thinking?
2. Are American songs popular in other countries? Why do you think this is so?

VOCABULARY

Farsi the language of Iran

pop pop music (popular music)

to boot in addition (idiomatic expression)

tallied counted

mainstay a very important part

strategy technique or plan

stunning impressive, surprising

hone sharpen or make more effective

a shot in the arm something that creates a boost or an increase (idiomatic expression)

134

canvassed surveyed, asked questions

gauge measure or determine

elites people with high social status

intelligentsia intellectuals

bopping dancing or moving to the music

subversive intended to undermine the government

WOLFMAN IN FARSI?

Broadcasting Britney Spears to young Iranians may get their ear. But will it capture their minds?

Millions of Iranians flooded the streets to torch American flags and chant "death to America" last winter after Presi-dent Bush implicated their country in his "axis of evil." So you might not expect those same folks to welcome a new radio station that mixes contemporary Persian songs with western pop from the likes of Britney Spears and Enrique Iglesias—and that's funded by Uncle Sam to boot.

2   You might be wrong. Since beaming its AM signal into Iran last month from two nearby transmitters, Radio Farda (*Farsi* for Radio Tomorrow) has tallied more than a thousand E-mails from its fans. "It has been really nice to hear a radio which is nonstop music," writes a 19-year-old from Tehran. "Our young Iranian generation is tired of these hellish politics [that have] made a black Iran, full of sorrow."

3   Hellish politics were a mainstay of Radio Azadi (Radio Freedom), a U.S. government-sponsored service launched in 1998 and replaced in December by Radio Farda. While Azadi pumped five hours of original news, analysis, and cultural programs into Iran each day, Farda offers a round-the-clock diet of pop music sprinkled with hourly 12-minute newscasts and two half-hour daily programs of news analysis. The broadcast hopes to attract 20 percent of all Iranians—up from the roughly 2 percent who tuned in to Azadi—by targeting listeners under 30, fully 70 percent of the population. "We wanted the largest possible audience," says Norman Pattiz of the Broadcasting Board of Governors, the presidentially appointed panel that supervises U.S. broadcast efforts abroad. "So we had to marry our mission to the market."

4   The strategy has met with stunning success in the Middle East, where Voice of America's talk-heavy Arabic service was replaced last March by a musically inclined broadcast called Radio Sawa. The information-driven VOA model didn't work there, says Pattiz: "If listeners don't like our policies, you can't lead with them." Instead, Radio Sawa relies on weekly audience research to hone a playlist of Arabic and western pop tunes. News reports are kept short and punchy—and the result has been a shot in the arm for listenership. In a recent survey from Jordan, 39 percent of young people cited Sawa as their most trusted news station, about double the number who picked state-run radio.

5   **No Escape.**   But because anti-Americanism runs so much lower among Iranians than among Middle Eastern Arabs, Radio Farda has come under fire for playing more music than necessary to retain Iranian audiences. Azar Nafisi, an Iranian literary scholar and author of the forthcoming *Reading Lolita in Tehran*, would prefer a combination of Farda's snappy pop-culture sensibility and Azadi's hourlong public-affairs shows. "We don't want the music to be just an escape for Iranians," she says. "We need to explain why

the act of choosing to listen to music is vital to the creation of a democratic society."

6   But Farda steers clear of didacticism. It seeks to give the people what they want and has canvassed Iranians outside their country to gauge their tastes, a total departure from the Azadi model. "We aimed for Iranian elites—professors, activists, even some reform-minded members of the clergy and government," says Stephen Fairbanks, Radio Azadi's former director. "These were people who were more effective in bringing about change in the country." Farda management holds that the intelligentsia still listen to its hourly news reports and to VOA's *Farsi* service. But a University of Tehran political science professor who requested anonymity doubts that elites listen to either. "Radio Farda is going to lose a very influential audience" to international broadcasters like the BBC," the professor says. "And youth are going to enjoy the music and ignore the news."

7   So far, Radio Sawa's surveys in Jordan suggest otherwise. And Farda news director Ali Farhoodi cautions that bopping to western pop in Iran isn't as mindless as it may seem, with the vice police enforcing bans on much western music and restrictions on women singing in public. "Listening to pop in Iran isn't like listening to American FM," he says. "It's a political statement with a risk involved." Which makes Britney and Enrique sound downright subversive.

A . C O M P R E H E N S I O N

1. What types of programming does Radio Farda offer?

2. What percentage of the Iranian population does Radio Farda hope to attract? What age are the listeners who are targeted?

3. How does Radio Sawa differ from previous Arabic programming by Voice of America (VOA)?

4. What are some of the criticisms that some people have of Radio Farda?

B . C R I T I C A L T H I N K I N G

1. Why does news director Ali Farhoodi say, "Listening to pop in Iran isn't like listening to American FM. It's a political statement with a risk involved"?

2. Do you think that some of the programs on Radio Farda, Radio Sawa, or Radio Azadi could be considered propaganda? (If you are unsure of the meaning of *propaganda*, look it up before answering this question.)

3. According to the former director of Radio Azadi, why did Azadi programming target professors, clergymen, and other high-ranking "elite" citizens? Do you think this was the most effective approach, or does the newer Radio Farda's approach seem to be more effective?

4. To what extent do you think American-sponsored radio programs are trusted by young people in Iran, Jordan, or other Middle Eastern countries?

C. LANGUAGE AND VOCABULARY

1. At the end of paragraph 3, a member of the Broadcasting Board of Governors is quoted as saying, "We had to marry our mission to the market." What do you think this means? Have you previously heard or seen the word *marry* used in this way rather than referring to an actual marriage?

2. What does the word *didacticism* mean in the next to the last paragraph? Try to figure out the meaning of the word from the context (surrounding ideas) before looking it up. In what kinds of broadcasting situations could didacticism be useful? In what kinds of broadcasting situations do you think didacticism would be ineffective? Why?

D. STYLE, STRUCTURE, AND ORGANIZATION

1. Who is or was Wolfman, who is referred to in the title? Look up the answer on the Internet if you don't know. Do you think the title of the article is effective? Why or why not? Why isn't Wolfman mentioned anywhere else in the article?

2. Do you think that author Dan Gilgoff's style and approach to the topic are pro-American, pro-Middle Eastern, or relatively neutral, showing both sides? Point out specific parts of the article that support your answer.

E . TOPICS FOR DISCUSSION OR JOURNAL WRITING

1. To what extent do you think song lyrics can influence how people think? Can you think of examples of some lyrics that might influence listeners in either positive or negative ways?

2. If you were in charge of planning a radio program to be broadcast in Iran or any other Middle Eastern country, what kinds of things would you include in the program? Why?

3. Do you think that broadcasting American programs in the Middle East or other parts of the world is a good idea or not? Give reasons for your answer.

4. Would you like to listen to radio or television programs that are broadcast by Middle Eastern stations (with English translations available)? Why or why not? What kinds of programs would you expect to hear?

5. Which other contemporary musical artists in addition to Britney Spears and Enrique Iglesias do you think are popular in a variety of different countries? Why?

F . WRITING TOPICS FOR PARAGRAPHS OR ESSAYS

1. Write a speech that you would like to broadcast to the young people of Iran, Iraq, Jordan, Saudi Arabia, or another Middle Eastern country. Think carefully about what you could tell them that might promote international peace and understanding.

2. Choose one of your favorite CDs that you think people of other countries or from different backgrounds would enjoy. Play one selection from the CD for your class and explain why the lyrics and music would be appealing to the listeners of an international radio station such as the ones mentioned in this article. Also write down the lyrics and your explanation if your teacher asks you to.

3. Write a persuasive paper either for or against the use of radio programming to influence people in foreign countries.

4. Learn more about Radio Farda in Iran or Radio Sawa by doing some Internet research or using the library (if your library has

current sources) and write a paper about what you learn. You may want to start with some of these Web sites: **www.clandestineradio .com**, **www.iran-press-service.com**, or **www.radiosawa.com/ english_sp.cfm**.

5. Visit the official Voice of America Web site at **www.voa.gov/ index.cfm** and learn about programs that the United States sponsors in other countries. Write an informative report about one of the VOA stations or programs, including the kinds of programming offered and the audience that it is intended to appeal to.

Elvis Culture

ERIKA DOSS

Although Elvis Presley died in 1977, his popularity continues. He is considered by many to be "The King," the most popular rock star in the history of American music. His first hit song, "Heartbreak Hotel," skyrocketed him to fame in 1956, and during the next few years almost all of his recordings made the "Top 10" list. Why do fans still adore and admire Elvis? In her book *Elvis Culture,* from which this reading is taken, Erika Doss examines this cultural phenomenon.

PREREADING QUESTIONS

1. Why was Elvis Presley one of the most admired performers of the twentieth century?

2. Why do some people enjoy collecting special items, or memorabilia, related to a famous person, such as a sports figure or a movie star?

VOCABULARY

sanctified considered sacred

quasi-religion resembling a religion

martyr a person who dies or suffers greatly for a cause or belief

icon symbol

J. F. K. John Fitzgerald Kennedy

mass-produced manufactured in large quantities

prevail dominate, have greater influence

pivotal of vital importance

rocket-fueled in this context, full of energy

rockabilly a combination of rock and roll and "hillbilly," or country, music

repertoire the range of music that a person performs

sensual involving the senses, seductive

captivating enchanting, capturing an audience's emotions

phenomenal exceptional, extraordinary

vibrato a vibrating or pulsating quality

conventions customary or usual ways of doing things

aura an intangible quality

flamboyant showy, elaborate, colorful

glitzy glamorous, flashy

ELVIS CULTURE

Why Elvis? Why has Elvis Presley become sanctified as the central figure in what some are calling a quasi-religion? Why not some other popular culture martyr who died young, like John Lennon, Buddy Holly, Janis Joplin, Jimi Hendrix, or, more recently, Kurt Cobain or Selena? Why is Elvis—more so than Malcolm X, Martin Luther King, Jr., and J.F.K.—consistently held up as an "icon of the twentieth century"? Why is it Elvis's image that we see on the surface of every conceivable mass-produced consumer item, from black velvet paintings and ceramic statuettes to laminated clocks, liquor decanters, ashtrays, oven mitts, address books, earrings, checks, flags, key rings? Why does Elvis's image prevail in contemporary visual culture?

2   More to the point, why should any of this be taken seriously— why should any of us even bother with looking at and trying to make sense of Elvis Culture? The answer, quite simply, is that Elvis Presley occupies a big space in the daily lives of many Americans. For some, the space that he—or, more specifically, his image— occupies is not especially broad or deep. But for others, especially for fans, Elvis has sweeping significance in terms of personal, social, and even national identity: Elvis is who they want to be, who they most admire, who they mourn for; Elvis is their image of an ideal American. In a contemporary culture where images dominate (some estimate we receive three-quarters of our knowledge from visual sources), it is worth wondering why Elvis's image seems to dominate most of all.

3   Many fans were turned on to Elvis when they first saw him on television. Elvis turned up thirteen times on TV in 1956, each time drawing more viewers, more critical attention, more teenage fans. His first appearance on *The Ed Sullivan Show* in September drew the highest ratings in then-TV history, with over 82 percent of the American viewing public (54 million people) tuning in to watch Elvis sing "Don't Be Cruel" and "Love Me Tender." By the time of the second Sullivan show in October (the third aired in January 1957), Elvis's records were selling at the rate of $75,000 a day (accounting for more than half of RCA's profits). Fans mobbed his concerts (he performed live 161 times in 1956), followed him everywhere, ripped bits of upholstery from his pink and black Cadillacs, and organized "I Love Elvis" clubs.

4   Elvis's music was, of course, absolutely pivotal to his popularity. If he had been only a teen heartthrob and B-movie star, Elvis would never have attracted the adulation that continues unabated. From the start, he courted a singing style that bound his fans and himself in an intensely emotional relationship. From the rocket-fueled and raw-voiced rockabilly energy of the 1950s performances to the gospel reportoire of his 1967 album *How Great Thou Art* and the

slick pop of his 1970s arena acts, Elvis's music was always sensual (if not downright erotic) and utterly captivating.

5   Sight is the dominant sense in modern Western culture—how else can we explain the phenomenal popularity of television compared with radio?—and Elvis, perhaps more so than any other performer in the 1950s, recognized this. Just as he skillfully mixed black and white musical forms to create his own influential brand of rock and roll, Elvis consciously blended sound (the rhythm and pulse of his music, the vibrato of his voice) and sight (the look of his body, the style of his movements) into sensual and seductive spectacles.

6   Shattering musical and theatrical conventions, Elvis set the pace for the predominantly visual aura of contemporary popular culture: within a decade or so of his mid-1950s debut, flamboyant stage acts with Spectra-Color light shows and glitzy special effects became the norm for rock bands ranging from the Rolling Stones to the Grateful Dead. Today we talk about going to "see" Sting or Prince or Madonna, which tells us a lot about how profoundly visualized contemporary popular music has become.

A. COMPREHENSION

1. Why was Elvis Presley's music so appealing to fans?

2. According to the author, why is Elvis still very important in the lives of many Americans?

3. How did Elvis's style of performing influence other musicians during the last half of the twentieth century?

B. CRITICAL THINKING

1. Why do fans do things that could be considered vandalism, such as ripping pieces of upholstery from Elvis's cars?

2. Why does the author describe the relationship between Elvis and his fans as "intensely emotional"? Do you think this type of relationship exists between all performers and their fans? Why or why not?

3. How important are visual elements to contemporary popular music? Give reasons for your answer.

4. Why do you think some people believe that Elvis is still alive?

C . LANGUAGE AND VOCABULARY

1. This reading mentions several types of music, such as *pop* and *gospel*, as well as a few other musical terms, such as *vibrato*. Select at least three other musical terms that appear in the reading, and look up their meanings if you do not already know them.

2. In the last paragraph, the author calls readers' attention to our typical word choice of *see* rather than *hear* to refer to attending a live performance: "Today we talk about going to 'see' Sting or Prince or Madonna. . . ." Why do you think people tend to choose the visual verb *see* rather than *hear* or *listen to*?

D . STYLE, STRUCTURE, AND ORGANIZATION

1. Why does the first paragraph consist entirely of questions? Does the author answer all of these questions somewhere in the reading?

2. In informative and persuasive writing, body paragraphs often begin with a *topic sentence* that expresses the main idea of the paragraph. Choose paragraph 3, 4, or 5 of the reading and underline or highlight the main idea of the paragraph—either the first sentence or a portion of the first sentence.

E . TOPICS FOR DISCUSSION OR JOURNAL WRITING

1. Which performers of today do you think will still be enthusiastically admired 40 or 50 years from now? Why?

2. Do you think that Elvis might still be alive? Why or why not?

3. How do you think it would feel to sing in front of a live audience, with thousands of screaming fans captivated by your music?

4. What difficult challenges might a popular rock musician face?

5. Who is your favorite singer or musical group? What is special about that person's or that group's music?

F. WRITING TOPICS FOR PARAGRAPHS OR ESSAYS

1. Have you ever attended a live concert? If so, write about your experience, including details about the performance and the fans' reactions. How do you think this concert compared with one of Elvis's?

2. Write a paper about another popular musician who died young, such as Jimi Hendrix, Selena, Richie Valens, Rick Nelson, or Janis Joplin. (See the first paragraph of the reading for more suggestions.) In addition to writing about the person's life and accomplishments, include how fans reacted to the musician's death and how it affected his or her popularity. You will probably need to do some research at the library or on the Internet in order to find enough information.

3. Watch a movie about the life of a well-known musician or performer, such as *Selena, The Buddy Holly Story,* or *La Bamba* (Richie Valens). Then write a review of the movie. In your paper, include a summary of the main events, an evaluation of the movie, and your personal reactions.

4. Have you ever sung, danced, or played a musical instrument in front of an audience? If so, write about your experiences as a performer and how you felt about being on stage. If you have never performed in public, you may interview someone else who has and write about that person's experience instead.

5. Watch (and listen to) a music video. Which element of this video do you think is more important to the viewing audience, sight or sound? Are there any special visual effects that grab your attention? Write a review of the music video, including what you like and dislike about it.

Dressing Down

JOHN BROOKS

Most people don't know that when they put on a pair of Levi's® they are wearing a style of clothing that is more than 100 years old. Although Levi Strauss first produced denim jeans in 1874, they did not achieve wide popularity until the mid-twentieth century. This article by John Brooks, which was originally published in *Atlantic Monthly* magazine, examines the amazing worldwide popularity of jeans.

PREREADING QUESTIONS

1. Why do so many people like to wear jeans?
2. What types of situations or social occasions are jeans appropriate for?

VOCABULARY

phenomenon something that is unusual or unexplainable

seismic startling, earthshaking (as if caused by an earthquake)

postwar after World War II

differentiation distinguishing one group from another, showing them to be different

Williams College a college in Williamstown, Massachusetts

chino-wearing wearing a type of pants made of a cotton twill material called chino

untrammeled not limited

banning prohibiting

ideological baggage an association with certain ideas and beliefs

propel cause something to move forward

dissent disagreement

emulate try to be like

indulgent lenient, tolerant

anomic lacking in purpose

posture in this case, attitude or point of view

post exchanges stores for
service personnel on military
"posts" or bases

ersatz fake, imitation

perennially again and again,
continually

Benelux nations Belgium, the
Netherlands, and Luxembourg

avidly eagerly

blatant obvious and offensive

saturation point the point at
which the market is flooded
because too many items are
being produced

attire clothing

DRESSING DOWN

Beyond doubt, the jeans phenomenon is a seismic event in the
history of dress, and not only in the United States. Indeed, the habit
of wearing jeans is—along with the computer, the copying machine,
rock music, polio vaccine, and the hydrogen bomb—one of the
major contributions of the United States to the postwar world at
large.

2   Before the nineteen-fifties, jeans were worn, principally in the
West and Southwest of the United States, by children, farmers,
manual laborers when on the job, and, of course, cowboys. There
were isolated exceptions—for example, artists of both sexes took to
blue jeans in and around Santa Fe, New Mexico, in the nineteen-
twenties and -thirties; around 1940, the male students at Williams
College took them up as a mark of differentiation from the chino-
wearing snobs of Yale and Princeton; and in the late forties the
female students of Bennington College (not far from Williams)
adopted them as a virtual uniform, though only for wear on
campus—but it was not until the nineteen-fifties, when James Dean
and Marlon Brando wore jeans in movies about youth in revolt
against parents and society, when John Wayne wore them in movies
about untrammeled heroes in a lawless Old West, and when many
schools from coast to coast gave their new symbolism a boost by
banning them as inappropriate for classrooms, that jeans acquired
the ideological baggage necessary to propel them to national fame.

3   After that, though, fame came quickly, and it was not long before
young Americans—whether to express social dissent, to enjoy
comfort, or to emulate their peers—had become so attached to their

jeans that some hardly ever took them off. According to a jeans authority, a young man in the North Bronx with a large and indulgent family attained some sort of record by continuously wearing the same pair of jeans, even for bathing and sleeping, for over eight months. Eventually, as all the world knows, the popularity of jeans spread from cowboys and anomic youths to adult Americans of virtually every age and sociopolitical posture, conspicuously including Jimmy Carter when he was a candidate for the presidency. Trucks containing jeans came to rank as one of the three leading targets of hijackers, along with those containing liquor and cigarettes. Estimates of jeans sales in the United States vary wildly, chiefly because the line between jeans and slacks has come to be a fuzzy one. According to the most conservative figures, put out by the leading jeans manufacturer, Levi Strauss & Company, of San Francisco, annual sales of jeans of all kinds in the United States by all manufacturers in 1957 stood at around a hundred and fifty million pairs, while for 1977 they came to over five hundred million, or considerably more than two pairs for every man, woman, and child in the country.

4   Overseas, jeans had to wait slightly longer for their time to come. American Western movies and the example of American servicemen

from the West and Southwest stationed abroad who, as soon as the Second World War ended, changed directly from their service uniforms into blue jeans bought at post exchanges started a fad for them among Europeans in the late nineteen-forties. But the fad remained a small one, partly because of the unavailability of jeans in any quantity; in those days, European customers considered jeans ersatz unless they came from the United States, while United States jeans manufacturers were inclined to be satisfied with a reliable domestic market. Being perennially short of denim, the rough, durable, naturally shrink-and-stretch cotton twill of which basic jeans are made, they were reluctant or unable to undertake overseas expansion.

5   Gradually, though, denim production in the United States increased, and meanwhile demand for American-made jeans became so overwhelming that in parts of Europe a black market for them developed. American jeans manufacturers began exporting their product in a serious way in the early nineteen-sixties. At first, the demand was greatest in Germany, France, England, and the Benelux nations; later it spread to Italy, Spain, and Scandinavia, and eventually to Latin America and the Far East. By 1967, jeans authorities estimate, a hundred and ninety million pairs of jeans were being sold annually outside the United States; of these, all but a small fraction were of local manufacture, and not imports from the United States, although American-made jeans were still so avidly sought after that some of the local products were blatant counterfeits of the leading American brands, complete with expertly faked labels. In the late nineteen-seventies, estimated jeans sales outside the United States had doubled in a decade, to three hundred and eighty million pairs, of which perhaps a quarter were now made by American firms in plants abroad; the markets in Europe, Mexico, Japan, Australia, and other places had come so close to the saturation point that the fastest-growing jeans market was probably Brazil; Princess Anne of Great Britain, and Princess Caroline of Monaco, had been photographed wearing jeans, and King Hussein of Jordan was reported to wear them at home in his palace; the counterfeiting of American brands was a huge international undertaking, which the leading American manufacturers combated with world-ranging security operations. In Russia, authentic American Levis were a black-market item regularly commanding eighty or more dollars per pair. All in all, it is now beyond doubt that in size and scope the rapid global spread of the

habit of wearing blue jeans, however it may be explained, is an event without precedent in the history of human attire.

A. COMPREHENSION

1. Before the 1950s, who wore jeans? in what parts of the country?

2. When did jeans first become popular in the United States? What factors helped make them popular?

3. What were the sales figures for jeans in 1957 and 1977? Why did sales of jeans increase so much during that time?

4. Where, when, and why were large numbers of counterfeit jeans produced and sold?

B. CRITICAL THINKING

1. Do you think that the sales of jeans have increased or decreased since this article was written? Give reasons for your answer.

2. Are jeans still worn as a symbol of "revolt against parents and society"?

3. Why was the popularity of jeans slower to develop in Europe than in the United States?

4. Why were truckloads of jeans, liquor, and cigarettes the most common targets for hijackers at one time?

5. Why does the author give examples of several famous people who wore blue jeans in public? Which of these people do you think would have had the most influence on clothing trends in the United States? Why?

C. LANGUAGE AND VOCABULARY

1. Had you ever heard the term *black market* before you read it in this article? What do you think it means? Look up the meaning if necessary. Can you think of any other kinds of products besides jeans that have probably been sold on the black market?

2. What is a *fad*? Can other things besides clothing be fads? Look up the meaning of *fad* if necessary. Then write two or more sentences about certain styles of clothing or other things that you think are current fads.

D. STYLE, STRUCTURE, AND ORGANIZATION

1. Find two sentences that express the main idea of the article: one in the introduction and one at the end of the last paragraph.

2. To what extent does the author use *chronological order* (time order)? Is this an effective method of organization for this topic?

E. TOPICS FOR DISCUSSION OR JOURNAL WRITING

1. Do you think that jeans will continue to be as popular in the future as they are now? Why or why not?

2. How often do you wear jeans? Are there any situations for which you consider jeans inappropriate? What is the most formal occasion you have ever worn jeans for? How did you feel wearing jeans on that occasion?

3. Do people in your area and your age group tend to wear jeans frequently? Are jeans currently the most popular style of pants for men and/or women, or are other types of pants and slacks more popular now?

4. Should dress codes for public schools permit students to wear Levis and other types of jeans? Would school uniforms create a better educational environment?

F. WRITING TOPICS FOR PARAGRAPHS OR ESSAYS

1. Write about a current style of clothing that you like or dislike. Include a description of the style and why you like or dislike it. If possible, give some reasons for its current popularity. Also, predict whether this style will remain popular in the years to come.

2. Find out more about Levi Strauss, whose company produced the first denim jeans, and write about how he became successful.

3. Using library resources or the Internet, research the clothing styles of one particular decade of the twentieth century: 1920s, 1930s,

1940s, 1950s, 1960s, 1970s, 1980s, or 1990s. Write a report on what people were wearing during that decade.

4. Take a stand on the issue of dress codes or uniforms in public schools, and write a persuasive paper that explains and gives reasons for your viewpoint. You may choose to take a stand against dress codes in general, in favor of a specific dress code, or for or against school uniforms.

5. How many categories or types of clothing do most people need? Write a classification paper about the various types of clothing that should be an essential part of every man's or woman's wardrobe. Your classification should include at least three categories. Be sure to give each category a name, explain its purpose, and give some examples of types of clothes that belong in this category.

P A R T

5

FITNESS AND HEALTH

Strive to Be Fit, Not Fanatical

TIMOTHY GOWER

The author of this selection, Timothy Gower, is a newspaper columnist who writes on men's issues and men's health. He has also written health and fitness articles for several popular magazines, including *Esquire, Men's Fitness, Walking,* and *American Health.* In his book, *Staying at the Top of Your Game,* Gower offers a practical guide on how to stay in peak condition at any age, including realistic workout plans, nutritional guidelines, answers to numerous health questions, and resources for additional information.

As you read "Strive to Be Fit, Not Fanatical," which originally was published as a column in the *Los Angeles Times,* identify the author's intended audience—who he is writing for.

PREREADING QUESTIONS

1. How important is exercise?
2. How much exercise is enough to maintain good health?

VOCABULARY

fitness Nazi a person who is fanatical about physical fitness

scold admonish, chastise, tell people about their bad points

biohazard a dangerous biological substance

beat in this case, the area a reporter covers

unabashedly unashamedly, without any shyness or apology

chinks in the armor vulnerabilities (in this case, potential health problems)

grueling long-lasting and difficult

malarkey nonsense

bum out make someone (or something) unhappy or depressed

palate in this case, one's sense of taste

retch vomit, throw up

ticker a slang word meaning the heart

crash weight-loss plans diets that promise rapid results

splurge a moment of going off a strict diet

blasé boring

Camel a brand of cigarette

to weasel to get what you want by being sneaky

orb circle

chromosomes tiny structures in body cells that determine what characteristics we inherit from our parents

STRIVE TO BE FIT, NOT FANATICAL

I know what you're thinking. Who's this clown? Another fitness Nazi with a word processor who's going to scold and call me a girly-man if I don't do 150 chin-ups before breakfast? Or maybe he's one of those camera-hogging doctors who's always turning up on TV news shows, insisting that if I eat one more bacon cheeseburger my body will be declared a biohazard?

2   Nope. I'm just a reporter whose beat for much of the last decade has been health and medicine, with a particular focus on the care and feeding of the male animal. My interest is unabashedly personal: I just turned 38 and have begun to notice a few chinks in the armor. Chances are you have, too.

3   And if you're reading this column, maybe you've also picked up your share of health books and magazines that are targeted at men. Me, too, and you know what I've noticed? Some contain a lot of valuable information, but they all seem to have two things in common: (1) they avoid using big words, and (2) they take the old "no pain, no gain" philosophy very seriously. All that talk about "getting ripped" and "feeling the burn"—ouch!

4   Of course, "no pain, no gain" is hardly a new idea. Many men grew up hearing it from coaches who insisted that if you didn't

collapse in a puddle of protoplasm at the end of practice, then you obviously weren't hustling. We've been led to believe that working out isn't supposed to be fun; it's supposed to leave your muscles aching and stomach rolling. Is it any wonder that only about one in five U.S. men exercises regularly?

5   The thing is, getting enough exercise and eating right aren't as hard as you might think. The idea that it takes long, grueling workouts to get in shape is malarkey. Believe it or not, more isn't always better when it comes to exercise. And if you're tired of diets that leave you with a fridge full of icky cabbage soup, then tuck in your napkin: Healthy eating doesn't have to bum out your palate.

6   Let's start with exercise. If you know that a little jogging is good for your heart, then you might assume that doing laps till you're dizzy and ready to retch would make your ticker indestructible. But you would be incorrect. A 1997 Harvard study determined that the cardiovascular benefits of an intense aerobic workout peak at about 24 minutes; pound the pavement longer if you like, but your heart won't get any stronger.

7   Ditto for strength training. According to the gospel of the weight room, you must do a minimum of three sets of bench

presses, curls, or any other strength-building exercise, to build up a muscle. But studies at the University of Florida show that's just not true; doing one set of an exercise produces more than three-quarters of the muscles you get from doing three. You gain a little less in the biceps department, maybe, but you get the heck out of that stinky, sweaty gym in one-third of the time. Sounds like a good deal to me.

8   Unless you are obese, forget about dieting. (And if you are dramatically overweight, see a doctor who specializes in obesity.) Nutrition experts say crash weight-loss plans that require you to stop eating certain foods don't work; you'll lose weight, but inevitably your willpower crumbles, and the pounds return. Instead, eat a balanced meal plan that includes lots of fruit, vegetables, whole grains and an occasional splurge. Add regular exercise, and eventually you'll attain a manageable, healthy weight.

9   Bottom line: Modest lifestyle changes can make a huge difference. Consider the evidence. Exhibit A: me. In high school my classmates gave me the nickname "Blaze." At first, I thought they were mispronouncing "blasé," but it turns out they were poking fun at me for being a slow and easily winded runner. During forced-jogging sessions in gym class, I'd bring up the rear, gasping like I was born sucking a Camel. Though I managed to weasel my way on to a few sports teams, few people mistook me for an athlete.

10   In the two decades that followed, I wasn't much of a Healthy Man. I'd go running occasionally, but only if it was getting close to 11 p.m. and the liquor stores were closing. Then, a few years ago, I began to notice a pale, flabby orb forming where my flat stomach used to be. It had to go; I started jogging for half an hour every other day and have never looked back.

11   Last winter I injured my back and went to the hospital. As a nurse took my heart rate, she suddenly arched her eyebrows.

12   "Are you an athlete?" she asked. It turns out my resting heart rate was 56 beats per minute. The average guy's heart rate is about 70, but with regular aerobic training, the cardiovascular system becomes more efficient, and the heart doesn't have to work as hard.

13   I lay back on the exam table and thought of that lonely teenager, huffing and puffing behind the pack during gym class, and how I could totally humiliate him in a race today. See ya, Blaze! If I can become a Healthy Man, anyone with the right chromosomes can, too.

A . C O M P R E H E N S I O N

1. According to the author, what kinds of food should people eat to be healthy?

2. How much exercise is necessary to improve our health?

3. What is one important benefit of regular exercise?

4. Is the author in better physical condition now, or was he in better shape in high school?

B . C R I T I C A L T H I N K I N G

1. Who is the author's intended audience—in other words, who is he primarily writing this column for?

2. What is the main message (main idea) of this reading?

3. Do you think that the author's advice is reasonable for most people? Would his advice be useful for women as well as for men?

4. How do you think the author feels about fitness fanatics?

C . L A N G U A G E A N D V O C A B U L A R Y

1. What does the word *cardiovascular* mean in the sentence "A 1997 Harvard study determined that the cardiovascular benefits of an intense aerobic workout peak at about 24 minutes; pound the pavement longer if you like, but your heart won't get any stronger"?

2. In this selection, the author uses several informal or slang expressions, such as *icky* and *see ya*. Find two or three more informal or slang expressions and highlight or underline them.

D . S T Y L E , S T R U C T U R E , A N D O R G A N I Z A T I O N

1. Does the informal style of this column work well for this topic?

2. How many sections does this newspaper column have, and how many paragraphs are in each section? (Hint: Look for the extra space between sections.) Is this normal academic style, such as you would use in most college classes? If not, how is it different?

3. Where is the main idea of this reading stated—in the first paragraph, in the middle, or in the conclusion?

E. TOPICS FOR DISCUSSION OR JOURNAL WRITING

1. How would you describe your own level of health and physical fitness?

2. What physical activities do you enjoy doing?

3. If you wanted to take the author's advice, what would be your first step?

4. Why is it so difficult to change our lifestyles to become more fit or lose weight?

5. In your opinion, what is the most important single thing a person can do to be healthier?

F. WRITING TOPICS FOR PARAGRAPHS OR ESSAYS

1. Describe your own lifestyle, especially what kinds of food you eat and how much exercise you get.

2. This reading gives advice on physical fitness. Write a persuasive paper to convince people to follow this advice.

3. Interview a doctor, a nurse, a dietitian, a coach, a physical trainer, or another health or fitness professional. Ask for advice on improving your health, and write about it.

4. Compare your own fitness now and when you were in high school.

5. Choose one of the following topics. Find out more about the topic by searching online or in a library; then write about it.
   a. What are the best, proven ways to lose weight and keep it off?
   b. What are some of the best sports for life-long fitness, and why?

Procrastination and Stress

LESTER A. LEFTON

At the start of the twenty-first century, many people feel that there is a shortage of one extremely important resource: *time*. Procrastination—putting things off, waiting until the last minute to do something—sometimes seems as if it's the easy way out, but only temporarily. As you read this selection, compare the benefits of doing things on time to the shorter-term benefits of procrastinating.

PREREADING QUESTIONS

1. Do you think that most people put things off until the last minute?

2. Which do you think is less stressful for most people in the long run—procrastinating or completing things on time?

VOCABULARY

habitually usually, regularly

assert to insist

stress a feeling of emotional pressure, with physical effects

deadline date by which something must be finished, due date

assessed evaluated

ascertaining determining, deciding

hypothesized predicted

term paper a long paper based on information from several sources, a research paper

thus as a result

SOURCE: "Procrastination and Stress" by Lester A. Lefton. From Lefton, Lester A. *Psychology,* Seventh Edition. Copyright © 2000 by Allyn & Bacon. Reprinted/adapted by permission.

blind in this case, anonymous

negatively correlated in this case, two things moving in opposite directions: when one increases, the other decreases

impact effect

tardiness lateness

outweighed by in this case, not as important as

a causal effect a cause and effect relationship (one causes the other)

tendency inclination

impulsive emotional and spur-of-the-moment

postponement putting off, delaying

scant very little

adaptive useful, beneficial

PROCRASTINATION AND STRESS

Why do now what you can put off until tomorrow? The answer is that if you habitually put things off, your work will suffer and so may your health.

2   Getting work done on time is considered proper, rational adult behavior, especially in Western culture. But an awful lot of us procrastinate occasionally, and some people put off, delay, and make excuses for lateness very often. Critics of procrastinators call them lazy or self-indulgent and argue that their work performance suffers from the high stress levels they experience. Defenders—and many procrastinators themselves—assert that work performance is the same, sometimes better, because of heightened pressure to get the job done. They'll argue, "I do my best work under pressure." But do they?

3   Diana Tice and Roy Baumeister investigated the effects of procrastination on performance, stress, and illness. Students were given an assignment with a deadline. Procrastinators were identified using a standard scale. The students' well-being was assessed with self-reports of stress and illness. Finally, task performance was checked by ascertaining whether students turned in assignments early, on time, or late.

4   The researchers hypothesized that procrastination might show poorer performance and health and higher stress levels. Alternatively,

they acknowledged that there might indeed be benefits from intense, last-minute efforts.

Participants and Method

5   The participants were volunteers from a class of students taking a health psychology course. They were assigned a term paper and were told that if they could not turn the paper in on the due date they would automatically be given an extension. Researchers recorded when students turned in their papers and then asked them to fill out questionnaires about health and stress. The instructor who graded the papers did not know who turned in which paper and when; the research design was thus blind.

Results

6   As expected, procrastinators (as identified at the beginning of the study) turned in their papers late; procrastinators also received lower grades than nonprocrastinators did. Interestingly, procrastinators' scores were negatively correlated with stress and reporting of symptoms—that is, the more of a procrastinator a student was, the fewer stress and wellness problems he or she reported. The procrastinators thus reported feeling better but had poorer grades.

Discussion

7   It appears that procrastination brings short-term health benefits. Procrastinators benefit from the carefree, casual situation they create for themselves—stress is lowered and illness is reduced. But when Tice and Baumeister did another study to assess whether these effects were the same at all points in the semester, they found that the procrastinators experienced much more stress late in the semester than the nonprocrastinators did. In fact, when the impact of procrastination is considered relative to the time (early or late in the semester), the effects are negative—total stress and illness are higher for procrastinators. As the researchers put it, the early benefits of tardiness were outweighed by the later costs of stress and ill health. Especially important is the finding that procrastinators

wound up doing inferior work—postponing work seemed to lead to compromises and sacrifices in quality.

8   The researchers acknowledge that this study was not perfect. Participants were not randomly assigned. That stress, illness, and procrastination are related does not prove a causal effect. Further, some people wind up doing their work late for reasons other than procrastination, such as family emergencies. And, of course, university students are not representative of the general population.

Implications

9   The study suggests that procrastination should be considered a self-defeating behavior because it leads to stress, illness, and inferior performance. The tendency to prefer a short-term benefit *may* identify people who make other self-defeating mistakes such as abusing alcohol or drugs or committing other impulsive acts. Of course, some procrastinators mistakenly believe that they can improve performance by postponement, but the evidence to support this view is scant. In the end, procrastination is not adaptive— procrastinators end up suffering more and performing worse than other people. Procrastinators of the world, organize now!

A. COMPREHENSION

1. Who were the participants in the study?
2. What short-term health benefits did procrastinators experience?
3. What bad results can procrastination lead to in the end?

B. CRITICAL THINKING

1. What is the author's purpose in writing about this research study— to inform, to entertain, to persuade, or a combination of these?
2. How can procrastination reduce stress at some times?
3. Do you think the author is using clear logic, or does he seem biased?
4. Do you think the author is sometimes a procrastinator? Are there any clues in the reading that make you think so?

C . LANGUAGE AND VOCABULARY

1. What are some *synonyms* (words with close to the same meaning) for *wound up* and *wind up* in the following phrases from the reading: "procrastinators wound up doing inferior work" and "some people wind up doing their work late"?

2. This selection contains many sentences written in the passive voice, such as "procrastination *should be considered* a self-defeating behavior" and "the early benefits of tardiness *were outweighed* by the later costs of stress and ill health." Does this technique make the paper feel somewhat formal and scientific?

D . STYLE, STRUCTURE, AND ORGANIZATION

1. Where is the main idea of this reading stated—in the introduction, the conclusion, or both?

2. Highlight or underline the heading of each of the sections of the reading. Are these types of headings common in readings, or are they mainly for certain kinds of reports about research?

3. Does the paper flow smoothly from one section to another, and does each section seem complete?

E . TOPICS FOR DISCUSSION OR JOURNAL WRITING

1. Are you a procrastinator (almost always, sometimes, almost never)?

2. Which is more stressful for you, to work hard and complete something on time or to put it off until later?

3. How do you feel about your use of time on a typical day? Do you usually have time to do everything you want or need to do?

4. Do you have any advice for people who are usually procrastinators? What do you recommend?

F . WRITING TOPICS FOR PARAGRAPHS OR ESSAYS

1. Describe a typical day in your life, from the time you get up to the time you go to sleep, and analyze how well you use your time.

2. Describe someone you know who has an extreme attitude toward time—either very rigid or very relaxed. Would you like to be able to treat time the way that person does?

3. Write about a time when you were late turning something in or arriving somewhere. How did it make you feel to be late? What can you do to avoid being late in the future?

4. Make a list of people you know who are successful in school, at work, or in their personal lives, and interview one of them. Ask if he or she has any advice on the subject of managing time and avoiding procrastination, and write a report of the interview, together with your own opinion or reaction.

5. Choose one of the following topics. Look up information on the topic online or in a library; then write a short report on what you find out.

   a. Various personality types and how each type manages stress differently.

   b. Attitudes toward time in various cultures. (For example, compare Swiss or Japanese ideas of time with Arabic or Latin American ideas of time.)

Managing Time

REBECCA J. DONATELLE AND LORRAINE G. DAVIS

Time, the subject of both this reading and the previous one ("Procrastination and Stress"), is an important topic because people are busier now than ever before. The Internet, cell phones, pagers, and hand-held computers keep us connected with work, information, and people around the clock. As you read the following practical instructions for making the most of your time, look for tips that you think would be helpful.

PREREADING QUESTIONS

1. Do you think that most people are good at managing their time and balancing their lives?
2. Do you think that time management can be learned, or are some people just born with the gift of managing time well?

VOCABULARY

obligations necessary duties or responsibilities

stress management program a plan for reducing the negative effects of stress

toss in this case, throw away

prioritize put in order of importance

categorize put into categories of related items

post put up (a notice or sign)

energize fill with energy

precious extremely valuable

potential possibilities

restorative strength-building

assess judge, evaluate

MANAGING TIME

 Time. Everybody needs more of it, especially students trying to balance the demands of classes, social life, earning money for school, family obligations, and time needed for relaxation. The following tips regarding time management should become a part of your stress management program:

- *Clean off your desk.* According to Jeffrey Mayer, author of *Winning the Fight Between You and Your Desk,* most of us spend many stressful minutes each day looking for things that are lost on our desks or in our homes. Go through the things on your desk, toss the unnecessary papers, and put papers for tasks that you must do in folders.

- *Never handle papers more than once.* When bills and other papers come in, take care of them immediately. Write out a check and hold it for mailing. Get rid of the envelopes. Read your mail and file it or toss it. If you haven't looked at something in over a year, toss it.

- *Prioritize your tasks.* Make a daily "to do" list and try to stick to it. Categorize the things you must do today, the things that you have to do but not immediately, and the things that it would be nice to do. Prioritize the Must Do Now and Have to Do Later items and put deadlines next to each. Only consider the Nice to Do items if you finish the others or if the Nice to Do list includes something fun for you. Give yourself a reward as you finish each task.

- *Avoid interruptions.* When you've got a project that requires your total concentration, schedule uninterrupted time. Unplug the phone or let your answering machine get it. Close your door and post a Do Not Disturb sign. Go to a quiet room in the library or student union where no one will find you. Guard your time and don't weaken.

- *Reward yourself for being efficient.* If you've planned to take a certain amount of time to finish a task and you finish early, take some time for yourself. Go for a walk. Start reading something you've wanted to read but haven't had time for.

- *Reduce your awareness of time.* Rather than being a slave to the clock, try to ignore it. Get rid of your watch, and try to listen more to your body when deciding whether you need to eat, sleep, and so on. When you feel awake, do something productive. When you are too tired to work, take time out to sleep or to relax to try to energize yourself.

- *Remember that time is precious.* Try to value each day. Time spent not enjoying life is a tremendous waste of potential.

- *Become aware of your own time patterns.* For many of us, minutes and hours drift by without our even noticing them. Chart your daily schedule, hour by hour, for one week. Note the time that was wasted and the time spent in productive work or restorative pleasure. Assess how you could be more productive and make more time for yourself.

A . C O M P R E H E N S I O N

1. What are some of the many demands on a student's time?

2. What are the three levels of priorities listed in the reading selection?

3. How can people become more aware of their own time patterns?

B . C R I T I C A L T H I N K I N G

1. Who is the authors' intended audience—in other words, who are the writers primarily directing this reading selection to?

2. How can good time management affect a person's health and mental attitude?

3. Do you think that time management is more important today than it was in the past? Why?

4. How well do you think the authors manage time themselves? Does knowing these time management techniques guarantee that a person will always be good at managing time?

C . L A N G U A G E A N D V O C A B U L A R Y

1. What do the authors mean when they write, "reduce your awareness of time"?

2. In this selection, the authors give many instructions on how to manage time better. Some of them are to *categorize, prioritize, schedule,* and *assess.* Find three or four more of the authors' instructions. If you are unsure of the meaning of any of the words in these instructions, look them up in a dictionary.

D . S T Y L E , S T R U C T U R E , A N D O R G A N I Z A T I O N

1. Does the introductory paragraph give the reader a clear idea that the rest of the reading selection will include instructions and advice to help people manage their time better?

2. Highlight or underline the heading of each of the eight body paragraphs. Do the headings provide a good indication of the information in each paragraph?

3. Is there a conclusion? Would the selection be more effective if it had one?

E. TOPICS FOR DISCUSSION OR JOURNAL WRITING

1. Describe your own time management skills and how you feel about them.

2. What are some things you would do if you had more free time?

3. If you wanted to take the authors' advice, which one or two time management tips would you try first?

4. Why is it especially challenging to manage projects that involve many people, such as planning a wedding, building a highway, or starting up a new business?

5. In your opinion, are people going to have more free time in the future or less free time? Why?

F. WRITING TOPICS FOR PARAGRAPHS OR ESSAYS

1. Compare this reading selection with the previous one, "Procrastination and Stress." How are they similar and how are they different?

2. Choose three of the tips in the reading, and make an effort to use them for several days. Then write a report about your experience, and evaluate the techniques you chose. Which techniques seem to work best for you?

3. Go to an office supply store or a college bookstore, or find an office supplies site online. Investigate three to five time management tools, such as organizers or calendars, and write about the benefits and possible drawbacks of using each of them.

4. Choose one of the following instructions topics. Find out more about the topic by searching online or in a library; then write a short instructions paper on how a person can improve one of these important areas of his or her life.

    a. What are some of the most important steps people can take to improve their health?

    b. What are some useful tips on how to relate well with other people in a specific situation, such as at work, in a social situation, or in a relationship?

Computer Addiction
Is Coming Online

WILLIAM J. CROMIE

The use of computers both at home and in the workplace has
increased tremendously during the last several years. New software
offers a variety of entertainment options, video games are more
exciting than ever, and the Internet has broadened our horizons in
every direction. As a result, many people are spending more and more
time in front of their video screens. For some, the computer has
become addictive, distracting them from the real world of family,
friends, and daily living.

In this article from the *Harvard University Gazette,* well-known
science writer William J. Cromie examines the effects of being a
computer addict. (The *Gazette* is available online at
www.news.harvard.edu.)

PREREADING QUESTIONS

1. What attracts people to spend a lot of time surfing the Internet or
    playing video games?

2. How can people tell the difference between a healthy pastime and
    an unhealthy addiction?

VOCABULARY

absorbing interesting, capable of
holding someone's full
attention

the Web, the Internet the
network linking millions of
computers together

aberrant not normal

addicted to something unable
to control your desire for
something or to function
without it

anecdotal evidence other people's stories, not scientifically validated

pathological harmful

self-esteem how a person feels about himself or herself

incorrigible unable to reform or behave well

therapist in this context, a psychologist, counselor, or other professional who can help patients work through an addiction

relapses recurrences of the addictive behavior

COMPUTER ADDICTION IS COMING ONLINE

Luci could not wait to get in front of her computer. It took the divorced mother away from two demanding children and the drudgery of housework. She could play absorbing games, chat with appealing people, "travel," gamble, even have fantasy sex.

2   When her ex-husband visited their children, he saw that they were being neglected. He discovered that Luci (not her real name) spent 10 or more hours a day on the Web.

3   The husband sued for custody of the children. The court agreed with his claim that Luci's excessive use of the computer was abnormal. She lost custody of the children.

4   Maressa Hecht Orzack, a Harvard University psychologist, cites this true case as an example that computer addiction is real and a growing problem. As founder and director of Computer Addiction Services at McLean Hospital, a Harvard-affiliated teaching hospital in Belmont, Mass., she receives messages every day from people who ask for help or want information about the signs of computer addiction. "It's an emerging disorder," Orzack says, "suffered by people who find the virtual reality on computer screens more attractive than everyday reality. Health-care specialists, school counselors, corporate executives, and families have begun to notice the aberrant behavior and mental health problems of computer addicts. They feel unhappy when they are away from the machine. Some try unsuccessfully to stop using it. Many of them spend constantly-increasing amounts of time and money on computers,

often neglecting their families and work. Then they compound the problem by denying it."

5   "It's a new and serious addiction not too many people know about," says Carol Steinman of Harvard University's Faculty and Staff Assistance Program. "In the past year and a half, we have seen this problem among people of all ages."

Symptoms and Surveys

6   Orzack herself knows how easy it can be to become addicted. A few years ago, she was trying to teach herself to use a new software program. When frustrated with trying to understand the manuals, Orzack escaped to playing solitaire on the machine.

7   "I've always liked the game and I started spending more and more time with it," she recalls.

8   Soon, Orzack avoided her primary reason for being on the machine. She started staying up late and spending less time at work.

9   "I have a lot of experience with impulse control problems, like gambling and eating disorders, so I realized what I was getting into," she admits.

10   Orzack started treating herself by placing limits on the amount of time she played, rather than staying at a game until rewarded by winning. "It's one of the strategies I use with patients," she notes.

11   At first, people thought Orzack was crazy when she talked about people becoming addicted to computers. But several articles in scientific journals and newspapers, as well as anecdotal evidence, convinced her that other professionals were concerned about the problem. Recently, a new scientific journal devoted to this subject, called *Cyber Psychology and Behavior,* was started.

12   No one knows how big the problem is. Several research groups have tried to measure it but without notable results. "Many addicts don't admit it," notes Orzack, "or they're not aware of it. There isn't a good definition of what is normal and what is pathological use."

13   Here is Orzack's list of the signs and symptoms:

- Using the computer for pleasure, gratification, or relief from stress.
- Feeling irritable and out of control or depressed when not using it.

- Spending increasing amounts of time and money on hardware, software, magazines, and computer-related activities.
- Neglecting work, school, or family obligations.
- Lying about the amount of time spent on computer activities.
- Risking loss of career goals, educational objectives, and personal relationships.
- Failing at repeated efforts to control computer use.

14   In addition, addicts often have problems such as skipping meals, repetitive stress injuries, backaches, dry eyes, headaches, and loss of sleep.

15   One 14-year-old boy e-mailed Orzack begging her for help. "I have been a computer addict since I was 11," he wrote. He said his grades went from 3.8, when he wasn't using the computer much, to 1.3. He told her he missed meals, suffered backaches, lost track of time, went to bed late, and fell asleep in school.

16   "I'm afraid that I will run away if my parents take my computer away," he continued. "It is almost like the computer owns me."

17   One of the few studies done on admitted addicts found they had other problems such as loneliness, shyness, depression, and low self-esteem. Orzack's observations agree with these findings, and she adds "lousy marriages, incorrigible kids, and boredom at school, home, and work."

18   Linda Welsh surveyed 810 college students at Northeastern University in Boston and found that 62 of them (almost 8 percent) fit the profile of those she labels "Internet dependent."

19   "That's consistent with other research I'm familiar with, most of which was done with college students," Welsh says. "These studies come up with a number between 6 and 10 for the percentage of people who are computer-addicted."

Treatment

20   Treatment is tricky, according to Orzack. "Like an eating disorder, you can't expect people to give it up completely," she says. "Tempting 'food' is all around at work, at school, and in their homes. You have to limit the time spent in front of a machine the

way you limit the time spent at the table. Moderation is important, especially for the new generation of kids who begin to use computers in the first grade, or even before then."

21   One of the hardest things is to get people to come in and talk face-to-face with a therapist. They want to do it all on the Internet.

22   Orzack describes one man who spent all night on the Internet. He couldn't get up to go to work or keep appointments. She kept contacting him by Internet to remind him of his obligations until he finally came to see her.

23   Orzack and other therapists use the same treatment methods as they do with gambling, alcohol, or eating addictions. In one technique, known as cognitive-behavioral therapy, people are taught to monitor their thoughts and identify those that trigger addictive feelings and actions. At the same time, they learn new skills to cope with the addiction and ways to prevent, or handle, relapses.

24   In another technique, motivational interviewing, patient and therapist work together to set goals such as learning to recognize the difference between healthy and addictive computer use. "The efforts of patients are constantly reaffirmed, and they are not scolded for slips or failures," Orzack explains.

25   She uses a combination of both techniques, making "contracts" with people to specify how much time they will spend in front of a computer screen. As an example, she encourages them to set an alarm, or two alarms if needed, to signal when to turn to other activities. Orzack tries to get them to devote more time to other pursuits, such as exercising, talking with family and friends, and developing new recreational or social interests.

26   The average treatment takes three months of regular sessions and telephone (not e-mail) checkups. But, Orzack acknowledges, some people require a year or more to deal with their bad habits.

27   "Nobody's ever cured," she says. "You just learn to deal with the problem."

A. C O M P R E H E N S I O N

1. What are some indications that someone might be a computer addict?

2. What are some of the methods of treating computer addiction?

3. How long is the average treatment time for computer addiction? Is anybody ever really cured, according to the article?

B . CRITICAL THINKING

1. What is the author's purpose in writing this article?
2. What is the main idea of this article?
3. Do the examples in the article provide good support for the main idea? Which examples do you think are most effective?
4. What should you do if you think you are addicted to computers, video games, or the Internet?
5. Do you think that in the future the number of computer addicts is going to increase or decrease? Why?

C . LANGUAGE AND VOCABULARY

1. Had you ever read or heard the expression *repetitive stress injuries* before? What is your best guess as to its meaning? What kinds of repetitive stress injuries do you think are likely to occur as a result of computer addiction?
2. In this article, the author includes quite a few technical words and expressions that health professionals use to describe addictions and other mental health problems, such as *abnormal* and *impulse control problems.* Find three or four more of these mental health terms and look up the meaning of any that you do not understand. Does using technical vocabulary make this article clearer and more specific?

D . STYLE, STRUCTURE, AND ORGANIZATION

1. Find the part of the reading where the author uses *narration*—the experiences that people have had with computer addiction. Mark it by running a marker or pen down the side of the reading.
2. Now find where the *definition* of computer addiction is given, and use a different color marker to highlight it.

3. Finally, mark all the sections that show the *effects* that computer addiction can have on people. Do you think that this combination of narration, definition, and cause-and-effect writing is effective for this article?

E. TOPICS FOR DISCUSSION OR JOURNAL WRITING

1. Do you spend a lot of time in front of a computer screen? Do you think you spend too much time online or at the computer?

2. What do you think it feels like to be addicted to something?

3. What is the first place or who is the first person you would go to for help if you thought you were addicted to something?

4. Would you like to be a counselor, psychologist, or therapist who helps people with their addictions? Why or why not?

F. WRITING TOPICS FOR PARAGRAPHS OR ESSAYS

1. Write about someone you know who might be addicted to computers or who may have another type of addiction. What would you recommend for that person?

2. Describe some of your favorite computer activities, software, or Web sites.

3. Tell the story of computer addiction from the addict's point of view.

4. Research the career of psychologist or therapist. What are the job duties, working conditions, pay ranges, and required education for this career?

5. Choose one of the following topics and find out more about it by searching online or in a library; then write about it. If possible, use a combination of types of writing in your paper.
   a. What are some of the most common addictions in our country today, and how do they affect individuals and our society?
   b. What are the best and most successful treatments or strategies for overcoming an addiction?
   c. Write about one type of addiction. What are the effects of this addiction? How can a person overcome it?

---⚜---

Playing for Keeps

ANDY STEINER

Linda Mastandrea has succeeded in ways that no one thought she could, not even Linda herself. Most people do not expect a person with cerebral palsy to play basketball, to compete in track and field events, or to serve on the United States Olympic Committee. Andy Steiner, senior editor for the magazine *Utne Reader*, tells the story of this amazing woman.

PREREADING QUESTIONS

1. Why do many people enjoy participating in college or high school athletics?

2. What kinds of sports are available for athletes with disabilities to participate in?

VOCABULARY

sprinter a runner, a competitor in short races at top speed

cerebral palsy a disorder characterized by impairment of muscles and coordination

sidelines (on the) watching rather than participating

profile in this context, image or public awareness

perception a point of view or way of perceiving something

marketable saleable, capable of bringing in money

attest to give testimony or affirm that something is true

squad team

pale in this case, to be of lesser importance or value

perks extra benefits

dished out handed out, given

PLAYING FOR KEEPS

Sprinter Linda Mastandrea holds two Olympic medals, but she
didn't start racing until she was in her 20s. In fact, for the first part
of her life, no one, including herself, thought she could ever be
athletic.

2   "As a kid growing up with cerebral palsy, I couldn't run, I
couldn't jump, I couldn't even walk very well," Mastandrea, 35,
says. "So I spent a lot of time on the sidelines. People assumed
sports were out of the picture for me."

3   Today, she's leading a campaign to raise the profile—and
funding—of Paralympic athletics. An attorney and advocate in the
Chicago office of the nonprofit America's Athletes with Disabilities,
Mastandrea has been a member of the United States Olympic
Committee (USOC) board of directors since 1998, and is using her
position to be a "thorn in the side" of the other members, pushing
and prodding them to provide equal funding and recognition for
Paralympic athletes.

4   Her goals are numerous, but she's convinced they're attainable.
They include securing funding and training facilities for disabled
athletes, providing Paralympians with the option of joining the
health insurance plan provided to able-bodied Olympians, and
encouraging media attention and exposure for Paralympic events,
which are currently held immediately following the closing
ceremonies of the "real" Olympic Games.

5   "Paralympic athletes have struggled under the USOC leadership
for years," Mastandrea says. "In many ways, it comes down to
money. There's a perception that athletes with disabilities are not
marketable, and therefore supporting us is a charity thing. But I
think a lot of people—able-bodied or not—identify with people
with disabilities. An athlete is an athlete is an athlete. If you love
sports, you love sports. I'm here to attest that the thrill of the game
can change your life. It doesn't matter if you're in a wheelchair or if
you are standing."

6   Her own life changed when the coach of her university's
wheelchair basketball team encouraged her to join the squad. On
wheels, Mastandrea discovered that she was an athlete. "Before

college, sports was something for everybody else," she says. "But once I got in a chair and on the basketball court, it was like, 'Wow. I've never felt this great before. I'm playing basketball even though my legs don't work very well.' Once I realized I could be an athlete, I never looked back."

7   Track and field was next, and soon Mastandrea was competing— and winning—in 100-, 200-, and 400-meter races against other disabled athletes. In 1992 she joined the U.S. Paralympic team, traveling to the summer games in Barcelona, and later to Atlanta (where she earned her gold and silver medals) in 1996.

8   The Paralympic experience was exciting, but it was also expensive. Mastandrea, like her teammates, had to pay for her own coaches, rent her own training facilities, and find her own health insurance. Since 1994 the USOC has provided travel, housing, and uniforms for Paralympic athletes, but those benefits pale in comparison to the perks dished out to able-bodied competitors.

9   "It's a lot like where the women's sports movement was 25 years ago," Mastandrea says. "Disabled athletes are up against a lack of recognition, a lack of funding, a lack of opportunity."

A .   C O M P R E H E N S I O N

1.   When Linda Mastandrea was growing up, why did everyone assume that she could not participate in sports?

2.   How did Mastandrea first become involved in athletics?

3.   What athletic awards has Mastandrea won?

4.   What are Mastandrea's goals as a member of the United States Olympic Committee (USOC)?

B .   C R I T I C A L   T H I N K I N G

1.   Why do you think the Paralympics receive less publicity and public attention than the regular Olympics?

2.   What does Mastandrea mean when she says, "An athlete is an athlete is an athlete"?

3.   What makes the Olympics special and unlike any other type of athletic competition?

4. Do you think the Olympics have become too commercialized in recent years? Give reasons for your answer.

C. LANGUAGE AND VOCABULARY

1. The word *Paralympic* is not defined in the reading. What do you think it means? What two other words do you think were combined to create the word *Paralympics*?

2. Notice the expression *thorn in the side,* which is used in the third paragraph. Based on the *context* (other information in the same paragraph), what do you think this expression means? (Hint: To help figure out the meaning, think about how annoying an actual thorn stuck in someone's side would be.)

D. STYLE, STRUCTURE, AND ORGANIZATION

1. How does the introduction (the first paragraph) capture readers' attention? What were you curious about when you first read the introduction?

2. In writing this profile of Linda Mastandrea, why did author Andy Steiner include several statements from Mastandrea herself? Choose one of Linda Mastandrea's statements that you especially like and explain why you like it. What does it add to the reading?

E. TOPICS FOR DISCUSSION OR JOURNAL WRITING

1. Do you admire Linda Mastandrea? Why?

2. What are some of the biggest challenges that people with disabilities face?

3. Have you ever seriously competed in basketball, track and field, or another sport? In what way was the experience rewarding for you?

4. Can you think of any ways in which your school or local community could do more to provide equal opportunities for people with disabilities?

5. Do you know anyone who has either a physical disability or a learning disability? What are some of the obstacles that person has had to overcome?

F. WRITING TOPICS FOR PARAGRAPHS OR ESSAYS

1. Interview someone you admire and write a paper about that person. Use "Playing for Keeps" as a model for your writing.

2. Write about someone with a disability who has had to overcome many obstacles. How has that person succeeded in meeting challenges and coping with problems? Are there certain obstacles that remain? You may interview someone you know personally, or you may write about a well-known person.

3. Using library resources or the Internet, look up information about how the Olympics began and the history of the Olympic games. Write an informative paper about the most interesting information you find.

4. Using library resources or the Internet, look up information about the Paralympics or the Special Olympics, including how these special Olympic games began and their history. Write a paper about your findings.

5. Write a paper about a time in your life when you overcame an obstacle, a time when you proved yourself to be more capable than someone else thought you were, or a time when competing for an award made you feel good about yourself. Tell the story with interesting details, and include some of your feelings.

PART

NATURE AND
THE OUTDOORS

Journey of the Pink Dolphins

SY MONTGOMERY

Author and naturalist Sy Montgomery has traveled to and observed wildlife in Borneo, Zaire, India, Costa Rica, Southeast Asia, and many other places to research material for her books, articles, and films. Some of Montgomery's most popular books are *The Curious Naturalist, Spell of the Tiger,* and *Search for the Golden Moon Bear,* which tells about the discovery of a marvelous golden bear in Southeast Asia. *The Snake Scientist,* Montgomery's first book for children, received ten national awards, including one from the International Reading Association. She also produced a National Geographic documentary based on her observations of tigers in West Bengal.

To write her book *Journey of the Pink Dolphins,* from which this reading is taken, Sy Montgomery explored the Amazon and other connecting waterways in search of freshwater dolphins that live in the warm waters of the South American rivers. She has also written a children's book called *Encantado: Pink Dolphin of the Amazon* about her adventures among the people and the animals of the Amazon region.

PREREADING QUESTIONS

1. Why do many people consider dolphins to be special?
2. Do you know of any fables or legends about animals?

V O C A B U L A R Y

looking glass mirror

constellations formations of stars

boas large tropical snakes

sizzle a bubbling sensation (like drops of water dancing on the surface of a hot frying pan)

effusion an unrestrained outpouring

otherworldly from another world, mystical

eerily strangely, mysteriously

festas feasts, celebrations

ruddy reddish-colored

Shamans tribal religious leaders

twang a sharp vibrating sound, usually made by plucking strings on an instrument

pulses occurs at regular intervals

Shipibo a native South American tribe

traverses crosses or passes through

starboard the right side of a boat or ship (when facing toward the front)

port the left side of a boat or ship (when facing toward the front)

intangible not capable of being perceived by the senses

ballet a graceful classical dance

JOURNEY OF THE PINK DOLPHINS

The river is the looking glass into another world. By day, the water is a perfect mirror of trees and sky—and yet its glassy surface moves so quickly that if you enter the water without a lifejacket, the current will sweep you under. The river people speak of the Encante, an enchanted city beneath the water, ruled by beings they call Encantados. Those who visit never want to leave, because everything is more beautiful there.

2   At night, even the stars seem brighter in the water than in the sky. The constellations shine above, their starry reflections below, and from the trees, the glowing eyes of wolf spiders, tree boas, tree frogs. In your canoe, you feel like you are traveling through the timeless starscape of space.

3   But if you stop and wait, the Encantados will come. At first you may feel a sizzle of bubbles rising beneath zthe craft, an effusion of pearls cast up from below like a net of enchantment. If the night is moonless, you will only know their breath. But if the moon is full, you may see a form rising from the water, gathering into the shape of a dolphin. Inches from your canoe, a face may break the surface—a face at once otherworldly and eerily familiar. The forehead is clearly defined, like a person's. The long beak sticks out like a nose. The skin is delicate, like ours. Sometimes it is grayish, or white—and sometimes dazzlingly, impossibly *pink*. The creature turns its neck and looks at you, and opening the top of its head, gasps, "Chaaahhhhh!"

4   In Brazil, they call this dolphin "boto." They say the boto can turn into a person, that it shows up at festas to seduce men and women. They say you must be careful, or it will take you away forever to the Encante, the enchanted city beneath the water. In

Peru, they call the creature "bufeo colorado"—the ruddy dolphin. Shamans say its very breath has power, and that the sound it utters when it gasps can send poisoned darts flying, as from a blowgun. Scientists call it by the species name: *Inia geoffrensis.*

* * *

5   On the glass-smooth waters of Charro Lake, we wait for the moon.

6   A bat shoots by, a flying shadow. In the dark, frogs call in the clicking voices of bamboo chimes; others twang like rubber bands. Lightning pulses silently in the southern sky. But the moon hides behind dark billowing rain clouds, so we wait.

7   The Shipibo say that by moonlight, women are especially susceptible to spells cast by dolphins. The moon, it is said, is the sun of the underworld. It traverses the world of darkness, illuminating the Encante. That is why Dianne and I have come here now: with Moises and Graciella, with Jerry and Steve, we wait in our canoe for the moon to reveal the dolphins.

8   At 6:40, a glow pierces the clouds. By 6:45, it shines bright enough to write these words by. And still we wait.

9   Around us, bells, creaks, whistles, honks; the forest heaving and sighing, like a dream set to music. And then, at 7:04, we hear their breath: "Chaaahhhh!" A minute later, another gasp.

10   Another minute passes. And now, all around us, tiny bubbles begin to rise—behind us, in front of us, to starboard, then port. It is the expelled breath of dolphins—breath so close we can touch it.

11   I stop taking data. "This can't be happening," I say to Dianne. "Believe it—it's happening," she answers. I dip my hand in the water and feel the bubbles sizzle on my skin, intimate as a caress. It seems as unreal as a kiss from a ghost, and yet it continues: for four minutes, we touch the intangible and see the invisible, as the dolphins bless our canoe with their breath.

12   The bubbles disappear. In the seventeen minutes that follow, we can see, by moonlight, the glistening pink heads bobbing in the water. But still, more real than the visible are these breaths: a loud blow, a tail slap, a sigh; a gasp, a blow, a ballet of breath. And now the breaths grow fainter, more distant, as the dolphins move away.

A . C O M P R E H E N S I O N

1. Who or what are the Encantados?

2. What other names does the pink dolphin have in Brazil and Peru? What special powers are the dolphins said to have in those countries?

3. What are the beliefs of the Shipibo about moonlight and the dolphins?

4. Before Sy Montgomery and her companions can actually see the dolphins, how do they first learn that the dolphins have arrived?

B . C R I T I C A L T H I N K I N G

1. Why do you suppose some people believe in legends about the dolphins? Can you imagine how any of these legends might have begun?

2. Why did Sy Montgomery wait for the dolphins at night rather than look for them during the day? Do you think she believes any of the native legends?

3. How do you think the author felt about this experience? Why did she feel that way?

4. Based on what you learned about the pink river dolphins in this reading, in what ways do they seem similar to other dolphins that you have seen or read about?

C . L A N G U A G E A N D V O C A B U L A R Y

1. In the first paragraph, the author uses the Portuguese name *Encantados,* which the river people have for beings that live under the water and appear at night in the form of dolphins. The name for the place where they live is also Portuguese: the *Encante.* What do you think these words mean in English? Look for clues that the author gives us. You may also want to ask someone who speaks Portuguese or look up the words in a Portuguese-English dictionary.

2. When the author describes being on the river at night in a canoe, she writes, "You feel like you are traveling through the timeless

starscape of space." What do you think the word *starscape* means? You probably will not find *starscape* in a dictionary, so you will need to use clues in the reading. Also, think about similar words you may already know that use a combination of another word with *-scape,* such as *landscape* or *seascape.*

D. STYLE, STRUCTURE, AND ORGANIZATION

1. This reading has two distinct parts. What is the main topic of each part? Where does the second part begin?

2. At times, the author makes the dolphins seem almost human. At other times, they seem more like supernatural beings. Which descriptive details make them seem almost human? Which details make them seem supernatural?

3. Shortly before the dolphins appear in Charro Lake, what kind of mood (or *feeling*) does the author create through her description of the scene? Which details help establish that mood?

E. TOPICS FOR DISCUSSION OR JOURNAL WRITING

1. Would you enjoy going down the river and taking a canoe out on Charro Lake, as Sy Montgomery did? What do you think would be the best parts of the trip? Would anything seem scary or dangerous to you?

2. Have you ever seen a live dolphin or watched a movie in which trained dolphins played a significant part? Recall as many details as you can about the dolphins you saw.

3. If you could observe any animal that you wanted to anywhere in the world, which animal would you choose? Where would you go to see that animal, and what would the experience be like?

4. What legends, stories, superstitions, or religious beliefs can you think of in which animals are thought to have special powers?

F. WRITING TOPICS FOR PARAGRAPHS OR ESSAYS

1. Have you ever had an opportunity to go boating on a lake or river or to go river-rafting? If so, write about one or more of your experiences. Include descriptive details about the lake or river and any animals you observed.

2. Observe an animal at a zoo, an aquarium, or a marine park for at least half an hour. How would this animal's life be different in the wild? Write a paper from the animal's point of view, comparing life in captivity with life in the wild.

3. Find a newspaper column about nature, such as Sy Montgomery's column in *The Boston Globe,* or any other article about nature in a newspaper or magazine. Write a summary of the column or article, plus your own evaluation of it. Attach the column or article to your paper.

4. Write an informative paper about the Amazon River. Consult a good encyclopedia or other reference source to learn about the Amazon.

5. Use library resources or the Internet to find out more about dolphins. Then choose one of the following writing assignments:
   a. Compare and contrast marine dolphins with river dolphins.
   b. Identify and describe the four kinds of river dolphins and their habitats (where they live).
   c. Explain how dolphins communicate with each other.
   d. Report on how dolphins are trained and what they can be trained to do.

In the Shadow of Man

JANE GOODALL

Jane Goodall began her research on chimpanzees in 1960 when she went to their native habitat near Lake Tanganyika in East Africa to study them, an unusual venture for a twenty-six-year-old woman. During more than thirty years of observing and interacting with chimpanzees in the wild, Dr. Goodall has written several books, including *In the Shadow of Man* and *Through a Window,* as well as books for children, such as *Grub: The Bush Baby* and *My Life with the Chimpanzees.* Her wide-screen IMAX movie, *Jane Goodall's Wild Chimpanzees* (2002), has made millions of viewers aware of her work.

The Jane Goodall Institute for Wildlife Research, which she founded, is a leader in wildlife conservation, especially the protection of chimpanzees, and she has received many honors and awards, including the National Geographic Society's Hubbard Medal and the Ghandi/King Award for Nonviolence. In 2002 the Secretary-General of the United Nations honored Dr. Goodall as a "Messenger of Peace."

PREREADING QUESTIONS

1. What qualities or abilities make human beings different from animals?

2. What can we learn from observing animals in their natural surroundings?

V O C A B U L A R Y

weary tired, worn out

slight small

termite a hive insect that lives underground and builds mounds

casual observers in this context, people other than trained researchers

wandered moved around, not in a specific direction

swarm a moving mass of insects

discarded thrown away, rejected

mandibles in insects, similar to a jaw

a hide a small area screened off from view, also called a *blind*

IN THE SHADOW OF MAN

I had had a frustrating morning, tramping up and down three valleys with never a sign or sound of a chimpanzee. Hauling myself up the steep slope of Mlinda Valley I headed for the peak, not only weary but soaking wet from crawling through dense undergrowth. Suddenly I stopped, for I saw a slight movement in the long grass about sixty yards away. Quickly focusing my binoculars I saw that it was a single chimpanzee, and just then he turned in my direction. I recognized David Graybeard.

2   Cautiously I moved around so that I could see what he was doing. He was squatting beside the red earth mound of a termite nest, and as I watched I saw him carefully push a long grass stem down into a hole in the mound. After a moment he withdrew it and picked something from the end with his mouth. I was too far away to make out what he was eating, but it was obvious that he was actually using a grass stem as a tool.

3   I knew that on two occasions casual observers in West Africa had seen chimpanzees using objects as tools: one had broken open palm-nut kernels by using a rock as a hammer, and a group of chimps had been observed pushing sticks into an underground bees' nest and licking off the honey. Somehow I had never dreamed of seeing anything so exciting myself.

4   For an hour David feasted at the termite mound and then he wandered slowly away. When I was sure he had gone I went over to

examine the mound. I found a few crushed insects strewn about, and a swarm of worker termites sealing the entrances of the nest passages into which David had obviously been poking his stems. I picked up one of his discarded tools and carefully pushed it into a hole myself. Immediately I felt the pull of several termites as they seized the grass, and when I pulled it out there were a number of worker termites and a few soldiers, with big red heads, clinging on with their mandibles. There they remained, sticking out at right angles to the stem with their legs waving in the air.

5   Before I left I trampled down some of the tall dry grass and constructed a rough hide—just a few palm fronds leaned up against the low branch of a tree and tied together at the top. I planned to wait there the next day. But it was another week before I was able to watch a chimpanzee "fishing" for termites again.

* * *

6   On the eighth day of my watch David Graybeard arrived again together with Goliath, and the pair worked there for two hours. I could see much better: I observed how they scratched open the sealed-over passage entrances with a thumb or forefinger. I watched

how they bit the ends off their tools when they became bent, or used the other end, or discarded them in favor of new ones. Goliath once moved at least fifteen yards from the heap to select a firm-looking piece of vine, and both males often picked three or four stems while they were collecting tools, and put the spares beside them on the ground until they wanted them.

7   Most exciting of all, on several occasions they picked small leafy twigs and prepared them for use by stripping off the leaves. This was the first recorded example of a wild animal not merely *using* an object as a tool, but actually modifying an object and thus showing the crude beginnings of tool*making*.

A.   COMPREHENSION

1.   Who or what are David Graybeard and Goliath?

2.   What did David Graybeard do with a long grass stem? Why were his actions surprising to the author?

3.   In West Africa, how had observers seen chimpanzees using tools?

4.   Why did Jane Goodall keep watch at the termite mound? How long did she have to wait?

B.   CRITICAL THINKING

1.   What is the main idea or most important point of this selection?

2.   What range of emotions did the author and researcher, Jane Goodall, probably experience during her research?

3.   Does the reading include mostly opinion or mostly facts?

4.   What qualities would a researcher need in order to be a successful observer of animal behavior in the wild?

5.   Is *In the Shadow of Man* a good title for the book from which this selection is taken? Why do you think the author chose this title?

C.   LANGUAGE AND VOCABULARY

1.   Had you ever read or heard the expression *strewn about* before you read it in the fourth paragraph of this selection? What do you think it means?

2. In this reading, the author uses many -*ing* words and phrases (present participles and participial phrases), such as "Quickly *focusing* my binoculars. . . ." Find six -*ing* words or phrases in the first paragraph. Do they make the reading more descriptive?

D . S T Y L E , S T R U C T U R E , A N D O R G A N I Z A T I O N

1. Jane Goodall uses a lot of descriptive details in this selection. Highlight or list four specific details in the second paragraph that help the reader picture the scene. How does the author's use of descriptive details make this story interesting to read?

2. Where is the sentence that expresses the main idea of this selection—at the beginning, in the middle, or at the end? Is it effective where it is? Why?

E . T O P I C S F O R D I S C U S S I O N O R J O U R N A L W R I T I N G

1. Imagine the living conditions that Jane Goodall experienced while she studied the chimpanzees in the wild. What do you think it was like for her to spend so much time away from other humans?

2. What do think was the best thing about living in the wild and studying the chimpanzees?

3. Would you like to do this kind of research? Why or why not?

4. Do you think that many rare and endangered species of animals will become extinct in the near future? Why?

F . W R I T I N G T O P I C S F O R P A R A G R A P H S O R E S S A Y S

1. Write about a time when you had an adventure or witnessed something amazing.

2. Describe a wild place away from civilization that you have visited, heard of, read about, or seen on TV.

3. Use your imagination to describe the camp where Jane Goodall lived while she was doing her research with the chimpanzees.

Include details about things you might see, hear, smell, or feel if you were there.

4. Tell the story of Jane Goodall's adventures and research from the chimpanzees' point of view.

5. Read more about Jane Goodall's research in one of her books, on the Internet at **www.janegoodall.ca**, or in *National Geographic* articles. Then choose one of the following writing assignments:

a. Write about Jane Goodall's life. Include details about her research in Africa.

b. Write a short summary of what Jane Goodall learned about chimpanzees in her lifetime of work.

Life in the Treetops

MARGARET D. LOWMAN

Margaret D. Lowman writes about her experiences as chief scientist on a special expedition to the Blue Creek rain forest of Belize in 1994. This expedition was sponsored by the Jason Project for Education, which made it possible for Dr. Lowman and other researchers to share their discoveries with students in the United States, Canada, and several other countries by means of live broadcasts from their research sites. The author's two sons, Eddie and James, accompanied her on this expedition to Belize.

P R E R E A D I N G Q U E S T I O N S

1. What types of plants and animals would you expect to find in a rain forest?
2. Why would learning firsthand about a rain forest be a valuable educational experience?

V O C A B U L A R Y

donned put on

mode method or means

canopy in this usage, the dense upper area of the trees

shack a small, crudely constructed building

clambered climbed

commotion noisy disturbance

towheads people with very light blond hair

lavish excessive

traipsing walking about

preserve an area set aside for the protection and preservation of plants and/or animals

ecotourism tourism to places of ecological interest

venture a business

tract an area of land

neophytes beginners, those who are doing something for the first time

199

epiphyte a plant that does not need to have its roots in soil, absorbs moisture from the air, and is supported by a tree or another tall plant

emanating coming out of

reeling whirling, going round and round

spanning, spanned extending from one side across to the other

arborists tree specialists

agile able to move quickly and easily

jubilant very happy

emergent rising above the surroundings

sway a back-and-forth movement

awe amazement, wonder

reputedly supposedly

elation happiness, joy

LIFE IN THE TREETOPS

My children and I boarded a small six-seater plane with a simple propeller engine. Along its side the words *Maya Airways* were almost worn off. Our luggage was thrown casually into the back, and Eddie was invited to serve as copilot. He donned a pair of heavy headphones and we were off into the skies over Belize. I felt somewhat apprehensive about putting my precious children on this old propeller plane, but there was no other mode of transport to our field site. (Four years later both pilot and plane crashed into the Maya Mountains.)

2   My young sons were thrilled to be accompanying their mom on a tropical rain-forest expedition. Eddie was eight years old, James was six. (They had seen the Australian rain forest on numerous occasions as infants, but were too young then to remember any details.) Our destination was Blue Creek in southern Belize. Our mission was to set up the study site for the Jason Project, including the construction of a canopy walkway with several platforms upon which to conduct field research. I called this structure my green laboratory, but the boys called it their giant treehouse.

. . .

3   This was my second journey to the rain forests of Belize. Upon arriving at the Punta Gorda airport (one dirt runway and a small shack for shelter during rain or hot sun) we were met by an old

truck with some of the Jason Project crew. We clambered into the truck bed and bumped along from the coastal town of Punta Gorda about 20 miles west, into the interior. At Blue Creek village Eddie and James caused quite a commotion among the village children. The arrival of two towheads—probably almost of marriage age in their culture—aroused great curiosity. The girls brought samples of their bracelets and embroidery to show the boys. James (still in his antigirl stage) was horrified; Eddie (slightly older) was friendly, but did not know how to handle such lavish attention. They passed shyly into the forest, traipsing down the new trail built to access the canopy research station, future site of our giant treehouse.

· · ·

4   Blue Creek was a leased preserve, operated by a small ecotourism venture back in Boston. The site offered little except an outhouse and one shed that served as kitchen, library, dining room, and sleeping area. But it had a superb tract of primary forest and a captivating limestone cave just 500 meters upstream from the "lodge."

· · ·

5   We had reservations to stay at the Blue Creek "lodge" that night. Accommodations included the opportunity to lay out a sleeping bag on the floor of the open hut, or (in my fortunate situation) to tie a hammock between two posts. I had brought my faithful khaki hammock from the jungles of Cameroon, and the rest of the group was impressed. Everyone was in bed by 7:00 P.M. because there was no electricity and it was pouring rain. Sleeping in the rain forest was a new experience for most of our group. Several of the neophytes expressed concern about the risk of snakes while sleeping on the floor, and others looked about anxiously for bats. Only minutes after everyone had finally settled into his or her sleeping bag, we all leapt up at the sound of a loud explosion. A large fruit from the over-hanging bobo tree (similar in size to the cannonball tree, named for the obvious size and shape of its fruits) had fallen on the tin roof. Its fruits were slightly larger than coconuts, and weighed more. Everyone laughed nervously and settled back down for a relatively sleepless night.

· · ·

6   After that first night in the Belizean jungle, we awoke to a glistening green world. Each leaf was dripping water from the

evening storms, and every drip tip was functioning to funnel water off the leaf surface and onto the root system. I mapped trees at this site, examined the canopies with binoculars to estimate epiphyte diversity, and brainstormed with the crew about possible camera angles. We traveled back to Punta Gorda in the evening, slept in real beds, and absorbed the sounds of a tropical town—bicycles pedaling on bumpy streets, skinny dogs barking, frogs peeping, music and voices emanating from tiny open-air drinking huts, and a gentle drizzle cooling the sultry summer air.

7   I returned the next day to Belize City, and on to Miami and Sarasota. My brain was reeling with enthusiasm and ideas.

· · ·

8   Three months flew by. By the time they were over, my walkway partner, Bart Bouricius, and I had designed and created a budget for our green laboratory. We had assembled a team of six experts for the erection of the walkway. Huts had been built that more than quadrupled the space of the field station, and foam mattresses and bunk-bed frames were flown in at great expense.

· · ·

9   When my sons and I had settled into our camp site at the Blue Creek research station, we eagerly looked around us. The research station had changed dramatically since I had been there several weeks ago with Robin. Spanning the Blue Creek watercourse hung a stainless steel cable, and on either side a wooden platform had been built about 75 feet from the ground. Using our binoculars, we could observe the arborists, like a troupe of monkeys, "performing" overhead.

· · ·

10   Eddie and James were eager to climb. They had been given children's harnesses for Christmas, so each had his own canopy gear. We had practiced at home, but this was the big time. Ironically, I was very anxious and not looking forward to having them ascend 75 feet into the sky. Even though I did this sort of thing virtually every day, it seemed more dangerous when I contemplated the ascent for my children. I knew, however, that they were probably more agile than I! My brother Ed, an expert woodworker who had helped build the platforms, was part of the construction crew. . . . Ed generously offered to accompany the boys to the top and

promised to call me when they were on the bridge (so that I could open my eyes). In no time the three of them had ascended the ladder and reached the platform overlooking the creek. I hastily climbed up to join the jubilant crew.

· · ·

11   A look at the tranquil stream below gave us a vivid respect for our height. The people at ground level looked like ants. We saw the glistening sun leaves and felt the winds gusting over the emergent flame tree adjacent to our platform.

· · ·

12   The canopy was a whole new world for Eddie and James, and a whole new world for me to appreciate through their eyes. They cautiously crossed the bridge over the creek, which spanned approximately 72 feet and had a well-defined sway in the center. Once on the other side, they peered in awe at the white poisonwood tree (*Sebastiana* sp., family Euphorbiaceae), whose leaves reputedly inflict an irritating rash to human skin if touched.

13   After several exploratory hours in the canopy, the boys descended on the metal staples and ladders to the ground below. With elation they observed a hairy black tarantula on the tree trunk. It looked identical to our faithful pet spider, Harriet, at home. The day was a huge success. The boys did not even seem to mind their dinner of beans and rice, despite the fact that it was the fourth night of that menu.

A . C O M P R E H E N S I O N

1.   How did the village children at Blue Creek react to seeing Eddie and James? Why did they react this way?

2.   Why was it difficult to get a good night's sleep at the Blue Creek "lodge"?

3.   What changes did the author observe at the Blue Creek research station when she and her sons returned three months after their first visit?

4.   How did the boys and the author get to the observation platform? What could they see from the platform?

B . C R I T I C A L   T H I N K I N G

1. How did the boys feel about their experience in the treetops?

2. What does the author mean when she writes that it was "a whole new world for me to appreciate through their eyes"?

3. Do you think Eddie and James were in any real danger? Why or why not?

4. How would you describe the relationship between Margaret Lowman and her sons?

5. How do you think the Jason Project could contribute to worldwide understanding of rain forests?

C . L A N G U A G E   A N D   V O C A B U L A R Y

1. The author comments that, by using binoculars, they "could observe the arborists, like a troupe of monkeys, 'performing' overhead." When you read the author's comparison, what kind of scene did you picture in your mind? Can you figure out what the word *troupe* means? If not, look it up in a dictionary.

2. What do you think the term *rain forest* means? If necessary, look up *rain forest* in a dictionary or an encyclopedia to get a better understanding of the meaning.

D . S T Y L E ,   S T R U C T U R E ,   A N D   O R G A N I Z A T I O N

1. Which of the following scenes can you picture most clearly in your mind: the "lodge" at Blue Creek, the tropical town of Punta Gorda, or the view from the platform? Which details do you think are most interesting and effective in the description of the scene you have selected?

2. In addition to using description, this reading also uses *narration*, or storytelling, to relate what happened. Make a list of all of the important events in the story, beginning with the author and her sons boarding a plane for Belize. Be sure to keep the events in chronological order (time order).

E. TOPICS FOR DISCUSSION OR JOURNAL WRITING

1. What do you think was the most exciting part of the trip for the author's sons, Eddie and James? Why?

2. Does Punta Gorda seem similar to any towns that you have ever visited? In what ways? Describe any similar town that you know about.

3. Based on what you learned in the reading, would you like to visit Belize? Why or why not?

4. Did you ever have an opportunity to go along with one of your parents and observe or participate in his or her job activities? If so, what did you learn from that experience?

5. What do you think would be most interesting and rewarding about conducting research in tree canopies? What would be the biggest challenges of the job?

F. WRITING TOPICS FOR PARAGRAPHS OR ESSAYS

1. Write about an interesting or exciting experience you had in the outdoors. Use both narration and description.

2. "Job shadow" someone for a day—that is, spend a full day with someone at his or her job. Then write about your experience.

3. Describe the expedition to Belize from the viewpoint of one of the author's sons.

4. Find out more about rain forests by using library resources or the Internet, and write a persuasive paper about why rain forests should be preserved.

5. Use information from the Jason Project Web site at **www.jasonproject .org/** to write a report about one of the following topics:

   a. The current Jason Project or one of the other expeditions in previous years.

   b. One of the other research sites in Belize, such as the cave at Blue Creek or the Mayan city of Xunantunich.

   c. The life of author and scientist Margaret D. Lowman (Hint: Look for "Dr. Meg Lowman.").

Nature's R$_X$

JOEL L. SWERDLOW

Plants are something that we often take for granted, thinking of them merely as part of the landscape rather than as a source of medicines. Joel L. Swerdlow, an assistant editor for *National Geographic,* has investigated the effects of a number of medicinal plants from around the world, including the rosy periwinkle (scientific name *Catharanthus roseus*), which grows in Madagascar.

PREREADING QUESTIONS

1. Do you know of any plants or herbal remedies that are used to treat illnesses?

2. How do you think new medicines are discovered and developed?

VOCABULARY

chemotherapy a treatment for cancer that uses chemicals (drugs)

remission an inactive stage of a disease, disappearance of symptoms

chemotherapeutic used in chemotherapy

Hodgkin's disease a form of cancer affecting the lymph nodes, liver, and spleen

synthetic produced artificially, not from plant or animal sources

compounds combinations of two or more elements

chronic recurring or lasting for a long period of time

component an ingredient or a part

respiratory related to breathing

derived obtained or developed from a source

incentive a reward to create motivation

botanical related to plants

inconclusive not resulting in a definite conclusion

NATURE'S R$_X$

Party sounds float up from a swimming pool in Washington, D.C. Twenty children shout and splash, toss balls, and snack on sandwiches, cookies, chips, and sodas. The guest of honor is nine-year-old Audra Shapiro, who has just finished two years of chemotherapy and whose leukemia is in complete remission. Her recovery from this cancer depended on a plant that originated halfway around the world.

2   Until the early 1960s Audra's disease would have meant sure death. Now the long-term survival rate for childhood leukemia is above 90 percent, thanks in part to vincristine, a chemotherapeutic drug made from the Madagascar rosy periwinkle. Vinblastine, another drug made from the same plant, helps cure most cases of Hodgkin's disease.

3   Plants like the periwinkle have contributed to the development of 25 to 50 percent of all prescription drugs used in the United States, either directly or by providing biochemical models, or templates, used to make synthetic compounds. Digitalis, which is used to treat chronic heart failure, comes from the leaves of the foxglove plant, and ephedrine, a component of many commonly prescribed respiratory medicines, is derived from a chemical formula from the ephedra plant. But overall, in the past 40 years there has been little development of new plant-based pharmaceuticals. During that period the U.S. Food and Drug Administration (FDA) approved fewer than a dozen drugs derived from plants.

4   Part of the reason is simply bottom line. The development of a new FDA-approved drug costs as much as 500 million dollars. Manufacturers have found the route from plant to safe, reliable pill difficult and unpredictable, so there is limited incentive to base drug development on plants. Still, almost two-thirds of the

Earth's 6.1 billion people rely on the healing power of plants; for them nothing else is affordable or available. And even in industrialized countries where scientifically formulated drugs are readily available— Americans spent 103 billion dollars on retail prescription drugs in 1998—use of nonprescription botanical drugs is rising dramatically. In 1990, 2.5 percent of Americans purchased herbal remedies; in 1997, 12.1 percent spent roughly five billion dollars on them.

5   What part of that money was spent wisely is a matter of some debate. While many plants have been the subject of extensive study and their effects well documented, data on others are inconclusive. Scientists are often unable to determine which chemical or combination of chemicals within a plant is responsible for relieving pain or stimulating blood flow or creating a feeling of increased well-being. Trying to find the part of a plant that has a specific effect can be like disassembling a radio to search for the one part that makes the sound.

A.   COMPREHENSION

1.   Which diseases have been successfully treated with drugs made from the rosy periwinkle plant?

2.   How do plants contribute to the development of prescription drugs?

3.   According to the author, approximately how many people worldwide rely on plants for healing? Why?

4.   Why do scientists' studies sometimes not result in useful and reliable data about the healing effects of plants?

B.   CRITICAL THINKING

1.   How do you think the author feels about using plants as medicine?

2.   Why do you think Americans' use of herbal remedies is increasing?

3.   Do you think that herbal remedies are always reliable? Why or why not?

4.   Does knowing about the potential healing qualities of plants affect your attitude toward preserving rain forests or natural wilderness areas? Explain your answer.

C .   L A N G U A G E   A N D   V O C A B U L A R Y

1. What does the symbol R$_x$, which is in the title of the reading, mean? How did you figure out the meaning? Have you seen this symbol anywhere before?

2. The last sentence of the reading includes a *simile,* a comparison using *like* or *as,* to explain how difficult it is to find the specific part of a plant that has a healing effect. What is examining a plant compared to? Does this simile create a clear picture of the situation? Give reasons for your answer.

D .   S T Y L E ,   S T R U C T U R E ,   A N D   O R G A N I Z A T I O N

1. Where in the reading does the author include a personal story about someone who has recovered from leukemia? Why does the author include this story? Is this the best place for it, or should it be in a different part of the article? Why?

2. At what points in the reading does the author include statistics? Why does he include these statistics? Do you think any of the statistics will surprise or shock readers? If so, why?

E .   T O P I C S   F O R   D I S C U S S I O N   O R   J O U R N A L   W R I T I N G

1. Do you believe in using herbal remedies? homeopathic medicines? vitamin or mineral supplements that are not endorsed by the Food and Drug Administration (FDA)? any other medicinal substances not prescribed by doctors? If so, discuss (or write about) why you believe these substances or remedies are effective.

2. Share a true story about the healing effect of anything other than traditional prescription or drug-store medicines. In addition to herbal remedies, you may want to consider such things as exercise, relaxation, meditation, prayer, or any form of alternative medicine.

3. In what other ways are plants important to us (besides their medicinal value)?

4. Is there a wilderness area or a forested area near where you live, or have you ever visited one? What kinds of interesting plants can be

found there? Name as many native plants as you can and describe some of them.

5.   Walk around your college campus and observe all the different kinds of plants, including trees. What are some of the most interesting plants? Try to identify them. (Hint: Check out a plant identification book from your library to help you.) This project can be done individually or collaboratively in groups.

F. WRITING TOPICS FOR PARAGRAPHS OR ESSAYS

1.   Have you, or has anyone you know, used medicinal herbs or other plant remedies? If so, write a paper explaining which ones and how they have helped.

2.   Using library resources or the Internet, look up information about poisonous plants, and find one that grows in your area. Write a paper about that plant, including information about how to identify it, what part of the plant is poisonous, and what to do if you accidentally come in contact with it.

3.   Write a descriptive paper about any area that contains a variety of plants, either in their natural environment or in a landscaped area. Include plenty of visual details, as well as some details that use other senses, such as smell and touch.

4.   Research more information about the rosy periwinkle, the foxglove plant, or another plant that is used medicinally, such as the Pacific yew, ginkgo, qing hao, aloe, or echinacea. Write a paper about your findings.

5.   What disease or other health problem do you think is most threatening to the world's population in the twenty-first century? Why? What do you think should be done to find a cure or prevent the problem?

The Wild Within

PAUL REZENDES

Paul Rezendes, author of the book, *The Wild Within: Adventures in Nature and Animal Teachings,* is an expert in tracking animals and interpreting their actions through their tracks and other signs that they leave. His objective is not to hunt and kill the animals but to gain a greater understanding of the animals in their natural habitat. Rezendes is also a wildlife consultant and a professional photographer. His other books include *Wetlands: The Web of Life* and *Tracking and the Art of Seeing: How to Read Animal Tracks and Sign.* In this selection from *The Wild Within,* students who are participating in one of his tracking workshops have joined him to follow the trail of a bobcat in a wilderness area northeast of Springfield, Massachusetts.

PREREADING QUESTIONS

1. If you could observe an animal in the wild, which animal would you choose? What kinds of things would you like to learn about that animal's way of life?

2. In which parts of the United States do you think bobcats or other types of wild cats live in the wild?

VOCABULARY

domain home territory

emitted let out a sound

stifled repressed, held back

laurel a type of evergreen shrub or tree

napes backs of necks

clichéd commonplace, not original, stereotypical

buck a male deer

wary cautious

jutted extended outward,
  protruded

scree loose rock debris on a
  slope

bellied out bulged out in a
  rounded shape

padded moved quietly

blithely in a carefree manner

en garde on guard, watchful
  (French)

cubby (*pl.* **cubbies**) a small
  sheltered space

matted flattened

pristine undisturbed, pure

muck up mess up, damage

bogs wetland areas with soft,
  spongy ground

veered turned from a course

blotched spotted

matrix a complex pattern or
  network

THE WILD WITHIN

My students and I were getting to know this bobcat, learning how it hunted, where it liked to lay up, where it deposited its scent, how it moved through its territory. This was the cat's domain, heavy cover, perfectly suited to its slinking, secretive nature. We were learning that there is no better way to get to know an animal than to track it; but we were also learning that tracking, and knowing, are often hard work. My students had been grumbling behind me; every so often someone emitted a stifled curse.

2   Snow cascaded from the laurel tops down our napes and backs. We penetrated deeper into the laurel, and I felt the group become quiet and attentive. It was as if the ghost of the cat was out in front of us. We began to move like the bobcat, see like the bobcat. Its tracks were our tracks, its world, our world. We had found our inner bobcat! A part of ourselves that had been there all along. What a little suffering will do, I thought.

3   I've told my students that we don't expect to track the bobcat down. That's not the kind of tracking that I teach or practice. Tracking for me is not about the clichéd images of a hunter stalking a buck, or a Native American in a Western movie tracking a villain, troops following behind. For me, tracking is an educational process that opens the door to an animal's life—and to our own.

4   As my students and I moved deep into the laurel, I became wary. I had once found a bobcat den in exactly this kind of country, on the side of a steep hill, deep in laurel. I didn't want to intrude on another den site, especially with a big group—the cat might abandon the den. Bobcats usually don't den when they're done hunting. Instead they have lays throughout their territory. The lays are like motel rooms. They go from one to another—one day here, one day there (these cats are nocturnal). Or they may stay in a favorite lay three days running.

5   My students followed me onto the face of a wide spur that jutted from the hillside. We were approaching a steep incline scored by ledges. I sensed our bobcat was heading for those ledges, where it had a lay, and, sure enough, the cat led us out along shelves of rock, slick with ice and snow.

6   I cautioned my students to take care, to keep themselves mindful and in the present, to take the journey along the ledges step by careful step. The ledges were very slippery. The drop-off on our left is about twenty feet straight down to jagged rock outcroppings and a steep slope of snow-covered scree. The rock wall on our right

bellied out. We had to squeeze along it, making ourselves thin and flat, feeling the rock up against our shoulders and knees, pressing cold and hard against our faces, pushing us out toward the edge.

7   The cat's tracks padded blithely ahead. I almost called everything off and turned the group around when the ledges opened a bit and we had room to breathe. But I still kept the group tight behind me and *en garde,* because of the drop and the icy patches on the path. We came to a place of beautiful little semi-caves scooped out of the cliff face. Shelves of stone overhung these little snow-free cubbies. The bobcat had checked each one, until it came to a particularly attractive cubby carpeted with dead leaves. In the leaves was a small, matted impression where the cat had rested. It was a hard-to-approach, snug, hidden spot.

8   I've found more bobcat lays than I can remember, and almost every one had a scenic view. This one was no exception. It looked south, out over the rolling hills and dense woodlands. In the distance, I could see water. We were in northcentral Massachusetts, on the protected lands around Quabbin Reservoir, one of the wildest places in southern New England. There were no houses in sight. No sound of traffic. Only the moan of the wind.

9   We stood there, taking in the view, looking at the lay, all of us feeling very close to that cat and exhilarated that it had led us to one of its secret places. After our hard morning tracking, we had a sense of completion and closure, as though we had come to the end of a journey.

10   But the bobcat wasn't through with us yet. Its tracks led from the cubby along the ledges to where the ledges broke and the hillside sloped steep and slippery downward. The slope was snow-covered, and under the snow I knew were loose wet leaves, slick as banana peels, and shifting scree.

11   In my tracking workshops I usually have a rule that we don't disturb an animal's tracks. I like to leave them as pristine as possible. I want to make sure everyone in the group has the chance to read what's written in the tracks. But I also don't want to interfere because to me tracks are an animal's signature, a way in which it communicates to the world, an essential and dramatic part of the environment.

12   With our clumsy human movements, our whole day, so far, had disturbed the bobcat's trail. It was impossible not to muck up the

tracks through the laurels and on the ledges. And now it was impossible to get down the hillside without sending rocks avalanching in front of us, half standing, half sitting, making a racket, coming to the base of the scree and brushing each other off. We looked horrified at the slope that the bobcat had descended without disturbing a leaf. Now it looked like a herd of buffalo had stampeded down its side.

13   The cat continued to move down, down, down through the hardwood forest of beech, oak, and ash toward lowland marshes, wet meadows, shrub swamps, and bogs. This is typical. Bobcats will lay up in the highlands and hunt in the wetlands. The cat moved toward the shrub swamp but then veered westward. Had I been wrong about where it was going?

14   Behind me, a student asked why the cat had changed direction. From long experience tracking, I've found that it's better to wait and see, not to force explanations. Often my students are too anxious for answers. I tell them to be patient, to let the animals tell you about their lives.

15   The cat took us into an area of forest where young hemlock saplings had sprung up close together, their limbs almost interlocked. It was a dense, sheltered place, scruffy and remote. We picked our way through, slowly and carefully, pushing back branches, ducking low, shielding our eyes with our arms. We broke out into an opening. Big hemlocks towered overhead, dimming the winter light. The snow in front of us was blotched red and yellow from the spilled body fluids of a dead deer. Pieces of the deer's carcass were scattered about, its hair strewn in a twelve-foot radius. Half a leg, the spinal column, and the head with some hide clinging to it were all that remained, except for the deer's rumen (the stomach contents), which few animals will eat. The snow in front of us was completely matted with tracks of various animals—coyotes, fishers, and domestic dogs.

16   The group was shaken. Some of them turned away while others looked on, unable to take their eyes off the carcass. One student asked me what happened. They all fell silent, waiting for the reply. I glimpsed tears in one student's eyes, expressing the raw emotion that such a scene can evoke.

17   "Let's see if we can piece it together," I said. "A scene like this can be hard to take. But perhaps when we come to an understanding

of exactly what went on here, you may respond to it in a different way."

18   "Who killed the deer?" someone asked.

19   "There's no way to know that," I said. "The deer died here about two days ago, maybe less."

20   "Come on! There's hardly anything left!"

21   "Things can happen very quickly at a kill site. There have been many animals feeding here. Let me paint as full a picture as I can of what has happened here. To begin with, this deer, in essence, has grown up not only in the forest but *from* the forest." I saw I was getting blank stares, so I tried to explain. "When it was born it weighed only four to eight pounds. When it died, I would guess it probably weighed in just over 100 pounds, a young adult. It doesn't look like it was very big."

22   They stood there, next to the kill, taking it in. I explained that the deer was able to grow, gain mass, by feasting on acorns in the fall, putting on as much fat as it could to carry it through the winter. During the winter months, it browsed on hemlock, juniper, dogwood, viburnum, maple, oak, witch hazel, and many other types of woody plants and fungi. In summer, it gorged itself on all kinds of herbaceous plants and leaves, including some of its preferred foods, like jewelweed, wild lettuce, and dogwood leaves.

23   That organic mass contained in the trees and shrubs, in the light, air, water, soil, and microbes, is the living forest. The deer had, literally, materialized from *this*. The deer *was* the forest breathing, walking, mating, living, and dying.

24   The organic mass of the deer had come from thousands of elements, from all directions in the forest, to this one point at the kill site. Now it was returning to the forest in every direction through the animals feeding on the carcass. Our bobcat had come to the deer and taken a few scraps. Coyote, fisher, weasel, fox, raven, crow, even the chickadees flitting from branch to branch, had fed on the carcass.

25   It was evident to our scientific minds, looking at the kill site in this way, that on a fundamental level the deer was the forest and forest was the deer—both were inextricably part of the web of life. But the deer's carcass also exposed another facet of the web of life that was difficult for our intellects to grasp. There are some aspects of life that thought cannot understand. Thought works by

compartmentalizing, creating boundaries—dividing the whole into parts. In order to fully comprehend the meaning before us, we had to go beyond thought.

26   The deer's death had changed the direction of the bobcat that we had been following—not only the direction in which it was traveling, but its whole life. When a bobcat hunts, timing is critical. When and where the cat is in relation to its prey often determines whether the prey dies or the bobcat eats and lives. Whatever happens to the bobcat at a given moment changes everything else for the rest of the bobcat's life. The vast matrix of timing that affected the movement of the deer had affected the movement of the bobcat, too. Because the deer had died, the bobcat had veered from its path to the marsh and we had also veered.

27   Seen in this light, it comes clear that no movement on this planet is separate from any other movement. The planet moves as a whole. We, too, are part of this movement. What happened at that kill site and the path the bobcat was traveling were the same movement as all of us tracking, walking, living, and dying.

A . COMPREHENSION

1. Why didn't the author want to intrude on the bobcat's den?
2. What made the ledge dangerous to walk on?
3. Where did the bobcat go after he came down the hillside and left the highlands?
4. What was Paul Rezendes able to figure out about how and when the deer died? What do the tracks near the carcass tell the trackers?

B . CRITICAL THINKING

1. Why did Paul Rezendes and his students want to track the bobcat?
2. How do you think the trackers feel about protecting wild animals and preserving the environment? Give reasons for your answer.
3. Which parts of tracking the bobcat do you think were the most difficult or the most dangerous?
4. In what ways is tracking similar to hunting? In what ways is it different?

5. When the author says in paragraph 3, "For me, tracking is an educational process that opens the door to an animal's life—and to our own," what do you think he means?

C. LANGUAGE AND VOCABULARY

1. In the fourth paragraph, the author says that bobcats "have lays throughout their territory." What do you think the term *lays* means? Look for clues about the meaning in the surrounding sentences.

2. In some parts of the story the writer either directly or indirectly reports something that he said to the group or something that a student said. For example, in paragraph 6, he tells us, "I cautioned my students to take care. . . ." Find two other examples of something that the writer or another person said, either directly or indirectly. What do these statements add to the story?

D. STYLE, STRUCTURE, AND ORGANIZATION

1. Whose point of view is "The Wild Within" told from? In which parts of the story does the writer use the first person (I, we)? In which parts of the story does he use third person (he, she, it, they)?

2. Does the last paragraph make an effective ending for the story? Why or why not?

E. TOPICS FOR DISCUSSION OR JOURNAL WRITING

1. What did you learn about bobcats and their way of life from reading this narrative?

2. How did you feel when you read the description of the site where the deer had died? Did you respond differently after you read the author's explanation of how the deer's death meant that it returned to the forest?

3. Have you ever gone for a long hike in the snow or in very wild country? If you have, describe what it was like and how you felt. If you haven't, try to imagine what it would be like.

4. Do you think that the natural environment of bobcats and/or other wild animals is threatened by development in your area or anywhere in your state? How could you learn more about this situation?

5. Should predatory animals, such as bobcats, lynx, and mountain lions, be protected, or should hunters be allowed to kill them? Give reasons for your opinion.

F. WRITING TOPICS FOR PARAGRAPHS OR ESSAYS

1. Write a true story about something you did that was adventurous, exciting, or dangerous. Include details about things that you saw as well as the events that occurred.

2. Describe the most threatening or dangerous weather conditions that you have ever experienced personally, such as heavy snow, ice, thunderstorms, a hurricane, a tornado, a sandstorm, or any other extreme condition.

3. Pretend that you were one of the students in Paul Rezendes's group and write about your experience of tracking the bobcat from the student's point of view.

4. Using Internet resources or library materials, look up information about bobcats, such as their appearance, habitat, diet, range, tracks, behavior, and anything else that you find interesting. Then write an informative paper about what you have learned.

5. Look up the author's Web site at **www.paulrezendes.com/** and then write about one of the following topics:
   a. Tracking and nature workshops that are currently offered
   b. Books that Paul Rezendes has written
   c. Other animals that Paul Rezendes and his associates have tracked
   d. Any other topics of interest that you discover at this Web site or by following related links.

Heavy Traffic on the Everest Highway

GEOFFREY TABIN

Mount Everest, located between Nepal and Tibet, is part of the massive mountain system known as the Himalaya. Rising to an altitude of 29,028 feet, Everest is the world's highest mountain and presents special challenges for climbers. Geoffrey Tabin, who is well known as a mountain climber and a travel writer, describes the last part of the ascent in this excerpt from his book *Blind Corners*.

PREREADING QUESTIONS

1. Why are some people attracted to sports that are physically demanding and dangerous, such as mountain climbing?

2. Do you think there are still places on the earth that no one has ever seen? Where might they be?

VOCABULARY

sheer almost vertical, straight up or down

Hillary Step a steep notch in the ridge about 200 feet below the top of Everest

crampon a set of spikes that clamps onto a climber's boots for walking or climbing on ice

adrenaline a natural chemical

that the body releases into the bloodstream in response to sudden stress; it raises blood pressure and speeds up the heartbeat

ambient surrounding

summit the top or peak of a mountain

SOURCE: Reprinted from *Blind Corners* © 1998 by Geoffrey Tabin with permission from *The Globe Pequot Press,* Guilford, CT, 1-800-962-0973, **www.globe-pequot.com**.

cliché an expression that has been repeated so many times that it has become commonplace

vistas broad, sweeping views

plateau a large, relatively flat area that rises higher than some other nearby areas

savor enjoy

solo alone, by one person

to commemorate to honor the memory of, in honor of

post-monsoon season after the season of heavy winds and rain

siege tactics specific strategies for a well-planned, long-range attack

sponsorship financial support

bidding in this case, stating one's intention or proposing to do something

foray attempt or venture

ardent extremely enthusiastic and serious

synonymous with equivalent to, having the same meaning

HEAVY TRAFFIC ON THE EVEREST HIGHWAY

The ridge I am climbing is barely two feet wide. To the east is a sheer drop of twelve thousand feet into Tibet. Westward it is eight thousand feet down to the next landing, in Nepal. The angle increases from seventy degrees to vertical at the Hillary Step. Climbing unroped, I delicately balance the crampon points on my right foot on an edge of rock. I swing my left foot, with all my remaining strength, into the adjoining ice. Precariously balanced on quarter-inch spikes attached to my boots, I gasp for breath. Forty feet higher the angle eases. Adrenaline mixed with joy surges through me. After eight hours of intense concentration, I know I will make it. The seventy-mile-an-hour wind threatens to blow me off the ridge. The ambient temperature is far below zero. Yet, I feel flushed with warmth. Ahead stretches a five-foot-wide walkway angled upward at less than ten degrees. Thirty minutes later, just after ten o'clock in the morning, the path ends in a platform of ice the size of a small desk. Everything is below me. I am the two hundred and ninth person to stand on the summit of Mount Everest.

2   The sky is deep blue and cloudless. The cliché is true, the vistas do seem to stretch infinitely in all directions. I look down over Lhotse, the world's fourth highest peak, upon the endless chain of mountains in Nepal. The Tibetan plateau on the other side extends to the horizon, where I can see the curve of the world dropping away. For fifteen minutes I savor the view as the highest person on earth. Then the crowds start to arrive.

3   Within an hour climbers from three countries are taking turns being photographed on the summit of Mount Everest. An American woman arrives on top. A Korean makes the climb solo to commemorate the October 2 closing ceremony of the Seoul Olympics. On the way down the woman, Peggy Luce, becomes snow-blind and then takes a near fatal fall before being rescued by the heroism of Dawa Tsering Sherpa. And this is one of the dullest days of the season.

4   Thirteen teams from ten countries made at least one attempt on every face and ridge on Mount Everest during the post-monsoon season of 1988. It was the first time that the Nepalese and Chinese gave out multiple permits for a mountain. Climbing styles ranged from siege tactics utilizing fixed camps, Sherpa porters, and supplemental oxygen to a solo, oxygenless, nonstop attempt from base camp. Everyone was out to set a record or do something new. Without a "first" it is nearly impossible to obtain sponsorship.

5   I was with the Northwest American Everest Expedition. Our team of eleven climbers, led by Seattle attorney Jim Frush, included three women bidding to become the first American woman to climb Mount Everest. The media played up this angle, as did our sponsors. Having been there before gave me a realistic perspective on the task ahead. Any success would have to be a team effort. Diana Dailey, Peggy Luce, and Stacy Allison were all selected for their climbing ability, strength, and personal qualities. They just happened to be women. On the mountain we would all be equal.

6   Chomolungma treats everyone equally. The Sherpa people and Tibetans, who live in her shadow, call the Goddess Mother of the Earth Chomolungma. They believe she resides in the mountain bearing her name. In 1842 the British survey of India calculated the height of Chomolungma to be 29,002 feet above sea level (it is actually 29,028

by modern measurements), and proclaimed it the highest mountain in the world. In 1863 the English renamed her Mount Everest, after Sir George Everest, a former Surveyor General of India, and proposed that she should be climbed. They brought Sherpa people along on their initial foray and were amazed by their strength at altitude and natural mountaineering talent. Moreover, as ardent followers of Mahayana Buddhism who believe that true Nirvana should be delayed until everyone on earth finds happiness, they are a delight to be with. They have accompanied so many expeditions that the name "Sherpa" has become synonymous with the job of high-altitude porter. Thirty Sherpas accompanied our expedition.

A . C O M P R E H E N S I O N

1. What is the Sherpa name for Mount Everest, and what does it mean?

2. Based on what you learned in the reading, what are some of the challenges and difficulties involved in climbing Mount Everest?

3. How many other climbers besides the author were members of the same expedition, and how many Sherpas accompanied the expedition? What do we learn about some of the climbers on this team?

4. How many countries, nationalities, or ethnic groups are listed in this selection? List them and briefly explain what people of each country or nationality accomplished, or their connection with Mount Everest.

B . C R I T I C A L T H I N K I N G

1. Scan the selection (quickly glance over it) for the words *Sherpa* and *Sherpas*. What did you learn about Sherpas from the reading?

2. Based on the reading, what kind of physical conditioning do you think Everest climbers and explorers need in order to reach the top and return alive?

3. Besides physical conditioning, what other qualities would be important for a climber to have in order to reach such a difficult goal?

4. How did Geoffrey Tabin feel about standing on top of Mount Everest? Do you think that his feelings changed when other climbers started to arrive?

5. Is the author trying to convey a message to the reader? If so, what is the message?

C .   L A N G U A G E   A N D   V O C A B U L A R Y

1. In the first four paragraphs of the reading, the author uses several terms that refer to land or rock formations, such as *ridge, drop, summit, plateau,* and *face.* Do you know what all of these terms mean? If not, try to guess at the meaning, and look up any terms you don't know. Then write a definition or draw a picture to illustrate each of these five terms.

2. Had you heard the term *base camp* before reading it in "Heavy Traffic on the Everest Highway"? What do you think the term means? Why do you think Everest climbers would need a base camp?

D .   S T Y L E ,   S T R U C T U R E , A N D   O R G A N I Z A T I O N

1. What point of view does the author have—is he a mountain climber, a reporter, or someone else? How does this point of view affect the way he writes?

2. Two of the writing techniques Geoffrey Tabin uses in this reading are *narration* (telling a story) and *description.* Highlight or underline at least two narrative sentences or passages and two descriptive sentences or passages. Which one of the four sentences or passages that you have marked do you like the best? Why?

3. Why do you think most of the sentences in the reading use present tense verbs? Find two places where the author changed to past tense verbs, and explain the reason for these changes.

E .   T O P I C S   F O R   D I S C U S S I O N O R   J O U R N A L   W R I T I N G

1. What is the most adventurous thing you have ever done?

2. Would you like to climb Mount Everest someday? Why or why not?

3. Modern technology and the sheer number of people on earth mean that many special places will soon be overcrowded, if they aren't already. What is the most special outdoor place you have visited? Were a lot of people there? What was the most exciting or most rewarding part of your experience?

4. Have you ever experienced extreme weather conditions or an extreme physical challenge? If so, share your experience with the class or write about it in your journal.

F. WRITING TOPICS FOR PARAGRAPHS OR ESSAYS

1. Take a short hike, a bicycle ride, or a leisurely walk in an outdoor area near where you live. Describe what you saw, and include narrative details about anything interesting that happened.

2. Write about a place you visited where there was a crowd of people, but you would have preferred being alone.

3. Look up *global warming* on the Internet or in a library and write a cause and effect paper about it. Include either the causes of global warming or the results of global warming.

4. Read more about Mount Everest on the Internet or at a library. Then choose one of the following writing assignments:
   a. Write about the Sherpa people. Who are they, and what makes them special?
   b. Compare an early Everest expedition with a modern one.

5. Watch the IMAX film *Everest* about events on Mount Everest in 1996, when several experienced climbers lost their lives, or the movie *K2,* which is about an ascent of the world's second highest mountain, also located in the Himalaya. Then write a review that includes three sections: (1) a summary of the events; (2) details about the part you found most exciting, most shocking, or most interesting; and (3) your reaction and opinion.

Death Valley

DOUG AND BOBBE TATREAU

Doug and Bobbe Tatreau spent many of their vacations in national parks, monuments, and recreation areas, taking pictures and doing research for their travel books. One of these books is *Parks of the Pacific Coast,* which this reading is taken from.

Death Valley was first designated as a national monument in 1933, and in 1994 the Desert Protection Act officially made the area a national park. Death Valley National Park contains more than 3 million acres of wilderness and includes many spectacular rock formations.

PREREADING QUESTIONS

1. How do we benefit from having National Parks?
2. What kinds of natural settings are most appealing to campers, hikers, and other outdoor enthusiasts?

VOCABULARY

ominous threatening or suggestive of something negative

blistering extremely hot

austere severe or somber in appearance

stark bare

pastel light-colored

meager sparse, small in quantity

alkaline containing various mineral salts

paradoxes things that seem to contradict each other yet are both true

pinyon a variety of pine trees with edible seeds (also spelled *piñon*)

pinnacles tall, pointed formations

torrential swiftly flowing water, a heavy downpour

treacherous dangerous, hazardous

lavishly abundantly

phenomena remarkable or amazing occurrences (plural of *phenomenon*)

remnants remains

potpourri mixture, variety

plaque a sign or marker

inserted put into something

arrowweed a desert plant

shocks in this case, stacks of corn or grain in an upright position for drying

vulnerable exposed or susceptible to possible injury

DEATH VALLEY

Death Valley—the name is ominous, the weather blistering, the land deceptively austere. Nevertheless, most visitors love this stark, majestic landscape, returning frequently to study the curious splendor of pastel mudhills, salt flats and the meager vegetation surviving despite the rocky, alkaline soil. Others complain the region is ugly—an unrelieved, barren panorama of grays and browns without the green usually associated with natural beauty. The decision is split. But whether you love Death Valley or hate it, you will remember it.

2   A terrain of paradoxes, Death Valley is more than a valley and it is certainly not dead. Though 20 percent of its land is below sea level (the lowest is 282 feet below), several mountain ranges parallel this 120-mile-long valley. The 11,049-foot Telescope Peak often wears a snowy cap even in late April. Pinyon and juniper forests crowd these higher reaches which remain cool in summer when the valley floor is sizzling.

3   In the center of the valley, little grows naturally. The salt creates attractive, humped pinnacles, but leaves the soil poisoned. The infrequent, sometimes torrential rain can be treacherous but, at the same time, it scrubs off the gray/brown surface to reveal the pinks, greens and purples of the hillside called Artist's Palette; if the timing is right, the moisture produces delicate spring blooms that lavishly decorate the valley floor.

4   There is another side of Death Valley to explore—the mining-boomtown phase during which man and sometimes his machines

invaded the valley to reap its mineral riches. The unique natural phenomena and the remnants of the civilized invasion provide a potpourri of pursuits for the visitor. There is always much to see and do.

* * *

5   *Central Valley Region:* Between Stovepipe Wells and Badwater are the park's most popular features. Two miles east of Stovepipe Wells Village are the sand dunes, an unbroken display of sand hills that brings out the child in all of us. The dunes are for walking but only during the cooler morning hours or at sundown, as the sand can be very warm.

6   Just north of the picnic area is the old stovepipe well and a historical plaque explaining that, when the dunes began to cover these valuable water sources, stovepipes were inserted to mark their locations.

7   In the same area, on the south side of Highway 190 is the Devil's Cornfield where clumps of arrowweed look like fat, stumpy corn shocks only a devil might cultivate.

8   Another popular feature is the Devil's Golf Course. The Golf Course is formed by sodium chloride (similar to table salt) which

forms a crust over the mudfloor of what was once the ancient Manly Lake. The pinnacled artistry of salt and mud is intriguing but makes difficult walking as the salt can scratch vulnerable ankles. Five miles south of the Golf Course is Badwater, approximately 282 feet below sea level, the lowest point in the United States. It is actually a large salt pool tucked into the curve of the road bordering the valley.

A. COMPREHENSION

1. Why do visitors have differing opinions about Death Valley?

2. Why is there little vegetation in most parts of the park?

3. What are four of the most popular features in the Central Valley region of Death Valley?

4. What is the lowest point in the United States? What is its elevation?

B. CRITICAL THINKING

1. As the authors point out, "Death Valley is more than a valley and it is certainly not dead." Why, then, do you think the area is called Death Valley? Do you think the name is appropriate? Why or why not?

2. Could camping or hiking in some parts of Death Valley National Park be dangerous? If so, what precautions should visitors observe?

3. Based on what you learned in this reading, why do you think Death Valley was selected to be a national park?

4. Why is it important to preserve wilderness areas and places of special geological interest, such as Death Valley? Give reasons for your answer.

5. What do you think was the authors' purpose in writing "Death Valley?" Did the authors' purpose affect the way they wrote this selection?

C. LANGUAGE AND VOCABULARY

1. What do you think a "mining boomtown" is? Take a guess at the meaning, and then look up *boomtown* in a dictionary if necessary.

How do you suppose being a mining boomtown at one time affected the Death Valley area?

2.   Although readers may not be familiar with some of the terms used to identify features of the Death Valley area, such as *mudhills, salt flats, valley floor, pinnacles,* and *sand dunes,* in most cases it is possible to figure out the meaning. Choose two of these terms and explain what you think they mean. (Consult a dictionary if you need to check your answers.)

D.   STYLE,   STRUCTURE, AND   ORGANIZATION

1.   How does the introductory paragraph capture readers' attention? What part of the introduction makes you interested in finding out more about Death Valley?

2.   Notice that each paragraph of this reading (after the introduction) focuses on one topic or one aspect of Death Valley. Make a list of the main topics covered in paragraphs 2–8. Which one of these paragraphs do you like best? Why?

E.   TOPICS   FOR   DISCUSSION OR   JOURNAL   WRITING

1.   In what ways is Death Valley different from other areas you have visited or read about?

2.   After reading about Death Valley, do you think you would enjoy visiting the area? Why or why not?

3.   Have you ever visited any national parks, national monuments, or national historic sites? If so, share your experiences with the class, or write about them in your journal.

4.   If you could go anywhere in the United States for a vacation, where would you choose to go? What would you like to see there? What kinds of activities would you find most appealing?

5.   If the United States government did not set aside park lands to preserve and protect them, what do you think would happen to unique areas, such as Death Valley (California), Mesa Verde

(Colorado), the Grand Canyon (Arizona), Carlsbad Caverns (New Mexico), Mammoth Cave (Kentucky), or the Everglades (Florida)?

F. WRITING TOPICS FOR PARAGRAPHS OR ESSAYS

1. Write a descriptive paper about a place you have visited, including vivid details that will give readers a clear picture of the most interesting sights in the area. Use the Death Valley reading as a model for your writing.

2. Access a Web site that offers information about Death Valley National Park, such as **www.death.valley.national-park.com/info .htm**. Look for additional information about the history, geology, climate, and/or wildlife of the Death Valley area that was not included in the reading selection, and write a paper about what you learn. (If you do not have Internet access, try consulting encyclopedias, travel brochures, magazine articles, or any other available sources of information.)

3. Create a travel brochure for a park or recreation area that you are interested in. Your brochure should feature information that would attract people to the park, such as special things to see and activities for visitors. If possible, include a few pictures.

4. Write an instructional paper about hiking, camping, mountain biking, rock climbing, or any other outdoor activity you know how to do. Include the reasons people enjoy the activity, the equipment that is needed, and precautions that people should be aware of.

5. Using a library or Internet resources, locate information about a national park in the United States or Canada, and write a paper that is informative as well as descriptive. The following are just a few of the parks you may want to consider for your topic: Rocky Mountain National Park (Colorado), Denali National Park (Alaska), Mesa Verde National Park (Colorado), Carlsbad Caverns (New Mexico), the Everglades (Florida), Acadia National Park (Maine), Banff National Park (Alberta, Canada), Pacific Rim National Park (British Columbia, Canada).

VALUES AND CHOICES

The Good Old Summertime

CAROL TANNEHILL

This feature article was published in various newspapers around the country. Journalist Carol Tannehill, who is a feature writer for *The News-Sentinel* of Fort Wayne, Indiana, suggests that we should examine how our values have changed over the years, as reflected in the kinds of activities that our children enjoy today compared to the outdoor games that entertained earlier generations in "the good old summertime." The author also refers readers to Internet sites that promote the tradition of outdoor games and a book by Stephen Cohen called *The Games We Played: A Celebration of Childhood and Imagination*.

PREREADING QUESTIONS

1. Did you like playing outdoor games when you were a child? Which games did you enjoy most?

2. How do you think children should spend their free time: watching television, using the computer, playing outside with their friends, reading books, or participating in some other activity?

VOCABULARY

dusk the time just before it gets dark

swarm gather together in large numbers

baby boomer anyone in the generation that was born from 1946 to 1964, after World War II

nostalgic bringing back pleasantly emotional memories of earlier times

banned not allowed

urban characteristic of living in a city

suburban characteristic of residential areas close to cities

archives information from the past that is stored and organized as a reference source

spark bring to mind

pitching throwing

agility ability to move quickly and flexibly

maneuvers moves in whatever manner necessary

straddling with one foot on each side of something

variant variation

terrain land surface

resumes starts again

THE GOOD OLD SUMMERTIME

Come dusk, neighborhoods would be crawling with them. All summer, they'd swarm over lawns, under porches, behind hedges, through alleys. There was no stopping them . . .

2   At least not until "The Wonderful World of Disney" came on.

3   "We used to play all those games in the summer . . . kick the can, hide-and-seek, baseball in vacant lots — back when there still were vacant lots," recalled baby boomer Evalyn Fate, an Indiana homemaker. "We used to play until our parents made us come home. My mom would always call me in for 'Father Knows Best.'"

4   The outdoor games of boomers' childhoods are getting attention again, thanks to nostalgic books and Web sites and to news reports that tag and dodge ball are being banned from politically correct playgrounds throughout the country.

5   Stephen A. Cohen's "The Games We Played: A Celebration of Childhood and Imagination" pays tribute to stoopball and other deceptively simple pastimes. Internet sites—**www.streetplay.com** and **www.gameskidsplay.net**—are devoted to preserving the handed-down traditions of urban and suburban games by offering rule archives, discussion boards, an e-newsletter and coverage of related events, such as a recent adult stickball tournament in New York.

6   The goal is "to recall when it was OK to go outside, hang out with friends and have a great time playing activities that didn't require a coach, schedule or major amount of brand-name equipment," the founders of streetplay.com said. "We're also interested in encouraging parents to share some of these games and enjoyment with their kids."

7   If you're old enough to know what "onesies" and "twosies" are—or so young that you've never screamed "olly, olly oxen free"—then read on. Our guide to the good old games of summer may spark memories or help you make some new ones.

Horseshoes

- **Origin:** The game is thought to have started as a time-passer among blacksmiths and farriers, people who shoe horses.

- **Number of players:** Two to four

- **Equipment:** Pitching horseshoes in two colors and two stakes

- **Setting:** A court is made up of two stakes driven into the ground 40 feet apart. A pit of sand, dirt or clay surrounds each stake.

- **How to play:** Participants decide either to play to 40 points or to toss 40 shoes. Each player pitches two horseshoes in succession toward the opposite stake. Any horseshoe within a horseshoe's width of the stake can earn points. The player with the closest shoe to the stake gets one point. If he or she has two shoes closer than any of the opponent's, he or she gets two points. A ringer (a shoe that completely encircles the stake) gets three points, though an opponent cancels that out by landing a ringer on top of it. Leaners—horseshoes touching the stake but not encircling it—are worth one point and are considered closer than any other pitch except a ringer.

Jacks

- **Origin:** Unknown

- **Number of players:** Two to six

- **Equipment:** Fifteen jacks and one small rubber ball

- **Setting:** Any smooth surface

- **How to play:** The jacks are tossed gently onto the playing surface. Players sit on the ground. The first player throws the ball in the air, then tries, with one hand, to pick up one jack ("onesies") and catch the ball after one bounce. If the player succeeds, he or she tries to pick up two jacks ("twosies") and catch the ball after one bounce. If he or she misses, the turn passes to the next opponent. On the first player's next turn, he or she reattempts the number missed on the previous turn. The winner is the person who reached the highest number of jacks at quitting time.

Hopscotch

- **Origin:** Variations of the game were used in ancient times as agility exercises for Roman soldiers.
- **Number of players:** Two or more
- **Equipment:** Sidewalk chalk and a place marker, such as a stone, bottle cap or coin
- **Setting:** Players draw a hopscotch board (or use a ready-made board on a playground) featuring numbered squares—some single and some side-by-side.
- **How to play:** The players take turns. Each player tosses a marker toward a designated square (Square No. 1 on the first turn, Square No. 2 on the second turn and so on.) If the marker lands on the wrong square or on the chalk line, the player gives up a turn. If it lands on the correct square, the player maneuvers through the board by hopping, in numerical order, on single squares with one foot and by straddling double squares with both feet. When the player reaches the end of the board, he or she turns and heads back toward the start, picking up the marker on the return trip. The first person through the entire course wins.

Kick The Can

- **Origin:** A variant of tag and hide-and-seek
- **Number of players:** Three or more

- **Equipment:** An aluminum can, lid removed and filled with rocks
- **Setting:** Street or yard of any terrain, preferably one surrounded by hiding places.
- **How to play:** "It" stands by the can, closes his or her eyes and counts to a prearranged number, while the other players run and hide. "It" then seeks the other players. Once players have been discovered, they must run back to the can and kick it before "it" tags one of them.

Red Light/Green Light

- **Origin:** Unknown
- **Number of players:** At least three, and the more the merrier
- **Equipment:** None
- **How to play:** One person is the "stoplight" and the rest try to touch him/her. At the start, all the children form a line about 15 feet away from the stoplight. The stoplight faces away from the line of kids and says "green light," which allows the other kids to move toward the stoplight.

  At any point, the stoplight may say "red light!" and turn around. If any of the kids are caught moving after this has occurred, they are out.

  Play resumes when the stoplight turns back around and says "green light." The stoplight wins if all the kids are out before anyone is able to touch him/her.

  Otherwise, the first player to touch the stoplight wins the game and earns the right to be "stoplight" for the next game.

A. COMPREHENSION

1. What are some of the games that children used to play in vacant lots? What favorite television shows did they finally go inside to watch?

2. According to the article, which games are now banned from many playgrounds?

3. Where can people learn more about how to play traditional outdoor games?

4. What do the founders of streetplay.com say that they want to accomplish with their Internet site?

B . CRITICAL THINKING

1. How do you think the author feels about traditional outdoor games? Why do you think she feels this way?

2. Why do you think that some games, such as dodge ball, are not permitted on school playgrounds? Do you agree that these games should be banned?

3. What are some of the advantages of outdoor games that young people can play in their neighborhoods?

4. In what ways do you think society's values have changed since the days when outdoor games were popular?

5. Choose one of the five games that are explained in the article, and reread everything about it. Would you be able to play this game by following the instructions in the article? Do you have any questions about how to play it?

C . LANGUAGE AND VOCABULARY

1. Who do the pronouns "them" and "they" refer to in the first paragraph?

2. In paragraph seven, the author suggests that some readers may be too young to know the meaning of "onesies" and "twosies," or "olly, olly oxen free." Are you familiar with these words? What do you think they might mean? What kinds of games do you think they are associated with?

3. Kick the can, hide-and-seek, and several other group games require someone to be "It." Try to explain what "It" means. (Reread how to play kick the can for details about what "It" does.) If you were playing, would you want to be "It" very often? Give reasons for your answer.

D. STYLE, STRUCTURE, AND ORGANIZATION

1. What categories of information does the author include about each of the five games featured in the article? Are these categories an effective way to organize the information? Can you suggest any other categories that you would like to see added?

2. Notice that the author has used present tense verbs to explain how each game is played. For example, instructions for hopscotch begin with these directions: "Players *draw* a hopscotch board. . . . The players *take* turns. . . . Each player *tosses* a marker toward a designated square. . . ." Do you think this style is effective for writing instructions? Is this style more or less effective, or about the same, as using command forms of verbs, like *Draw* a hopscotch board. . . . *Take* turns. . . . *Toss* a marker . . .?

E. TOPICS FOR DISCUSSION OR JOURNAL WRITING

1. Have you ever played any of the games that are explained or mentioned in the article? Which ones would you like to play or would you encourage children to play? Give reasons for your answer.

2. Do you prefer indoor or outdoor games? What are some of your favorite games to play? What are some of your favorite games to watch?

3. What are some of the ways our society has changed compared to the way things were twenty or thirty years ago?

4. How can children benefit from playing active outdoor games with other children? Are outdoor activities sometimes healthier and more rewarding than indoor activities?

5. What outdoor games are still popular, either with young people or with adults? On what occasions do adults tend to participate in games?

F. WRITING TOPICS FOR PARAGRAPHS OR ESSAYS

1. Write instructions for playing an outdoor game that is not already explained in this reading, such as tag, stickball, dodge ball, statue,

marbles, or another game that you know about. Follow the same format used by the author, unless your teacher asks you to use a different format. Include enough details that readers could play the game by following your instructions.

2. Write a true story about something good or something bad that happened while you were either playing or watching a game.

3. Choose any kind of new game that you would like to play and try to get a group of your friends or family to play it with you. Write a paper about your experience. Include both the best and the worst things (if any) that happened.

4. Interview a parent, grandparent, or an older relative or friend. Ask questions about how this person spent his or her free time as a child, including games, favorite television programs, and other things that he or she liked to do. Then write a paper about what you learned about young people of that generation and the things they enjoyed.

5. Visit one of the Web sites mentioned in the article (**www.streetplay .com** or **www.gameskidsplay.net**) or another similar site that features games, and then write about one of the following topics:
   a. An overview and evaluation of the Web site
   b. Some of the most interesting games
   c. Something of interest that you discover at this Web site, such as the dodge ball ban, a personal narrative about one of the games, or advantages of certain kinds of games.

The Toll Road

N. SCOTT MOMADAY

Navarre Scott Momaday is a Kiowa Indian author and artist who has written many books, poems, and other works based on Native American oral traditions. Raised on reservations and in pueblo towns, he earned a Ph.D. from Stanford University and was awarded the Pulitzer Prize for Fiction for his first novel, *House Made of Dawn*. Since that time Dr. Momaday has been a professor of English at Berkeley, Stanford, and the University of Arizona. Other books he has written include *The Gourd Dancer* and *The Native Americans: Indian Country*, among many others.

PREREADING QUESTIONS

1. Do you have a special place that you call your own, even if you don't own it?

2. Have you ever heard or read any stories by Native American Indian authors?

VOCABULARY

foothills smaller hills at the foot of a mountain

silhouette the outline of something dark against a light background

regard view, or look at

barrier an obstruction

token a sign or symbol

keenly enthusiastically

riddle in this case, puzzle

deter prevent from continuing

impede slow or stop

antagonist opponent

deed in this case, a legal document that shows ownership

vagrant wanderer

eminently noticeably, conspicuously, notably

continuum in this case, a repeated, continuing event

intrusion unwanted entry

242

encroachment in this case, the taking of the right to pass over someone else's land

domain territory

skirmish battle

adversary enemy or opponent

sufficed past tense of *suffice,* to be sufficient or to be enough

THE TOLL ROAD

I know a man who runs every morning. He runs into the foothills, where there are deep, many-colored folds in the earth and there are many more rabbits than people. The running, it may be, satisfies some longing in his breast.

2   He told me this story, which I relate in his own words.

3   "For some time, several weeks, I ran on the road that lies in the hills to the south. I like to run early in the morning, as you know, when the skyline is a silhouette and there are long shadows in my way—shadows within shadows—like deep, dark pools of water. It is a wonderful time to regard the earth, and a wonderful way to be in touch with it; I tell you, it is a religious experience I'm talking about, a holy thing.

4   "Well, one morning, after I had been following the same course for many days and had established a clear right-of-way, so to speak, I was amazed to find that someone had placed a barrier across the road, a bundle of branches! Oh, it was nothing that I couldn't negotiate with ease, mind you—it was only a token, after all. But the point is, it was there. It threatened me in some way, stood against me, destroyed the rhythm of my running . . . and of my life. I had to deal with it, don't you see? I removed it."

5   He paused here. I had become keenly interested in the story. It had begun to take the shape of a riddle, I thought. I asked him to go on.

6   "At first I supposed that the barrier was a joke or an accident," he said. "I thought that perhaps it had fallen from a wagon. I didn't want to take it personally, you see. But it was there again the next morning, and again I removed it. Every day it was there, and every day I removed it. Then I had to admit that the barrier was *mine*, that

it was placed there every day for no other purpose than to deter, impede, irritate, and finally infuriate *me*.

7   "Well, at last I discovered who my antagonist was, an elderly Indian man who lived nearby. His father probably lived there before him, and his father's father. He had no deed to the land, you know, but it was his all the same, by right of possession. He had centered his whole life upon it. In his eyes I was merely some pest, some vagrant—but eminently more dangerous than most because I had set up a continuum of intrusion, a persistent encroachment upon his domain, spiritual as well as physical. I never saw him, and as far as I know he never saw me, but we were engaged in a skirmish of the soul.

8   "On Christmas morning I took a bottle of wine with me into the hills. I removed the barrier which, sure enough, my adversary had again laid in my way, and I left the bottle of wine in its place.

9   "Not since has there been a barrier there, and every morning now I have only the open road before me and the sunlight breaking upon the red earth. I am free to run on the road, having paid my

way, don't you see? And I have no complaints. It was a reasonable fee, after all—oh, a token—to be sure but, you know, there are times when nothing is so valuable as a token. I am convinced that a handkerchief or a robin's egg or a sack of tobacco would have sufficed as well. The important thing is that I acknowledged the old man's possession of the land. That's all he wanted."

A.   COMPREHENSION

1. Was the author the same person who experienced the events of the story?

2. Who placed the bundle of sticks in the road each time?

3. What did the runner think about the person who kept blocking his path?

4. How did the runner solve the problem?

B.   CRITICAL   THINKING

1. How did the bundle of sticks affect the runner, and why?

2. Why did the old Indian man consider the land to be his, even though he didn't actually own it?

3. What did the bottle of wine symbolize, according to the runner?

4. Do you think the old Indian man will block the road again? Why or why not?

5. What lesson or message about how people should act toward each other can be learned from this story?

C.   LANGUAGE   AND   VOCABULARY

1. In the first paragraph, the author states that running "satisfies some longing in [the runner's] breast." What does he mean by this? In what way does this information preview the rest of the story?

2. In the sixth paragraph, where the runner is talking about the purpose of the bundle of sticks on the road, he uses the words "*deter, impede, irritate*, and finally *infuriate*. . . ." Why do you

think he used four different words to describe the effect of the barrier, instead of just one?

D. STYLE, STRUCTURE, AND ORGANIZATION

1. Most of this story is told using *dialogue* (or *quotations*)—the exact words that were spoken. Why do you think the author used dialogue to tell this story?

2. Reread the conclusion (the last paragraph of the story). Do you think this conclusion is effective? Why or why not? What is the main point that the storyteller makes in the conclusion?

E. TOPICS FOR DISCUSSION OR JOURNAL WRITING

1. Do you have a special place where you like to go and be alone?

2. How would you have reacted to the message of the bundle of sticks if it had been directed at you?

3. Do you think the old Indian man had the right to block the runner's path?

4. Have you ever known a person whom you considered an antagonist? In what way was this person an opponent or adversary?

F. WRITING TOPICS FOR PARAGRAPHS OR ESSAYS

1. Write a cause-and-effect paper about a time when you felt competitive or angry at someone. Explain why you felt competitive or angry and how these feelings affected you. You may also want to include the story of what happened, as the storyteller in "The Toll Road" did.

2. Write a narration paper telling about one time when you were able to get out of a difficult situation with a happy ending.

3. Search a library database or the Internet for more information about N. Scott Momaday. Write a short biography of his life and career.

4. Go to the Internet Public Library's Native American Authors Web site at **www.ipl.org.ar/ref/native/** and explore some of the materials found there (organized by author, title, and tribe). Write a short review of the Web site. Be sure to include some examples of authors, titles, and tribes that are represented on this site.

5. Write either a true story or a fictional story that offers a lesson or insight for readers, similar to "The Toll Road." If you wish, you may write the story in a style that is appropriate for young readers rather than for adults.

They Know Where You Are

DAVID LAGESSE

In the last few years, cellphones have become extremely popular, especially among the younger generations. Nowadays we see people using cellphones everywhere— in stores, on the street, on college campuses, even on the highways in areas where cellphone use is permitted. In the following reading selection, David LaGesse, a writer for *U. S. News & World Report*, reveals some amazing advances in technology for locating people by means of their cellphones, as well as discussing privacy issues related to the use of cellphones and Global Positioning Systems. He also provides information on the use of special chips or radio tags to locate and track people, vehicles, or merchandise.

PREREADING QUESTIONS

1. Why are cellphones so popular today? Do you think some people use cellphones more often than they use their home phone lines?

2. Do you like the idea of technology that would allow you to track where friends and family are and would also allow them to track you?

VOCABULARY

whereabouts approximate location

ubiquitous being everywhere

pervasive widespread, existing all over

monitor to observe and keep track of

nab catch

nagging annoying

mandated required

advocates people who support a cause

stir in this case, a commotion

streamline make simpler

implantable can be "implanted" or inserted under the surface of the skin

revamp reorganize or reconstruct

incapacitated having inadequate strength or ability; disabled

dubbed nicknamed

pacemakers electronic devices to control the rhythm of the heart

spooked alarmed, frightened

prototype an original or preliminary version of something

THEY KNOW WHERE YOU ARE

Just about any parent of a teenager would envy Seattle attorney Pat Char. She can track her son's whereabouts without even having to make a phone call. All it takes is a glance at her cellphone. Not long ago, 17-year-old Matt was at ski training in nearby Redmond. Char watched him make his way from practice, checking as he crossed the bridge toward home. After seeing that he had arrived safely back in their neighborhood, she headed out of the office to join the family for dinner. All because Matt carries a cellphone that broadcasts where it is.

2   Unknown to many Americans, most of our cellphones are capable of doing the same thing. Nowadays these ubiquitous little communicators quietly and persistently signal their location like electronic beacons. It takes sophisticated technology to find them, and commercial tracking services like the one Char uses are still uncommon. The real pioneers in location technology are local emergency services. After a slow start, authorities are putting into place gear to find wireless handsets, often much more precisely than Char can trail her son—so that ambulances, firetrucks, and police can be sent to the right spot when 911 calls come in from cellphones.

3   Street-smart phones are only the most pervasive in an emerging wave of new technologies designed to track us, our cars, and the goods we buy. Authorities are increasingly using toll tags, those radio transmitters that let drivers fly past toll gates, to monitor cars along an entire route as a measure of traffic flows. Major retailers like Wal-Mart are pushing for tiny radio tags on merchandise, which would let them trace goods in warehouses and, ultimately, all

the way to store shelves. And chips that get coordinates from the military's global positioning system satellites, already built into some cellphones, may soon be standard equipment in cars. Many rental cars already have GPS systems, which help nab customers who speed or travel outside the authorized zone.

. . .

4   In short, the new phones, tags, and chips will keep you from ever getting lost. The nagging fear is that they'll let others find you, whether you like it or not.

5   Yet it's hard to dispute the need for some kind of cellphone tracking. Perhaps half of all 911 calls now come from cellphones, often in waves. A single accident on Interstate 75 in Charlotte County, Fla., can spur 20 or 30 cell calls, says county 911 director Janet Hamilton. "It adds up [when dispatchers] have to ask every caller where they are," she says. Around the country, an inability to trace wireless 911 calls has had horrific consequences: a Philadelphia man tortured and murdered, his ordeal monitored over a cellphone line by helpless dispatchers; the deaths of four

youths lost in the mists of Long Island Sound, pleading for help to saviors who had no idea where to look. As early as 1996, the Federal Communications Commission saw the problem emerging. It mandated that by 2005, wireless carriers develop systems that would tell emergency dispatchers where most calls originate, to within 50 to 150 meters.

6   One way companies are satisfying the FCC mandate is by equipping new phones with GPS chips. When a caller dials 911, the carrier's network tells the phone where to look for the closest satellites. The phone then returns its precise latitude and longitude, which the carrier relays to the 911 center. A second approach is to install gear on cellphone towers that times the arrival of a handset's radio signal. Tiny differences in the arrival time at three different towers reveal the phone's position.

. . .

7   Even before the emergency systems are fully up and running, cellphone carriers are eyeing the commercial potential of "location services." The idea is to profit from the tracking ability, for example by alerting users to a nearby store having a sale or—in a widely cited fantasy—sending a Starbucks coupon to customers passing one of the coffee shops.

. . .

8   These prospects don't thrill privacy advocates. Congress in 1999 said cellphone users must give prior authorization before their location can be used for anything but emergency purposes. "Nobody knows what that really means," says David Sobel of the Electronic Privacy Information Center. Must a consumer push a button that says "find me," or can a carrier include the OK in a contract's fine print?

. . .

9   Sprint, for one, leaves it to customers to turn on the GPS beacon in its phones for any purpose other than 911 calls, and AT&T customers must specifically authorize others to track them through its Find Friends service. In the Char family everyone agrees to be found by others in the family. "It's a quid pro quo," says mom Pat. "The kids get a cellphone, and I get a little peace of mind."

. . .

10   In five or 10 years, the car seat itself—or the driver's shoe or sweater—may also have a chip that can be scanned by nearby readers. The world's largest retailer, WalMart, created a stir this summer by saying it wanted crates and pallets of goods arriving at its warehouses in 2005 to carry radio frequency identification, or RFID, chips. The tags, which broadcast a burst of data when scanned with a radio signal, store much more detailed information than conventional bar codes do and can be read from up to 10 feet away. By making goods easier to identify and trace, the chips could cut waste, theft, and loss and drastically streamline delivery, says retail consultant Scott Lundstrom of AMR Research.

· · ·

11   Farmers already use such chips to identify livestock, and pet owners increasingly tag their dogs and cats. One company is even selling them as implantable IDs for humans. But it will most likely be five years before the chips are widespread in warehouses and even longer before they appear on retail shelves. Before that happens, their current cost, about 50 cents, will have to drop to a fraction of a cent, says Jeff Woods, a retail consultant with the Gartner research firm. Also, retailers, shippers, and warehouse operators will have to revamp their systems to benefit from the tags. Nonetheless, "I think there's something huge here," says Woods. "It's going to have a major impact on retailing over the next 20 years."

· · ·

12   David Clement of Houston sees more serious benefits to the new era of automated tracking, which brought an ambulance to his wife when she was incapacitated while driving across town. Her Chevrolet Suburban came equipped with OnStar, a system that combines a cellphone with a GPS receiver, with private operators ready to offer assistance. When his wife became ill and had to pull over with their three kids in the car, 9-year-old Victoria pushed the OnStar button to summon help. "Up until then, I'd just thought it was a toy," says Clement. "I'm a believer now."

· · ·

An ID Card That You Can Never Lose

13   Pets have them; soon products will too. So why not radio tags for people? A Florida-based company called Applied Digital

Solutions is injecting a rice-grain-size ID chip under the skin of a few willing pioneers, including a Florida family dubbed the "Chipsons." Acquaintances raised their eyebrows, says mom Leslie Jacobs, 47. "But people thought pacemakers were weird at first."

. . .

14   Privacy experts, however, are spooked by the idea that people's personal data could be scanned without their knowledge. They're even less comfortable with another Applied Digital Solutions implant, still a prototype, that would include a global positioning system chip and could be tracked remotely.

A . COMPREHENSION

1. What are most cellphones capable of doing (in addition to their functions as phones)?

2. Why do emergency services, such as 911 centers, need cellphone tracking?

3. How can radio tags help retail stores and other types of businesses?

4. Who are the "Chipsons"?

B . CRITICAL THINKING

1. What do you think the author's viewpoint is? Is he in favor of or against the use of phones, tags, and chips to locate and keep track of vehicles, pets, livestock, various types of merchandise, and people?

2. Why are many privacy advocates not in favor of some of these new tracking technologies?

3. How does the title, "They Know Where You Are," relate to the reading? Who does "they" in the title refer to?

4. Why does the Federal Communications Commission want wireless phone companies to develop systems that can identify where calls originate?

5. Why are some people opposed to implanted ID chips or radio tags for humans? Why are some people in favor of them? Which side of this argument makes the most sense to you?

C . LANGUAGE AND VOCABULARY

1. Were you familiar with the terms *latitude* and *longitude*, which are used in paragraph 6? What do these words mean? What is the difference between the two? Take your best guess first, and then consult a dictionary if necessary.

2. Certain terms or phrases are commonly referred to by the first letters (or other key letters) of each word, such as ID, GPS, FCC, AT&T, and RFID, all of which are used in this article. What does each of these stand for? Can you think of other terms or phrases that are commonly represented by letters?

D . STYLE, STRUCTURE, AND ORGANIZATION

1. What is the purpose of the heading "An ID Card That You Can Never Lose," which appears just before the last two paragraphs?

2. Does the story in the first paragraph about Seattle attorney Pat Char and her 17-year-old son capture your attention and get you interested in the topic? Is this an effective introduction for the reading? Why or why not?

E . TOPICS FOR DISCUSSION OR JOURNAL WRITING

1. What are the advantages of cellphones? Are there any disadvantages?

2. What new developments in cellphone technology do you expect to see during the next ten years?

3. Would you like to be able to find out where friends and family members are by tracking their cellphones? Would you like them to be able to locate you by your cellphone? Give reasons for your opinions.

4. To what extent do you depend on your cellphone for daily use or for emergencies? Do you think that most people (or some people) are too dependent on their cellphones?

5. In what ways do you think the invention of the telephone has affected society and changed people's lives? What would our lives be like without telephones?

F. WRITING TOPICS FOR PARAGRAPHS OR ESSAYS

1. Write a personal narrative about a time when having a cellphone helped you or a friend get out of a difficult situation, or about a time when you would have been better off if you had one.

2. Using library resources or the Internet, look up information about the history of the telephone, and choose one interesting part of that history to write about. You might choose Alexander Graham Bell's invention, other early telephone inventors, early models of telephones, the development of cordless phones, fiber-optic technology, or the invention of cellphones. Write a summary in your own words of what you learn about the topic.

3. Write an argumentative paper in favor of or against the use of cellphones for tracking people. Include something about both sides of the argument, but be sure that your side comes out on top.

4. Write a comparison/contrast about two different cellphones or two different cellphone service providers. You can get information online, call for information, or visit sales offices or kiosks in person. You should give readers enough details so that they can easily decide which phone or service provider would be best for them.

5. Write a process paper explaining one type of technology mentioned in the reading, such as GPS systems, radio tags, or implantable ID chips, and how this technology works. Before you begin writing, research your topic on the Internet, in current library sources, or by checking with companies that make or use this technology.

Do Tell / Beware of Gossip That Knows No Bounds

R. J. IGNELZI

This lesson features two readings by R. J. Ignelzi, a staff writer for the *San Diego Union-Tribune*. Both articles are on the topic of *gossip*, that is, personal or sensational information that has not been confirmed. As you read each article, consider the choices that people make when they listen to gossip or pass it on to others, and how these choices may reflect our values. Also, notice the similarities and the differences between the two articles and think about the advice that is provided.

PREREADING QUESTIONS

1. What feeling do you get when you hear the word "gossip"?
2. What are the differences between beneficial gossip, harmless gossip, and destructive gossip?

VOCABULARY

scuttlebutt rumors or gossip

sociologists scientists who study human society

bond to establish a connection between two or more people

intimate close, personal

get a real grasp on fully understand

infidelities betrayals of someone's affection by

becoming intimate with another person

status a person's position within a group

perversely in a somewhat wicked way

blundered erred, made a mistake

lot in this case, our situation in life

angst anxiety or apprehension

256

tongue wagging gossiping

pernicious destructive

prattle babble, talk a lot about things that aren't very serious

liaisons in this case, affairs

mavens experts

embellish in this case, to add something interesting, even though it isn't true

implications in this case, the possible results or effects

gut check a test based on deep feelings

refute contradict, to prove something false

impunity with no punishment or penalty

reciprocity mutual give and take

DO TELL

Vegetarian or carnivore, everyone's favorite dish is "dirt."

2   People love to gossip, no matter if it's across the backyard fence, at the office water cooler or on the computer.

3   In fact, 65 percent of all conversations involve gossip, says the Social Issues Research Centre in Oxford, England.

4   If we aren't whispering about a neighbor or co-worker, then we're watching or reading about the latest celebrity scuttlebutt. Just look at the popularity of *People* magazine, "Entertainment Tonight" and Internet chat rooms.

5   "It's like breathing," says *New York Post* gossip columnist Cindy Adams. "Gossip is impossible not to do."

6   "We've been gossiping forever. Centuries ago, women were talking about each other as they beat clothes against the rocks at the river," she says. "They still do it today, but now it's over coffee."

7   So, why are we so obsessed with gossip?

8   Aside from its entertainment value, sociologists say gossip serves a powerful function in our society.

9   "Gossip supports the human impulse to bond," says Jack Levin, sociology professor at Boston's Northeastern University and author

of "Gossip: The Inside Scoop." "It aids in forging intimate ties and helps define who's in and who's out of a group."

10   It's impossible to be a success unless you understand your social environment, Levin says. And, the only way to get a real grasp on what's going on around you is to tune in to the latest gossip.

11   "In every job and anything you do in life, you have to be able to get along with others and be sensitive to their needs and desires. Gossip helps you understand what motivates others to behave the way they do," he says.

12   Nobody can afford to ignore office gossip.

13   "At work, we learn more about the company at the water cooler than in the official company handbook," Levin says. "Gossip is how you find out about who to go to for advice. How long it really takes to get a promotion or raise. How likely it is the company will go out of business."

14   Gossip about infidelities and rumors of improper behavior—no matter if it's Russell Crowe or your co-worker—help build a social map for what is accepted and what is not. We can learn what will improve our status and what will not.

15   "Gossip is simply a sharing of common values," says Leah Garchik, gossip columnist for the *San Francisco Chronicle* for the past 20 years.

16   Perversely, gossip can sometimes make us feel better about ourselves and others.

17   "We don't like perfection in human beings," Levin says. "So when we hear gossip that someone has blundered and made mistakes, it gives them credibility and makes us only like that person more."

18   Misery loves miserable company, according to Levin, who says there's an appeal to hearing about the misfortune of others, especially when they're important, successful and wealthy.

19   Knowing about other people's lives and troubles can make our own problems seem small by comparison. And, just realizing that the rich and famous don't have perfect lives makes our ordinary lot more bearable.

20   "To ease our own angst, we can think, well, Demi Moore had to get rid of Bruce Willis because it wasn't working. And, Jennifer Lopez has already had two failed marriages," Adams says.

21   Besides that, a little scuttlebutt can just be plain fun.

22   "Gossip is like lipstick," she says. "It's a cheap and fast way to make yourself feel good."

BEWARE OF GOSSIP THAT KNOWS NO BOUNDS

1   Pssst. Have you heard the latest?

2   Gossip, that age-old favorite pastime, may actually be good for us.

3   A study at the Research Centre for Economic Learning and Social Evolution at University College London says tongue wagging helps people bond and creates strong social networks.

4   Social scientists on this side of the pond agree.

5   "If gossip is not pernicious, it serves a valuable function," says Phillip Gay, sociology professor at San Diego State University. "People get to know each other through gossip. They can express their values and opinions. Gossip is a way of introducing yourself to other people."

6   But, there's got to be limits. While it's OK to pass judgment on Michael Jackson's facial transformation, is it in good taste to talk about your co-worker's suspected nose job? Although we loved to prattle on about the Clinton-Lewinsky affair, is it all right to whisper about your neighbor's sexual liaisons?

7   Since there's no written rules for gossip etiquette, we turned to gossip mavens and researchers for some guidelines.

8   Don't spread gossip that you know to be false.

9   "That makes you a liar instead of a gossip," says Jack Levin, sociology professor at Boston's Northeastern University and author of "Gossip: The Inside Scoop."

10   If you can't verify a rumor and you know it's hurtful, don't pass it along.

11   "Break that 'telephone tree' (of gossip) if you don't know it to be fact," says Peter Post, great grandson of Emily Post and co-director of the Emily Post Institute in Burlington, Vt.

12   It's unethical to spread negative gossip to intentionally damage someone.

13   "The rule of good gossip is you don't hurt or draw blood on purpose," says Cindy Adams, gossip columnist for the *New York Post* and author of "The Gift of Jazzy." "You can prick someone a bit, but don't deliberately wound them."

14   While it's tempting to exaggerate or embellish the tale you're passing along, try not to make up details.

15   "You can't tart up the naked bones of a story if you don't have it," Adams says.

16   Gossip should never be used to determine someone's character or human worth.

17   "You can't really judge someone based on gossip," Gay says. "Most gossip is speculation with no confirmation."

18   Think through the implications of your gossip before you let it spread.

19   "Before you talk about another person, give some thought to what damage it could cause. If there's the risk it could bring pain or hurt, don't spread it," says Rabbi Philip Graubart, of Congregation Beth El in La Jolla.

20   As a gossip columnist, it's Adams' job to reveal the latest scuttlebutt. However, she keeps her lips sealed when it comes to marital infidelities.

21   "I worry there might be children involved, and too many people could get hurt," she says. "If someone's having an affair, I won't be the one to break (the story)."

22   Speak up if someone is telling gossip you think is hurtful or untruthful. "It doesn't have to turn into a confrontation, but you should say this kind of gossip makes you uncomfortable," Post says. "Try to change the gossip's behavior."

23   Don't talk about someone's illness or health.

24   Gossiping about someone's sexual orientation is unacceptable.

25   "Don't speculate about someone's sexuality. You could be wrong, and it could be very hurtful," Post says.

26   If unsure whether a piece of gossip is appropriate to pass on, ask yourself if you could say it to the person it's about.

27   "It's a great gut check," Post says. "If you can't tell them to their face, then keep quiet."

28   If you think someone is not aware they're the target of gossip, let them know.

29   "Tell someone when others are talking about them, especially when the gossip is negative and/or false," Levin says. "You have to give the target a chance to refute the rumors. Otherwise, it can go on indefinitely."

30   Be careful of gossiping in Internet chat rooms. The information is often false and sometimes hurtful.

31   "Chat rooms give the illusion of anonymity, and people are more likely to be malicious in their gossip and spread nasty rumors with impunity," Levin says.

32   If you gossip about others, be willing to have others gossip about you.

33   "There needs to be a norm of reciprocity when it comes to gossip," Levin says.

34   If you're a victim of gossip, confront it directly and immediately.

35   "Don't assume the gossip will die of its inaccuracy," Levin says. "Silence infers guilt. The best thing you can do is to confront it, refute it and give your side of the story."

A. COMPREHENSION

1. According to the first article, what are some of the beneficial effects that gossip can have?

2. What are some harmful effects of gossip?

3. Which of these two articles provides advice on how *not* to gossip?

4. Who are Phillip Gay, Jack Levin, Peter Post, Cindy Adams, and Philip Graubart?

B. CRITICAL THINKING

1. Why do so many people enjoy listening to gossip and passing it on to others?

2. What is the difference between *gossip* and *news*?

3. Is it morally OK to gossip about someone if it's not harmful?

4. Do you think the "rules for gossiping" in the second article provide good advice?

C .   L A N G U A G E   A N D   V O C A B U L A R Y

1.   In these two articles, the author uses the words *pernicious* and *hurtful*. What are some other synonyms for these two words? If you can't think of any, look up these words in a thesaurus.

2.   In the first article, Cindy Adams is quoted as saying, "You can't tart up the naked bones of a story if you don't have it." What does she mean by that?

D .   S T Y L E ,   S T R U C T U R E , A N D   O R G A N I Z A T I O N

1.   What information is similar in the two articles on gossip? What information is included in one article but not in the other one?

2.   In the second article, the author quotes several authorities on gossip and ethics. Do these quotations give the reading more authority on the subject of gossip?

3.   How does the author end the second article? Do you think this is an effective conclusion?

E .   T O P I C S   F O R   D I S C U S S I O N O R   J O U R N A L   W R I T I N G

1.   Have you had any experiences with gossip, either good or bad? What did you learn from the experience?

2.   Do you like to read gossipy stories in magazines or newspapers? Do you like to watch gossipy TV shows about celebrities? Why or why not?

3.   What would you recommend to someone who was the subject of some harmful gossip?

4.   If you have a job, do you ever hear rumors at work? How do you feel when you hear rumors about your boss, your coworkers, or business decisions?

F. WRITING TOPICS FOR PARAGRAPHS OR ESSAYS

1. Write a narration paper telling about one or more of your own experiences with gossip. If you learned a lesson, include it in the body of the paper or in the conclusion.

2. Write an instructions paper that advises a victim of gossip what to do. Include detailed, step-by-step instructions.

3. Write a short paper telling about the most interesting gossip you ever heard. Include some of the details that made it interesting.

4. Search the Internet or a library database for other materials written by R. J. Ignelzi and write a paper comparing one or two of them to these gossip articles. Include information on how long the articles are, the topics, the main ideas included, how easy to read they are, and which articles you liked best.

5. Check out some of the gossip columns listed at **www.gossipcentral .com/**, other online gossip pages, or gossip columns and articles in newspapers or magazines. Write an evaluation of two or three of these columns or articles. Provide some information about the topics they cover, whether they are harmless or destructive, and whether they were interesting to read.

Choosing Virginity

LORRAINE ALI AND JULIE SCELFO

This thought-provoking excerpt from a *Newsweek* magazine article
features interviews with several of today's teenagers who express a
variety of reasons for saying no to sex before marriage. Their values
and choices may reflect a trend among an increasing number of young
people to wait longer before becoming sexually active. In response to
Lorraine Ali and Julie Scelfo's questions, many teens were willing to
discuss sex-related issues openly and frankly for this article. Both
authors are well-known to readers of *Newsweek* magazine. Lorraine Ali
is a general editor at *Newsweek,* as well as a music critic. She has also
written articles for several other magazines, including *Rolling Stone*,
GQ, and *Mademoiselle*. Also an experienced correspondent for
Newsweek, Julie Scelfo has written or contributed to a wide variety of
articles about society and culture.

PREREADING QUESTIONS

1. Do most young people that you know consider virginity before
   marriage an important value?
2. What is your opinion about sex education classes for high school
   students?

VOCABULARY

chaste morally pure, abstaining
from sex

ethos fundamental values

counterculture a secondary
culture with views opposed to
those of established culture

peddle sell

beleaguered harassed

proponents people in favor of
something

inherent existing as an essential
part

cacophony harsh or unpleasant
sounds

semblance outward appearance

prudish excessively concerned
 with proper behavior

STDs sexually transmitted
 diseases (abbreviation)

perilous dangerous

chaotic full of confusion, in a
 disordered state

smack-dab precisely (slang)

reclaiming taking back

compromising in this case,
 exposing to danger or
 temptation

dire urgent

hitched up in this case, involved
 with someone (slang)

CHOOSING VIRGINITY

There's a sexual revolution going on in America, and believe it or
not, it has nothing to do with Christina Aguilera's bare-it-all video
"Dirrty." The uprising is taking place in the real world, not on "The
Real World." Visit any American high school and you'll likely find a
growing number of students who . . . have decided to remain
chaste until marriage. Rejecting the get-down-make-love ethos of
their parents' generation, this wave of young adults represents a new
counterculture, one clearly at odds with the mainstream media and
their routine use of sex to boost ratings and peddle product.

2   According to a recent study from the Centers for Disease
Control, the number of high-school students who say they've never
had sexual intercourse rose by almost 10 percent between 1991 and
2001. Parents, public-health officials and sexually beleaguered teens
themselves may not be relieved by this "let's not" trend. But the new
abstinence movement, largely fostered by cultural conservatives and
evangelical Christians, has also become hotly controversial.

3   As the Bush administration plans to increase federal funding for
abstinence programs by nearly a third, to $135 million, the
Advocates for Youth and other proponents of a more comprehensive
approach to sex ed argue that teaching abstinence isn't enough.
Teens also need to know how to protect themselves if they do have
sex, these groups say, and they need to understand the emotional
intensity inherent in sexual relationships.

4   The debate concerns public policy, but the real issue is personal
choice. At the center of it all are the young people themselves,

whose voices are often drowned out by the political cacophony. Some of them opened up and talked candidly . . . about their reasons for abstaining from sex until marriage. It's clear that religion plays a critical role in this extraordinarily private decision. But there are other factors as well: caring parents, a sense of their own unreadiness, the desire to gain some semblance of control over their own destinies. Here are their stories.

The Wellesley Girl

5   Alice Kunce says she's a feminist, but not the "army-boot-I-hate-all-men kind." The curly-haired 18-year-old Wellesley College sophomore—she skipped a grade in elementary school—looks and talks like what she is: one of the many bright, outspoken students at the liberal Massachusetts women's college. She's also a virgin. "One of the empowering things about the feminist movement," she says, "is that we're able to assert ourselves, to say no to sex and not feel pressured about it. And I think guys are kind of getting it. Like, 'Oh, *not* everyone's doing it.'"

6   But judging by MTV's "Undressed," UPN's "Buffy the Vampire Slayer" and just about every other TV program or movie targeted at teens, everyone *is* doing it. Alice grew up with these images, but as a small-town girl in Jefferson City, Mo., most teen shows felt alien and alienating. "You're either a prudish person who can't handle talking about sex or you're out every Saturday night getting some," she says. "But if you're not sexually active and you're willing to discuss the subject, you can't be called a prude. . . ."

7   Alice, a regular churchgoer who also teaches Sunday school, says religion is not the reason she's chosen abstinence. She fears STDs and pregnancy, of course, but above all, she says, she's not mature enough emotionally to handle the deep intimacy sex can bring. . . .

The Dream Team

8   Karl Nicoletti wasted no time when it came to having "the talk" with his son, Chris. It happened five years ago, when Chris was in sixth grade. Nicoletti was driving him home from school and the subject of girls came up. "I know many parents who are wishy-

washy when talking to their kids about sex. I just said, "No, you're not going to have sex. . . ."

9   Today, the 16-year-old from Longmont, Colo., vows he'll remain abstinent until marriage. So does his girlfriend, 17-year-old Amanda Wing, whose parents set similarly strict rules for her and her two older brothers. "It's amazing, but they did listen," says her mother, Lynn Wing. . . .

10   "Society is so run by sex," says Chris, who looks like Madison Avenue's conception of an All-American boy in his Abercrombie sweat shirt and faded baggy jeans. "Just look at everything—TV, movies. The culture today makes it seem OK to have sex whenever, however or with whoever you want. I just disagree with that." Amanda, who looks tomboy comfy in baggy brown cords, a white T shirt and chunky-soled shoes, feels the same way. "Sex should be a special thing that doesn't need to be public," she says. "But if you're abstinent, it's like *you're* the one set aside from society because you're not doing it." . . .

11   To most abstaining teens, marriage is the golden light at the end of the perilous tunnel of dating—despite what their parents' experience may have been. Though Amanda's mother and father have had a long and stable union, Karl Nicoletti separated from Chris's mother when Chris was in fifth grade. His fiancée moved in with Chris and Karl two years ago. . . . Chris and Amanda talk about marriage in the abstract, but they want to go to college first, and they're looking at schools on opposite sides of the country. "I think we could stay together," Chris says. Amanda agrees. "Like we have complete trust in each other," she says. "It's just not hard for us." . . .

The Survivor

12   Remaining a virgin until marriage is neither an easy nor a common choice in Latoya Huggins's part of Paterson, N.J. At least three of her friends became single mothers while they were still in high school, one by an older man who now wants nothing to do with the child. "It's hard for her to finish school," Latoya says, "because she has to take the baby to get shots and stuff."

13   Latoya lives in a chaotic world: so far this year, more than a dozen people have been murdered in her neighborhood. It's a life

that makes her sexuality seem like one of the few things she can actually control. "I don't even want a boyfriend until after college," says Latoya, who's studying to be a beautician at a technical high school. "Basically I want a lot out of life. My career choices are going to need a lot of time and effort."

14   Latoya, 18, could pass for a street-smart 28. She started thinking seriously about abstinence five years ago, when a national outreach program called Free Teens began teaching classes at her church. The classes reinforced what she already knew from growing up in Paterson—that discipline is the key to getting through your teen years alive. Earlier this year she dated a 21-year-old appliance salesman from her neighborhood, until Latoya heard that he was hoping she'd have sex with him. "We decided that we should just be friends," she explains, "before he cheated on me or we split up in a worse way." . . .

15   Her goal is to graduate and get a job; she wants to stay focused and independent. "Boys make you feel like you're special and you're the only one they care about," she says. "A lot of girls feel like they need that. But my mother loves me and my father loves me, so there's no gap to fill."

The Beauty Queen

16   Even though she lives 700 miles from the nearest ocean, Daniela Aranda was recently voted Miss Hawaiian Tropic El Paso, Texas, and her parents couldn't be prouder. They've displayed a picture of their bikini-clad daughter smack-dab in the middle of the living room. "People always say to me 'You don't look like a virgin,'" says Daniela, 20, who wears supersparkly eye shadow, heavy lip liner and a low-cut black shirt. "But what does a virgin look like? Someone who wears white and likes to look at flowers?"

17   Daniela models at Harley-Davidson fashion shows, is a cheerleader for a local soccer team called the Patriots and hangs out with friends who work at Hooters. She's also an evangelical Christian who made a vow at 13 to remain a virgin, and she's kept that promise. "It can be done," she says. "I'm living proof." Daniela has never joined an abstinence program; her decision came from strong family values and deep spiritual convictions.

18   Daniela's arid East El Paso neighborhood, just a mile or so from the Mexican border, was built atop desert dunes, and the sand seems to be reclaiming its own by swallowing up back patios and sidewalks. The city, predominantly Hispanic, is home to the Fort Bliss Army base, breathtaking mesa views—and some of the highest teen-pregnancy rates in the nation. "There's a lot of girls that just want to get pregnant so they can get married and get out of here," Daniela says.

19   But she seems content to stay in El Paso. She studies business at El Paso Community College, dates a UTEP football player named Mike and works as a sales associate at the A'gaci Too clothing store in the Cielo Vista Mall. . . .

20   Daniela has been dating Mike for more than a year. He's had sex before, but has agreed to remain abstinent with her. "He's what you call a born-again virgin," she says. "Or a secondary abstinent, or something like that. We just don't put ourselves in compromising situations. If we're together late at night, it's with my whole family." . . .

The Ring Bearer

21   Leneé Young is trying to write a paper for her Spanish class at Atlanta's Spelman College, but as usual she and her roommates can't help getting onto the subject of guys. "I love Ludacris," Leneé gushes. "I love everything about him. Morris Chestnut, too. He has a really pretty smile. Just gorgeous." But Leneé, 19, has never had a boyfriend, and has never even been kissed. "A lot of the guys in high school had already had sex," she says. "I knew that would come up, so I'd end all my relationships at the very beginning." Leneé decided back then to remain a virgin until marriage, and even now she feels little temptation to do what many of her peers are doing behind closed dormitory doors. "I feel that part of me hasn't been triggered yet," she says. "Sex is one of those things you can't miss until you have it."

22   Last summer she went with a friend from her hometown of Pittsburgh to a Silver Ring Thing. These popular free events meld music videos, pyrotechnics and live teen comedy sketches with dire warnings about STDs. Attendees can buy a silver ring—and a

Bible—for $12. Then, at the conclusion of the program, as techno music blares, they recite a pledge of abstinence and don their rings. "My friend, who's also a virgin, said I needed to go so I could get a ring," Leneé says. "It was fun, like the music and everything. And afterwards they had a dance and a bonfire." . . .

The Renewed Virgin

23   Lucian Schulte had always planned to wait until he was married to have sex, but that was before a warm night a couple of years ago when the green-eyed, lanky six-footer found himself with an unexpected opportunity. "She was all for it," says Lucian, now 18. "It was like, 'Hey, let's give this a try.'" The big event was over in a hurry and lacked any sense of intimacy. "In movies, if people have sex, it's always romantic," he says. "Physically, it did feel good, but emotionally, it felt really awkward. It was not what I expected it to be."

24   While the fictional teens of "American Pie" would have been clumsily overjoyed, Lucian, raised Roman Catholic, was plagued by guilt. "I was worried that I'd given myself to someone and our relationship was now a lot more serious than it was before," he says. "It was like, 'Now, what is she going to expect from me?'" Lucian worried, too, about disease and pregnancy. He promised himself never again.

25   Lucian, now an engineering major at the University of Alberta in Canada, is a "renewed virgin." His parents are strong proponents of chastity, and he attended school-sponsored abstinence classes. But the messages didn't hit home until he'd actually had sex. "It's a pretty special thing, and it's also pretty serious," he says. "Abstinence has to do with, 'Hey, are you going to respect this person?'" He has dated since his high-school affair, and is now hoping a particular cute coed from Edmonton will go out with him. "But I'll try to restrict myself to kissing," he says. "Not because I think everything else is bad. But the more you participate with someone, the harder it's going to be to stop."

26   It's not easy to practice such restraint, especially when those around him do not. Lucian lives in a single room, decorated with ski-lift tickets and a "Scooby-Doo" poster, in an all-male dorm, but he says most students "get hitched up, sleep around and never see

each other again." . . . Lucian figures he can hold out until he's married, which he hopes will be by the time he's 30. "I'm looking forward to an intimate experience with my wife, who I'll truly love and want to spend the rest of my life with," says Lucian. "It's kind of corny, but it's for real."

A. COMPREHENSION

1. What are three of the main reasons young people give in the article for abstaining from sex before marriage?

2. What view of sex education does the organization called Advocates for Youth support?

3. Choose any two of the young people who were interviewed and explain what their views are about sex before marriage.

4. According to the article, is the number of teenagers who say they are virgins increasing or decreasing? What do statistics show about changes in attitudes between 1991 and 2001?

B. CRITICAL THINKING

1. Do you agree with the authors' statement that TV programs and movies aimed at young people convey the message that "everyone is doing it"? Cite some examples of current programs or movies that support your view.

2. To what extent have the authors examined both sides of the question of virginity? Does the article seem completely fair and unbiased, or do the authors at times seem to be promoting the viewpoint that they agree with? Give reasons for your answer.

3. Which one of the young people who were interviewed for this article do you admire most? Why? Do you agree or disagree with that person's views? (If you prefer, you may choose someone whom you do not admire at all.)

4. Judging from statements in the article as well as your own experience, to what extent do parents play a role in teenagers' decisions about whether or not to have sex?

5. What do you think is the authors' main point? Is that idea well-supported in the article?

C. LANGUAGE AND VOCABULARY

1. What does the term "born-again virgin" mean? Had you ever heard the term before reading this article?

2. As used in this article, what is the meaning of the word *abstinence*? Does it have a similar meaning in other situations that do not relate to sexual activity? Are there any other kinds of activities that a person might choose not to participate in? Could the word *abstinence* also be used appropriately to describe these decisions?

D. STYLE, STRUCTURE, AND ORGANIZATION

1. Why did the authors include a large number of quotations from the people who were interviewed? In what way do these quotations add to the effectiveness of the article? Do you think the authors interviewed too many people, too few, or just the right number?

2. Do you think the introduction to the article is effective? Why or why not? How does the introduction capture readers' attention?

E. TOPICS FOR DISCUSSION OR JOURNAL WRITING

1. What are your own views on virginity and the question of sex before marriage?

2. Do you think there is pressure on young people to engage in sexual activity? Where does this pressure come from—friends, dating partners, attitudes of society, movies and television programs, or other sources? Explain your answer.

3. What trends do you think will develop during the next five or ten years in teenagers' attitudes toward sex and marriage?

4. Were sex education programs offered in the high school that you attended? Do you think these programs were effective? If not, what changes would you suggest?

5. Can you think of any arguments in favor of the opposing point of view? What reasons might some people give for supporting the idea of sexual experimentation among teens?

F. WRITING TOPICS FOR PARAGRAPHS OR ESSAYS

1. Interview three or four young people about their attitudes toward virginity or sex before marriage and write about what you learn from them. Use some direct quotations from the people you interview, as Ali and Scelfo did for this article.

2. Imagine an argument between any two people on the topic of virginity: you and a parent, you and your boyfriend or girlfriend, two friends, or any other combination. The people may be either real or imaginary. Write a scene using dialogue to dramatize their argument. You may write it like a scene from a play or like a short story.

3. Interview a parent, grandparent, or other relative or friend who is at least ten years older than you are. Find out what young people's attitudes toward virginity were when this person was growing up. Write about what you learn from the interview, including whether attitudes seem to have changed since this person was in high school.

4. Look up an informative article on the Internet or at a library on a topic that is related to "The New Virginity," such as virginity pledges, sex education programs, abstinence, or teenage pregnancies, and write a one-page summary of the article in your own words.

5. Write a persuasive paper for or against one of the following topics: virginity until marriage, birth control, sex education in schools. Include at least three reasons to support the point of view that you support.

The Ambitious Generation

BARBARA SCHNEIDER AND DAVID STEVENSON

Barbara Schneider, a professor of sociology at the University of Chicago, and David Stevenson, assistant director for social and behavioral sciences in the U.S. government Office of Science and Technology Policy, have collected and analyzed a great deal of information about the teenage experience and how it has changed over the years. As you read the following selection from their book, *The Ambitious Generation,* consider how the social world of adolescents during the 1950s differed from the social world of today.

PREREADING QUESTIONS

1. In what ways do you think today's teenagers are different from the teenagers of 50 years ago?

2. What qualities make some people more popular in school than others? Does being an athlete, a cheerleader, or a member of certain organizations contribute to a person's popularity in high school or college?

VOCABULARY

bounded having specific boundaries

booster clubs clubs that promote and support certain school activities

social status in this context, a high social position

peer group people of approximately the same age and social position

---

markers indications or signs

confer to award an honor or a
position

elite considered to have a high
social position; above others

Sloan sample a reference to
participants in a survey called
the Sloan Study of Youth and
Social Development, which
the authors used as a source
of information

misperception an inaccurate
perception or viewpoint

fostered encouraged

prevalent common or
widespread

fluid in this context, frequently
changing

criteria guidelines or
requirements

THE AMBITIOUS GENERATION

The social world of adolescents in the 1950s was very different from
that of adolescents today. Public high schools then drew their
students primarily from bounded residential communities where
families were likely to know their neighbors' children, as well as the
children's grandparents, other relatives, and close friends. Some
families lived in the same communities for several generations, and
it was not uncommon for children to attend the same schools their
parents had and even to have the same teachers. In these
communities, parents and their children shared common
understandings of what it meant to be popular and successful in
adolescent society.

2   Adolescents in the 1950s lived in a world where participation
in certain activities, such as athletics and booster clubs, could give
one social status in the school as well as among adults within the
community. Other school organizations, such as the honor society
and debate club, were for "good students," but participation in these
activities did not result in popularity among teenagers at school.
Academic excellence was rarely helpful in achieving peer-group
popularity; only about a quarter of high school seniors would enroll
in college. School dances and other social activities were important,
and "dating" and "going steady" were highly valued by most
teenagers. The social life of the high school was an important part of

courtship, because most boys and girls married soon after high school.

3   The social world of today's teenagers is very different, and the markers of adolescents' social status are not as clear or as widely held by them or their parents. Being an athlete, a cheer-leader, or homecoming queen does not necessarily confer high social status. For the increasing number of young people who plan to attend college, getting good grades and participating in such organizations as academic clubs are important for college admission. And being admitted to a competitive college is an important marker of social status.

4   Peer groups have changed substantially since the 1950s. There are few dominant elite crowds that most students desire to become members of. There are, however, numerous smaller social groups whose composition changes from year to year. These changes in peer groups are reflected in adolescents' views of themselves. Adolescents in the 1990s are more likely to see themselves as popular. Ten percent of students in the Sloan sample considered themselves very popular, 65 percent reported that they were somewhat popular, and 25 percent said they were not popular. Considering oneself popular is probably not a misperception if one is referring to a smaller friendship group.

5   The creation of numerous small groups is fostered, in part, by large high schools that draw students from many different neighborhoods. Because school friends often live far apart, it can be difficult to get together outside school. Some young people have school friends whom they eat lunch with and talk with but do not see otherwise. During the past decade, many facilities like recreational parks and programs that cater to adolescents after school have closed. With fewer places to go after school other than work, adolescents can spend long periods of time alone at home.

6   The tight, closed peer groups so prevalent in the 1950s have been replaced by fluid friendship groups. Students often move from one group to another, and friendships change over a period of a few weeks or months. Best friends are few, and students frequently refer to peers as "acquaintances" or "associates." Building close, intimate ties with a special boyfriend or girlfriend that could lead to long-term commitment or marriage is viewed as undesirable. Few

teenagers "date"; instead, they "go out" with someone, which can mean anything from spending time together to a casual relationship that is recognized by the peer group as some form of special emotional attachment. Not only has the premise of dating changed, so have the criteria for whom one can go out with. Mixed-race couples and even same-sex couples are part of the teenage social world today.

A .   C O M P R E H E N S I O N

1. Describe high school social life in the 1950s. Which school activities helped certain teenagers become popular in the 1950s?

2. According to the authors, have attitudes toward getting good grades and attending college changed since the 1950s? In what ways have they changed?

3. How are peer groups and friendship groups different now than they were in the 1950s?

4. In what ways has dating or going out with someone changed since the 1950s?

B .   C R I T I C A L   T H I N K I N G

1. Why have young people's attitudes changed in so many ways since the 1950s?

2. Do you think that being popular is important to most teenagers? Why? Do people's attitudes about popularity tend to change as they grow older? If so, in what ways do they change?

3. Why do more people consider it important to attend college now than in the 1950s?

4. How did the authors acquire the information they used in writing *The Ambitious Generation*? In your opinion, how reliable is information obtained through surveys?

5. Which generation does the title *The Ambitious Generation* refer to? Do you agree with the authors' choice of title? Why or why not?

C . LANGUAGE AND VOCABULARY

1. In the next to the last paragraph of the reading, the authors make a distinction between the terms *date* and *go out*. What do these terms mean to you? Do you agree with the difference in meaning that the authors suggest?

2. Find two paragraphs that are written entirely in the past tense, and highlight or underline all of the verbs. Look for regular verbs that have an *-ed* ending (such as *lived*), verbs that have an irregular past form (such as *was*, *were*, and *drew*), and verbs that use "did not" to make them negative. Are the auxiliary verbs *could* and *would* also used to express something about the past?

D . STYLE, STRUCTURE, AND ORGANIZATION

1. Which sentence states the authors' main point? Is this an effective place to state the main idea of the reading selection? Why or why not?

2. One method of organizing a comparison/contrast is to go back and forth between the two items being compared. Another method of organization, called the block method, first presents a fairly long block of information about one of the items, followed by a block of similar information about the other item. Which of these methods serves as the primary organization for this reading?

E . TOPICS FOR DISCUSSION OR JOURNAL WRITING

1. Would you like to have been a teenager during the 1950s? Why or why not?

2. Do you agree with the authors' observations about friendships and popularity among teenagers of the 1990s and today? Why or why not?

3. What similarities or differences do you see between your own high school experiences and the types of experiences described in the reading?

4. Do you prefer getting acquainted with new people fairly often and making new friends or keeping the same friends for many years? Why?

5. Do you think that mixed-race couples are more likely to be accepted nowadays than in the past? What are the attitudes toward mixed-race couples in your community?

F. WRITING TOPICS FOR PARAGRAPHS OR ESSAYS

1. Write about the social world at the high school you attended.

2. Compare and contrast the social world of high school with the social world of college.

3. Write a comparison/contrast paper about the similarities and differences between two friends, two teachers, two family members, or two other people you know well.

4. Using library resources or the Internet, look up information about some aspects of life during the 1950s, such as clothing styles, popular movies, kinds of music, or television programs of that decade. Write a paper telling what you learn about the 1950s.

5. Interview someone who attended high school during the 1960s, 1970s, or 1980s. Ask about the kinds of things mentioned in the reading, such as friends, peer groups, popularity, college expectations, and relationships. Then choose one of the following writing assignments:

   a. Write about some of the high school experiences of the person you interviewed.

   b. Based on your interview, contrast the social world of adolescents in the 1960s, 1970s, or 1980s with the social world of adolescents today. Use the reading selection as a model for your writing.

The World After Cloning

WRAY HERBERT, JEFFERY L. SHELER, AND TRACI WATSON

This article originally appeared in *U.S. News & World Report,* not long after the widely publicized cloning of a sheep named Dolly. The authors ask and answer several questions about cloning that have been raised since Dolly first appeared, as well as considering some of the moral issues involved in cloning.

PREREADING QUESTIONS

1. In the past few years, what kinds of animals have been cloned successfully?

2. Do you think it will be possible to clone human beings in the future?

VOCABULARY

jaded cynical, having a negative view because of previous experiences

technophobe a person who is afraid of technology

in the wake of following directly afterward

scurried hurried

ethical moral

implications ideas that are suggested, implied, or closely connected

ramifications developments, consequences

debut first appearance

Source: "The World After Cloning" by Wray Herbert, Jeffery L. Sheler, and Traci Watson. Copyright, March 10, 1997, *U.S. News & World Report.* Visit us at our Web site at **www.usnews.com** for additional information.

ethicists persons who specialize in ethics, or standards of morality

pales becomes or appears less important

DNA the part of a cell that carries genetic information

intact unbroken, undamaged

membrane a thin layer of tissue

embryos fertilized eggs in the early stages of development

ewes female sheep

surrogate substitute

genes parts of each cell that are responsible for a person's characteristics

uterine referring to the uterus, the organ in the female body where embryos grow and develop

megalomaniac someone who is obsessed with power

unanimous in complete agreement

narcissistic focused on love of oneself

impoverished poor (in this case, without strength)

stigmatized marked as shameful or disgraceful, perceived as negative

apathetic uninterested

pedigree genetic inheritance

unscrupulous without moral principles

usurpation taking control of, taking over

from scratch from the beginning, using natural methods and/or ingredients

progeny offspring, other beings produced from one's genetic material

THE WORLD AFTER CLONING

At first it was just plain startling. Word from Scotland . . . that a scientist named Ian Wilmut had succeeded in cloning an adult mammal—a feat long thought impossible—caught the imagination of even the most jaded technophobe. The laboratory process that produced Dolly, an unremarkable-looking sheep, theoretically would work for humans as well. . . . It was science fiction come to life. And scary science fiction at that.

2   In the wake of Wilmut's shocker, government scurried to formulate guidelines for the unknown, a future filled with

mind-boggling possibilities. The Vatican called for a worldwide ban on human cloning. President Clinton ordered a national commission to study the legal and ethical implications. Leaders in Europe, where most nations already prohibit human cloning, began examining the moral ramifications of cloning other species.

3   Like the splitting of the atom, the first space flight, and the discovery of "life" on Mars, Dolly's debut has generated a long list of difficult puzzles for scientists and politicians, philosophers and theologians. And at dinner tables and office coolers, in bars and on street corners, the development of wild scenarios spun from the birth of a single sheep has only just begun. *U.S. News* sought answers from experts to the most intriguing and frequently asked questions.

Why Would Anyone Want to Clone a Human Being in the First Place?

4   The human cloning scenarios that ethicists ponder most frequently fall into two broad categories: 1) parents who want to

clone a child, either to provide transplants for a dying child or to replace that child, and 2) adults who for a variety of reasons might want to clone themselves.

5   Many ethicists, however, believe that after the initial period of uproar, there won't be much interest in cloning humans. Making copies, they say, pales next to the wonder of creating a unique human being the old-fashioned way.

Could a Human Being Be Cloned Today? What About Other Animals?

6   It would take years of trial and error before cloning could be applied successfully to other mammals. For example, scientists will need to find out if the donor egg is best used when it is resting quietly or when it is growing.

Will It Be Possible to Clone the Dead?

7   Perhaps, if the body is fresh, says Randall Prather, a cloning expert at the University of Missouri–Columbia. The cloning method used by Wilmut's lab requires fusing an egg cell with the cell containing the donor's DNA. And that means the donor cell must have an intact membrane around its DNA. The membrane starts to fall apart after death, as does DNA. But, yes, in theory at least it might be possible.

Can I Set Up My Own Cloning Lab?

8   Yes, but maybe you'd better think twice. All the necessary chemicals and equipment are easily available and relatively low-tech. But out-of-pocket costs would run $100,000 or more, and that doesn't cover the pay for a skilled developmental biologist. The lowest-priced of these scientists, straight out of graduate school, makes about $40,000 a year. If you tried to grow the cloned embryos to maturity, you'd encounter other difficulties. The Scottish team implanted 29 very young clones in 13 ewes, but only one grew into a live lamb. So if you plan to clone Fluffy, buy enough cat food for a host of surrogate mothers.

Would a Cloned Human Be Identical to the Original?

9   Identical genes don't produce identical people, as anyone acquainted with identical twins can tell you. In fact, twins are more alike than clones would be, since they have at least shared the uterine environment, are usually raised in the same family, and so forth. Parents could clone a second child who eerily resembled their first in appearance, but all the evidence suggests the two would have very different personalities. . . .

10   Even biologically, a clone would not be identical to the "master copy." The clone's cells, for example, would have energy-processing machinery (mitochondria) that came from the egg donor, not from the nucleus donor. But most of the physical differences between originals and copies wouldn't be detectable without a molecular-biology lab. . . .

Wouldn't It Be Strange for a Cloned Twin to Be Several Years Younger Than His or Her Sibling?

11   When the National Advisory Board on Ethics in Reproduction studied a different kind of cloning a few years ago, its members split on the issue of cloned twins separated in time. Some thought the children's individuality might be threatened, while others argued that identical twins manage to keep their individuality intact.

12   John Robertson of the University of Texas raises several other issues worth pondering. What about the cloned child's sense of free will and parental expectations? Since the parents chose to duplicate their first child, will the clone feel obliged to follow in the older siblings foot-steps? Will the older child feel he has been duplicated because he was inadequate or because he is special? Will the two have a unique form of sibling rivalry, or a special bond? These are, of course, just special versions of questions that come up whenever a new child is introduced into a family.

Could a Megalomaniac Decide to Achieve Immortality by Cloning an "Heir"?

13   Sure, and there are other situations where adults might be tempted to clone themselves. . . . On adult cloning, ethicists are more united in their discomfort. In fact, the same commission that

was divided on the issue of twins was unanimous in its conclusion
that cloning an adult's twin is "bizarre . . . narcissistic and ethically
impoverished." What's more, the commission argued that the
phenomenon would jeopardize our very sense of who's who in the
world, especially in the family.

What Are the Other Implications of Cloning for Society?

14   The gravest concern about the misuse of genetics isn't related to
cloning directly, but to genetic engineering—the deliberate
manipulation of genes to enhance human talents and create human
beings according to certain specifications. But some ethicists also
are concerned about the creation of a new (and stigmatized) social
class: "the clones." Albert Jonsen of the University of Washington
believes the confrontation could be comparable to what occurred in
the 16th century, when Europeans were perplexed by the unfamiliar
inhabitants of the New World and endlessly debated their status as
humans.

Could Cloning Be Criminally Misused?

15   If the technology to clone humans existed today, it would be
almost impossible to prevent someone from cloning you without
your knowledge or permission, says Philip Bereano, professor of
technology and public policy at the University of Washington.
Everyone gives off cells all the time—whenever we give a blood
sample, for example, or visit the dentist—and those cells all contain
one's full complement of DNA. What would be the goal of such
"drive-by" cloning? Well, what if a woman were obsessed with having
the child of an apathetic man? Or think of the commercial value of a
dynasty-building athletic pedigree or a heavenly singing voice. Even
though experience almost certainly shapes these talents as much as
genetic gifts, the unscrupulous would be unlikely to be deterred.

Doesn't Cloning Encroach on the Judeo-Christian View of God as the Creator of Life? Would a Clone Be Considered a Creature of God or of Science?

16   Many theologians worry about this. Cloning, at first glance,
seems to be a usurpation of God's role as creator of humans "in his

own image." The scientist, rather than God or chance, determines the outcome. "Like Adam and Eve, we want to be like God, to be in control," says philosophy Prof. Kevin Wildes of Georgetown University. "The question is, what are the limits?"

17   But some theologians argue that cloning is not the same as creating life from scratch. The ingredients used are alive or contain the elements of life, says Fletcher of Wheaton College. It is still only God, he says, who creates life.

Would Cloning Upset Religious Views About Death, Immortality, and Even Resurrection?

18   Not really. Cloned or not, we all die. The clone that outlives its "parent"—or that is generated from the DNA of a dead person, if that were possible—would be a different person. It would not be a reincarnation or a resurrected version of the deceased. Cloning could be said to provide immortality, theologians say, only in the sense that, as in normal reproduction, one might be said to "live on" in the genetic traits passed to one's progeny.

A .   C O M P R E H E N S I O N

1. How did the world react to the news that a sheep had successfully been cloned?

2. Would a cloned human being be identical to the original in appearance and personality?

3. What are some of the problems that could arise for cloned individuals?

4. What are the two sides of the religious controversy about cloning?

B .   C R I T I C A L   T H I N K I N G

1. Do you think the author is in favor of cloning humans or opposed to it? Find two or three statements in the reading that support your answer.

2. Why did the Vatican call for a worldwide ban on cloning?

3. Could cloning one day become a profitable illegal business?

4. Which possible uses of cloning seem useful and legitimate?

5. How do you think the clones would be treated by other members of society? Would they be considered a lower class of humans?

C . LANGUAGE AND VOCABULARY

1. Had you ever heard the term *sibling rivalry* before reading it in this article? What do you think it means? If you use a dictionary to find the meaning, try looking up the two words *sibling* and *rivalry* separately, and then put the meanings together.

2. This article uses a number of scientific terms, such as *DNA, molecular biology, cell, genes,* and *genetic engineering.* Make a list of six or more scientific terms from the reading, and find out the meaning of each. Then use two of these words in sentences of your own.

D . STYLE, STRUCTURE, AND ORGANIZATION

1. Unlike most academic essays, "The World After Cloning" is organized as a series of questions and answers. Is this an effective way to organize the article? Why or why not? Which questions do the best job of capturing readers' attention?

2. In several places, the authors present ideas from two different points of view. In the fourth paragraph, for example, the question "Why would anyone want to clone a human being in the first place?" is answered with reasons that sound good, but the next paragraph offers a contrasting viewpoint. Find at least one other section of the article that uses a similar pro-and-con technique. Do you think this technique is effective for writing about controversial topics? Why or why not?

3. Find at least two places in the reading where the authors quote or refer to experts to answer some of the questions about cloning. Does the information provided by experts make the answers clearer or more convincing? Why?

E. TOPICS FOR DISCUSSION OR JOURNAL WRITING

1. Would you ever want to clone yourself or someone else you know?

2. Do you think there should be a worldwide ban on the cloning of human beings? Why or why not?

3. How could cloning affect professional sports? Do you think these effects would be good or bad? Why?

4. In what ways could cloning be used for good purposes in the animal world? For example, what about cloning animal species that are endangered?

F. WRITING TOPICS FOR PARAGRAPHS OR ESSAYS

1. Imagine how you would feel about cloning if you were a clone. Write about cloning from the point of view of a clone.

2. Write an argumentative paper that takes a stand for or against cloning of human beings or in favor of cloning with certain restrictions. Consider what restrictions (if any) you think should be placed on cloning and how cloning should be used. In your paper, show that you are open-minded by presenting a little bit about the beliefs of those who have an opposing viewpoint, but be sure that your own side is more persuasive.

3. Which potential use of cloning, either of humans or of animals, do you think would be most beneficial? Write a paper about the benefits of using cloning for that purpose. Give clear, logical reasons for your opinion.

4. Using library resources or the Internet, find out more about Wilmut and his successful cloning of a sheep in 1997. Write an informative paper about what you learn.

5. Interview someone who is a twin (an identical twin, if possible). Ask questions about what it was like to grow up with a twin and whether or not he or she experienced any sibling rivalry. Write a paper about the twin you interviewed.

ACKNOWLEDGMENTS

TEXT
Strategies for Active Reading

"Tourist Trap" by James Hebert, which appeared in the *San Diego Union-Tribune,* January 1, 2000. Reprinted with permission from The San Diego Union-Tribune.

Cultural and Social Issues

"American Fish" by R.A. Sasaki, from *The Loom and Other Stories* by R. A. Sasaki. Copyright © 1991 by R. A. Sasaki. Reprinted by permission of Graywolf Press.

"Listen to Me Good" by Margaret Charles Smith and Linda Janet Holmes, from *Listen to Me Good: The Life Story of an Alabama Midwife.* Copyright © 1996 by Margaret Charles Smith and Linda Janet Holmes. Reprinted by permission of the publisher.

"Boomer Parents" by Sandy Banks, from the *Los Angeles Times* online, August 15, 2000, originally titled "What Are Boomer Parents Teaching Kids." Reprinted by permission of the Los Angeles Times Syndicate.

"Spanglish Spoken Here" by Janice Castro, from the July 11, 1988, issue of *Time.* Copyright © TIME INC. Reprinted by permission.

"Saffron Sky" by Gelareh Asayesh, from *Saffron Sky* by Gelareh Asayesh. Copyright © 1999 by Gelareh Asayesh. Reprinted by permission of Beacon Press, Boston.

"A Song Flung Up to Heaven" by Maya Angelou, from A SONG FLUNG UP TO HEAVEN by Maya Angelou, copyright © 2002 by Maya Angelou. Used by permission of Random House, Inc.

"Suspect Policy" by Randall Kennedy, from the September 13 and 20 issues of *The New Republic.* Reprinted by permission.

Fitness and Health

"Strive to Be Fit, Not Fanatical" by Timothy Gower, which originally appeared in the *Los Angeles Times,* June 7, 1999. Reprinted by permission of Timothy Gower.

"Procrastination and Stress" by Lester A. Lefton, from Lefton, Lester A., *Psychology,* 7/E. Copyright © 2000 by Allyn and Bacon. Reprinted/ adapted by permission.

"Managing Time" by Rebecca J. Donatelle and Lorraine G. Davis. From *Health: The Basics,* 3rd Edition, by Rebecca J. Donatelle and Lorraine G. Davis. Copyright © 1999 by Allyn and Bacon. Reprinted by permission.

"Computer Addiction Is Coming On-line" by William J. Cromie, which appeared in the *Harvard Gazette,* January 21, 1999. Reprinted by permission of William Cromie, Harvard University Gazette.

"Playing for Keeps" by Andy Steiner, which appeared in *Utne Reader,* January–February 2000. Reprinted by permission of Andy Steiner, senior editor at *Utne Reader.*

Nature and the Outdoors

"Journey of the Pink Dolphins" by Sy Montgomery, from JOURNEY OF THE PINK DOLPHINS: An Amazon Quest by Sy Montgomery. Copyright © 2000 by Sy Montgomery. Excerpted by permission of Simon and Schuster.

"In the Shadow of Man" by Jane Goodall, from IN THE SHADOW OF MAN by Jane Goodall. Copyright © 1971 by Hugo and Jane van Lawick-Goodall. Reprinted by permission of Houghton Mifflin Co. All rights reserved.

"Life in the Treetops" by Margaret D. Lowman, from Margaret D. Lowman, *Life in the Treetops: Adventures of a Woman in Field Biology,* published by Yale University Press. Copyright © 1999. Reprinted by permission of Yale University Press.

"Nature's R_x" by Joel L. Swerdlow, excerpted from Joel L. Swerdlow, "Nature's R_x," *National Geographic,* April 2000. Reprinted by permission of the National Geographic Society.

"The Wild Within" by Paul Rezendes from THE WILD WITHIN by Paul Rezendes. Copyright © 1998 by Paul Rezendes. Used by permission of Jeremy P. Tarcher, an imprint of Pengiun Group (USA) Inc.

Values and Choices

PHOTOS

INDEX

294